Distant Neighbours

A publication of the Graduate Institute of
International Studies, Geneva

Also by Harish Kapur:

*Soviet Russia and Asia, 1917–1929: Soviet Policy Towards Iran,
    Turkey, Afghanistan,* London, Michael Joseph, 1965
*Soviet Union and the Emerging Nations: A Case Study of Soviet Policy
    Towards India,* London, Michael Joseph, 1972
The Embattled Triangle: Moscow, Peking, New Delhi, New Delhi,
    Abhinav Publishers, 1973
China in World Politics, New Delhi, India International Centre, 1977
The Awakening Giant: China's Ascension in World Politics, Alphen
    Aan Den Ryn, Sitthoff and Noordhoff, 1981
The End of an Isolation: China After Mao, Dordrecht, Martinus
    Nijhoff, 1983 (available from Pinter Publishers, London)
China and the European Community: The New Connection,
    Dordrecht, Martinus Nijhoff, 1985 (available from Pinter
    Publishers, London)
As China Sees the World: Perceptions of Chinese Scholars, London,
    Pinter, 1987

Distant Neighbours

China and Europe

Harish Kapur

 Pinter Publishers, London and New York

© Pinter Publishers Ltd, 1990

First published in Great Britain in 1990 by
Pinter Publishers, 25 Floral Street, London WC2E 9DS
and P.O. Box 197, Irvington, New York 10533.

British Library Cataloguing in Publication Data

A CIP catalogue record for this book is available from the
British Library

ISBN 0 86187 122 7

Typeset by Florencetype Ltd, Kewstoke, Avon
Printed and bound in Great Britain by Biddles Ltd.

Contents

Preface

Research on the contemporary history of a country cannot be based solely on official documents: for one thing, they are relatively few; for another, they often reveal very little or even conceal the intentions, motivations or even the policies of the country.

A student of contemporary history, therefore, has to rely on a vast array of other published material—material that is issued by the media in printed form or electronically and material that is written by those who are involved, directly or indirectly, in the events that are covered in a study.

All these are very important as sources of information for research in contemporary affairs, for the volume of documentation available through such sources is sufficiently large to permit the historian to fill in the gaps in his research with which he is unavoidably faced. Though such documentation does not have the same credibility as classical source material, its magnitude and its diversity permit the historian to check and cross-check the reliability of the documentation. This is what I have done.

The other way I attempted to fill in the gaps was through interviews and off-the-record conversations with Chinese and European personalities, directly or indirectly involved in the events, whom I had the great fortune of meeting,

During my recent trips to China, I had the opportunity to meet many Chinese scholars and officials with whom I was able to review some of the important Sino-European developments which needed either further elaboration or some further interpretation. These people will remain nameless, since most of them wished to maintain anonymity. However, I must express my deep gratitude to the China Institute of Contemporary International Relations (my hosts in China), the Institute of West European Studies of the Chinese Academy of Social Sciences, the Foreign Affairs College, and the Institute of International Studies of the Chinese Foreign Ministery. The staff members of these institutes were kind enough to receive me and discuss the points I wished to raise.

I also benefited greatly from the discussions I had with many West Europeans involved in the relations of their respective countries with China. It would take too long to mention all of them, but I must mention specifically the late Christopher Soames, vice-president of the European Commission, Tran Van-Thinh, representative of the European Commission in Geneva and Sir Percy Craddock of the British Foreign Office. To all—named and unnamed—the author is greatly indebted. Needless to say, none of them should be held accountable in any way for the particular views and reflections in this study.

Harish Kapur
Aubonne, Switzerland

Introduction

China's relations with Europe may seem less important than her relations with other regions and other actors, for considerable space in the Chinese media and official declarations has been devoted to the two superpowers, to Japan and to the Third World. The facts and operational diplomacy tell a different story. Except for the first two years after the Chinese revolution, Europe has always occupied an important place in Chinese diplomacy for historical, strategic and economic reasons: historical because of all the difficulties, humiliations, etc. she had to face at the hands of many European colonial powers; strategic because of her geographical presence on the Western flank of the Soviet Union and economic because of all that Europe has had to offer, without political strings, towards China's modernization.

Europe has indeed meant a great deal to China, and the Chinese leadership has displayed a more stable and more benign interest in Europe, in what has been happening there and the extent to which Europe could play a more efficacious role within the international system.

This study is, therefore, devoted to forty years of China's relations with Europe, the forty years of interaction beginning in October 1949 and culminating in June 1989 when the events of Tiananmen Square generated a great deal of tension between the West Europeans and the Chinese—tensions that had previously arisen only during the Cultural Revolution.

The area of investigation chosen for this study is not only Western but also Eastern Europe. Although Europe was partitioned after World War II along ideological and political lines—with Eastern Europe under Soviet control, and Western Europe heavily influenced by the United States—de Gaulle and Willy Brandt, with their respective *détente* and *ostpolitik* policies, slowly and prudently initiated a process of interaction which bypassed these barriers. And now with the Gorbachevian revolution that has set in train a new and even more accelerated process of disengagement, the political barriers between Eastern and Western Europe are breaking down, encouraging many to conjure up visions of a new and non-partitioned Europe.

The Chinese leadership has been increasingly conscious of this process, which it has often discussed. Its response to this process has varied depending upon China's relations with the Soviet Union—against any East–West European interaction as long as Sino-Soviet relations were good, but for interaction when relations were bad. Although this pattern of thinking and behaviour is generally still valid, China seems to have become very concerned and even frightened by the process of democratization that has gripped Eastern Europe and by the new East–West relationships that dominate the European scene. China is frightened because of the horrendous ramifications this upheaval could have for its domestic situation, particularly after the events of Tiananmen Square.

If one were to examine, even briefly and impressionistically, the whole gamut of China's foreign relations, one element that would be most conspicuous is the constantly changing character of China's foreign policy.

1

Initially, China 'leaned' on the Soviet side, then made a sharp break with it, then slowly turned to the Third World, Western Europe and even the United States to forge an anti–Soviet international front, thereafter became neutral *vis-à-vis* the superpowers, finally once again opening up more and more to Moscow.

The priorities accorded to goals also continued to change. Basically four foreign policy goals—revolutions, security, modernization, integration of outlying areas—were viewed as important but each of these goals was at some point in the forefront only to be replaced by another depending on the mood of the country and the overall situation. At the decisional level, too, change was the rule. From a highly elitist foreign policy in which only a few top leaders were involved, the Chinese decisional process has slowly been broadened to include other elitist groups thus enlarging the number of people involved in the process.

Since China's foreign policy has constantly been in a state of flux, the most appropriate approach for this book for dealing with China's interaction with Europe is one that is historical and chronological. All the innovations introduced in China's foreign policy have been within a certain situation and time frame; remove it and the policies become incomprehensible. The organizational framework of this book has therefore been structured so that each chapter, representing a period, takes into account the context in which a given policy has been designed. Forty years of China's foreign policy have been broken up into ten sequential periods, each investigated within a certain context, highlighting the most important features in terms of issues and countries. Since the focus is on movement, each chapter attempts to answer the same questions as far as possible, centering on (a) the nature of a change, (b) the reasons for the change and (c) the decisional process used to introduce the change.

Chapter 1
'Leaning on one side': the early years

For slightly more than two years after the 1949 Revolution, Europe was at the lowest rung of the Chinese diplomatic ladder. In fact, it was, for the new revolutionary government of no interest; and there were no signs of any attempt to initiate a coherent and distinctive foreign policy or even, for that matter, any great eagerness to establish formal diplomatic relations even with those who were willing to do so.[1] Whatever interaction it had with what, to the Chinese at the time, seemed a faraway continent was really marginal and was closely anchored to the policy framework that had been designed by its senior partner, the Soviet Union—a partner with whom it had announced that it wished 'to form an international front'.[2] Several factors contributed to this conspicuous lack of any diplomatic interest in Europe.

First of all, this distant continent, at the hands of which China had experienced considerable humiliation and exploitation for more than a century, no longer really constituted a serious threat to its national security, undoubtedly a major foreign policy goal for the Chinese Communist Party (CCP) in the immediate aftermath of the Chinese revolution. This was not because European political behaviour had undergone a sudden sea-change, although some changes were discernible, but because the slow and irreversible process of historical decline, already visible after World War I, compounded with the ravages of World War II, had deprived the Europeans of the necessary clout to sway the world. In its place, there had emerged a weak, dependent and partitioned Europe that had been drawn into the spheres of influence of the two extra-European powers, the United States and the Soviet Union, both of whom had acquired a military power on a scale never enjoyed by any country before. In sum, the new European political landscape mirrored, at the time of the Chinese revolution, the often repeated historical phenomenon of the rise and fall of civilizations.

For the CCP, influenced by a very rigid and well-defined ideological framework and leaning on the Soviet Union, Europe could hardly be anything more than marginal in real foreign-policy terms. Having uncritically accepted the Soviet assessment of the international situation,[3] Europe was composed of a group of friendly Communist states and a cluster of generally unfriendly American-dominated capitalist countries. The main responsibility for diplomatic initiatives and revolutionary actions lay with the Soviet Union—the leader of the Communist bloc.

The acceptance of such a bi-polar picture of the international system in the immediate aftermath of the revolution was an implicit renunciation of the broad picture that Mao Zedong had drawn in 1946 in which 'a vast zone' had separated the United States from the Soviet Union, a zone that included 'many capitalist, colonial and semi-colonial countries in Europe, Asia and Africa'.[4]

Second, China was faced with more crucial problems on her periphery. There was, first of all, a military involvement in the Korean War in 1950 which had tied

3

China's hands to a large extent and which, after its termination, had left her severely battered. There was the unfinished task of integrating the outlying areas (Tibet and Taiwan) with the mainland—hardly an easy objective, given the potential risks of confrontation with neighbouring India and an interposed American naval presence between the mainland and Taiwan. There was the French colonial presence in Indo-China, the British in Hong Kong, the Portuguese in Macao, all of which needed the full and urgent attention of the Chinese leadership.

But more important and clearly more threatening was the American military encirclement of the mainland, and her effective military presence in all the strategic points that had hitherto been occupied by Japan. For China, whose recent history is studded with myriad examples of British, French, Russian and Japanese imperialism, the overwhelming American presence was perceived as extremely perilous, necessitating the mobilization of her diplomatic attention.

The measure of Chinese concern over such a presence can be discerned from the repeated references that Mao Zedong and Zhou Enlai made to the United States in most of their declarations. The main thrust of practically all of Mao's writings on foreign affairs just before and just after the revolution pertained to the threat that the United States constituted for China.[5] Perhaps even more reflective of this Chinese concern were Zhou Enlai's political reports to the different sessions of the Chinese People's Political Consultative Conferences. All the passages on foreign affairs that were included in his political report to the third session of the Consultative conference, for example, strongly castigated the United States and its threat to China's national security. While expressing this concern, he called for massive mobilization of China's defence forces against the United States. He declared:

> As already mentioned, in order to defend our motherland and peace in the Far East we must further consolidate and strengthen our national defence forces. On the basis of its glorious victorious traditions, the Chinese People's Liberation Army must study hard, strengthen the building up of all the armed forces, increase its modern equipment, improve its organization, introduce a unified system, intensify training, raise the level of discipline, and struggle for the establishment and building up of a strong and modernized defence forces . . . and intensify work in support of the great movement to resist American aggression and aid Korea.[6]

Third, the domestic task of rebuilding what was clearly a ravaged nation was indeed stupendous. Decades of civil war and years of Japanese occupation had severely damaged the economy, and had destabilized the already fragile political system. Hardly anything was actually functioning—and this had been true for decades. This scarcely left time for international affairs beyond the essential—especially after 1949, when the CCP had made it quite clear that it was not going to content itself with just governing the country, but would overhaul it—undoubtedly a time-consuming task. Admittedly, domestic preoccupations have rarely restrained nations from an active involvement in international affairs; in some cases they have even impelled decision-makers to instigate external events in the hope of diverting the attention of the population from domestic problems. But these diversions, it should be noted, have invariably been focused on issues of direct concern and not on those that are peripheral. In the case of China—engrossed as she was with important national and regional issues—distant, weak and non-threatening Europe could hardly figure as a major problem for Chinese diplomacy. In the face of all the real security concerns that China had *vis-à-vis* the United States, she did not have to raise issues that were clearly less important or even non-existent.

Fourth, there was an implicit geographical division of responsibilities between China and her senior partner—at least, that is how the Chinese projected it. While the principal burden for revolutionary and diplomatic initiatives in Europe was viewed as a Soviet responsibility, since the onset of World War II the task of inspiring and accelerating revolutionary movements in the Third World—particularly Asia—was considered by the Chinese leaders to fall on themselves.

In this connection it is important to note that the CCP had faithfully followed the Soviet line on all issues pertaining to Europe: whether it was the Soviet assessment of the European situation, or whether it was the German question, or the controversial Trieste issue or even the Soviet conflict with Yugoslavia, the CCP avoided having an autonomous position. On the other hand, when it came to Asian developments, China very clearly advanced her own position. As early as 1940, Mao Zedong, for example, had argued that since neither the bourgeois authoritarianism of the Western world nor the proleterian dictatorship of the Soviets were suitable for the developing countries, the Chinese revolutionary model of 'New Democracy', based on the alliance of four classes—the peasantry, the proleteriat, the petty bourgeoisie and the national bourgeoisie—should be emulated by like-minded nations.[7] Liu Shaoqi was even more categorical. In his view, the Chinese revolutionary model charted 'a way not only for the Chinese people but for the billion folk who live in colonial countries of Southeast Asia'.[8]

This line of thinking continued after the revolution. In fact, it was even more forcefully expressed. This was significant, for those who were expressing it were no longer simple revolutionaries but were now members of a government. The significance attached to such ideas can be gauged from the fact that they were openly aired at a conference of Asian and Australasian trade unions in November–December 1949. Holding such a meeting in the Chinese capital so soon after the revolution underlined the relevance of the Chinese model, and conveyed to Moscow China's determination to play a greater revolutionary role in Asia.

With this implicit division of labour, China made a point of abstaining from developing an independent strategy with regard to Europe. Apparently, she was content to play second fiddle to Moscow then in the hope that the latter would adopt China's attitude in Asia.

Lastly, since China had insignificant economic power and only very tenuous military strength, it was hardly possible for her to orchestrate a viable and coherent policy relating to a faraway continent. During the first two years after the Chinese revolution, there was, therefore, no real attempt at the globalization of China's foreign policy. Both interest and capacity were woefully lacking regarding Europe in China's operational diplomacy.

The European response

What about the Europeans' reaction to the emergence of a new China? Were they not interested? Did they not see the relative increase in China's international clout after 1949 as a major development to be reckoned with? And did they not take any initiatives?

The European response was neither unanimous nor independent. It could hardly be unanimous, given the important fact that the partition of Europe into two blocs had seriously divided the continent in their perceptions of the international system; and it could hardly be independent, given their dependence on the superpowers.

East European attitude

The East European response was clear, for all members of the bloc promptly established diplomatic relations with China and openly welcomed the new Communist government (see Table 1.1). This general decision to forge ties with China was influenced by two factors both of which were linked to the Soviet Union.

Table 1.1 Establishment of diplomatic relations between China and Eastern Europe

Bulgaria	4 October 1949
Romania	5 October 1949
Hungary	6 October 1949
Czechoslovakia	6 October 1949
Poland	7 October 1949
East Germany	27 October 1949
Albania	23 November 1949

The first was general East European subservience to Moscow. Once the Soviet Union had taken the decision to recognize China and welcome her as an important partner within the Communist bloc, the Soviet client states had hardly any choice but to follow suit. Actually, there was no reason why these countries would not recognize Beijing, since the emergence of Communist China, without any Soviet aid, was a confirmation of Communist vitality. The decision to recognize China was one of those few foreign-policy decisions where East European interests dovetailed with that of the Soviet Union. The second reason, perhaps, was the importance China had gained within the Communist bloc. The emergence of a Communist giant, which Moscow had to accept as much more of a co-equal than any Eastern European country, opened the prospects for these countries to play off one Communist giant against the other, thereby gaining a modicum of leverage that they had totally lost with their subordination after World War II.

But China's response to Eastern Europe, during the first two years after the revolution, was rather cautious at the political level. Though her response to the establishment of non-political relations was extremely forthright, she was indeed very careful to avoid any initiatives to forge independent political ties with any one of them. She did not, for example, conclude treaties of friendship, alliance and mutual assistance as she had done with the Soviet Union, and essentially limited her relations to the non-political sector by concluding a wide array of trade (see Table 1.2), cultural and technological agreements. In fact, in these sectors China was very active. For between October 1949 and Stalin's death in March 1953, China had signed twelve such agreements with Poland, fourteen with Hungary, nine with Czechoslovakia, fourteen with Bulgaria and nine with Romania.

Table 1.2 Trade agreements between China and
Eastern Europe, 1949–52

Poland	February 1950
Czechoslovakia	June 1950
East Germany	October 1950
Hungary	January 1951
Bulgaria	1952
Romania	1952

Thus, whatever internal views China may have had regarding the wisdom or the correctness of Soviet policies in Eastern Europe, the fact is that during the two years after the revolution, China had totally subordinated her policies to that of Moscow so far as Eastern Europe was concerned. There was really no attempt whatsoever either to challenge Soviet leadership or even to express a different view regarding the area.

The Chinese subordination became clearly evident from her decision to follow Moscow on the Soviet–Yugoslav conflict; so much so that she did not even deign to reply to Belgrade's formal proposal of 5 October 1949 to establish diplomatic relations with Beijing. In fact, according to the Yugoslavs, China not only 'adopted a negative attitude', but participated 'in the well-known campaign which was initiated in 1948 by certain East European countries and parties against Yugoslavia and her Communist Party'.[9] And yet if there was any country in Eastern Europe with which China had some degree of commonality it was Yugoslavia—commonality of having staged their own revolutions without Soviet aid, and commonality of having established relatively viable governments.

The measure of China's interest in Communist countries is discernible not only from the rapid establishment of diplomatic relations and the emergence of an identity of views on most international issues; it is also evident from the accelerated development of economic relations with most of them. The volume of China's trade with the Communist countries, for example, by 1951 accounted for 61.9 per cent of her total trade against only 25.9 per cent the year before.[10] With Eastern Europe specifically, trade also grew exponentially. While it was only $30 million in 1950, it shot up in 1951 and 1952 (see Tables 1.3 and 1.4).

Table 1.3 Foreign trade of China, 1950–2 (in US$ million)

Year	Trade with the West	Trade with the Soviet Union	Trade with Eastern Europe
1950	933	580	30
1951	919	809	220
1952	601	968	330

Source: Feng-Hwa Mah, *The Foreign Trade of Mainland China*, Edinburgh, Edinburgh University Press 1972, p. 16.

Table 1.4 Direction of trade towards Communist countries, 1950–2 (percentage of total trade)

Year	Soviet Union	Eastern Europe
1950	30.9	2.6
1951	48.7	14.6
1952	51.5	20.5

Source: Feng-Hwa, Mah, op. cit. p. 20.

The West European response

The West European attitude, on the other hand, was generally prudent towards Communist China. With the exception of a few small states, which had rapidly accorded recognition to the new government, most of them were rather hesitant or divided on the whole question (see Table 1.5).

Table 1.5 Recognition of China by West European nations, 1949–52

United Kingdom	6 January 1950
Norway	6 January 1950
Sweden	9 May 1950
Denmark	11 May 1950
Finland	28 October 1950

The Netherlands, for example, requested Great Britain not to recognize the new regime in China until after the Dutch transfer of power to the newly independent Indonesia on 27 December 1950. The French asked that British recognition be delayed until Emperor Bao Dai's new government in Indo-China could establish itself firmly. The Scandinavian countries informed Whitehall that they were prepared to accord recognition as soon as the United Kingdom. Italy and Portugal, on the other hand, waited for the clarification of the American position.

This general hesitation, disagreement and even lack of any coordination can be attributed to two factors. The first was the United States. American pressures against recognition were so great that it was hardly possible for the West Europeans to design autonomous policies on such a controversial issue. The intensity of the cold war and the establishment of a bi-polar situation did not lend themselves to the adoption generally of a positive attitude towards China—at least for those who were dependent on the United States. Even on the trade question, West European leverage was considerably reduced, particularly during the Korean war, the outbreak of which had resulted in the continuous expansion of the list of embargoed items—so much so that the Paris Coordinating Committee (COCOM), composed of thirteen NATO members plus Japan, which had been established for this purpose, had clamped down a far more restrictive list against China than against the Soviet Union.[11]

The second reason for this prudent attitude was China itself. The CCP's determination to overhaul the socio-economic system, to break up unequal ties with the Western countries, to seize Western economic interests and to forbid Western nations from continuing their mercantile interests within China hardly left them with any leeway for the type of economic activities they had hitherto sustained. Consider, for example, the determination with which the new leadership acted regarding foreign economic interests. Most of them were just taken over, and the few remaining in foreign hands were faced with so many constraints that they had little choice but to be abandoned.[12] And, even this could not be done, since exit permits were refused to those who wanted to leave. In the words of the British representative 'they were virtual prisoners, unable to do business, unable to leave, with all the privileges and pleasures of their old life disappearing round them'.[13]

In sum, the firm and very clear distinction that the CCP made between acceptable foreign trade and unacceptable foreign economic activity within China was disconcerting to the West Europeans. While they simply could not understand this decision, the Chinese, on the other hand, were determined to go ahead with their plans of completely taking over all foreign economic interests, apparently convinced that failure to do so would be incompatible with the Communist character of the new Chinese regime.

The restrictive Chinese attitude regarding diplomatic relations also did not help; it was made clear at the outset that the establishment of diplomatic relations was subject to negotiations and would be allowed only if they were based 'on equality, mutual benefit and mutual respect for territory and sovereignty'; if the foreign governments had severed all relations with the Guomindang; and if they 'adopted a friendly attitude towards the People's Republic of China'.[14]

Consider, for example, the establishment of relations with Britain which accorded a *de jure* recognition to China on 6 January 1950. Considering American opposition and West European reservation towards such a unilateral initiative, it was certainly a bold action in so far as it brought out in the open—for the first time—divergences within the Atlantic community. On the other hand, the half-hearted character of the British initiative also became increasingly evident. London, for example, continued to maintain a consular presence in Taiwan, declined to support the new regime's admission to the United Nations and spurned the mainland's claim to the former Chinese state property in Hong Kong. In Chinese eyes, the maintenance of a consular presence in Taiwan was in direct conflict with the conditions laid down for the establishment of diplomatic relations. The British reluctance to support China's admission to the United Nations was viewed as a half-hearted recognition, since recognition of China automatically carried with it, in her view, her right to be a member of the United Nations, and the British opposition to the Hong Kong claims was regarded as a sign of bad faith on London's part.

The Chinese government, therefore, decided not to pursue the negotiations with London regarding the resumption of diplomatic relations, and the British representative in Beijing was considered as the 'head of the British delegation for the negotiation of the establishment of diplomatic relations'.[15] Humphrey Trevelyan, the British Representative in Beijing at the time, had this to say about his status in China:

> After my first formal call, I could get no more interviews. They made it quite clear that I was not to be treated as *de facto* chargé d'affaires. The Vice-Minister only answered my letters when he wanted to be particularly offensive and to publish his replies; my requests for interviews were simply ignored. I had no formal ground for complaint, since I had not been recognized as head of the diplomatic mission and could not complain to be treated as such.[16]

The Chinese attitude towards the four other West European countries, which had promptly extended recognition to China in 1950 (Sweden, Denmark, Finland and Switzerland), and which had no conflict or even any major differences with China, was also restrictive. China declined to establish diplomatic relations right away with any of them and demanded a series of clarifications regarding their policies towards Beijing before recognizing their emmisaries as official representatives. When the Swedish Ministry of Foreign Affairs sent a note to China on 31 December 1949 on the Swedish decision 'to recognize *de jure* the Central People's Government as the Government of China', and to send its Consul General in Hong Kong, Sven Stiner, as its chargé d'affaires to Beijing, the Chinese government made it clear that it was accepting him in order 'to negotiate on the questions concerning the establishment of diplomatic relations'.[17] A similar fate awaited the Danish representative who was sent from Shanghai. He was not even allowed to open a consulate office. The Norwegian representative—despite Norwegian recognition—was rebuffed on the ground that his government had abstained from voting for The People's Republic's (PRC) admission to the United Nations.[18]

In the case of the non-socialist countries, particularly the West European states, the PRC was apparently making a clear distinction between recognition and the actual establishment of diplomatic relations. The second, in their view, did not automatically follow the first.[19]

The lack of Chinese interest in Western Europe, at the time, can also be discerned by the fact that the number of Chinese diplomatic personnel—once relations were finally established—was intentionally kept very small, and that they were strictly instructed to maintain only minimal official ties, but to maximize their unofficial contact with radical non-governmental organizations.[20]

Conclusion

Europe thus was marginal during the two years after the revolution. Whether it was Eastern or Western Europe, China systematically maintained a low profile and avoided designing an autonomous policy of her own. Though there were a number of factors—analysed in this chapter—that contributed to such a stance, the main element was the Soviet factor. Having accepted the Soviet Union as leader of the then monolithic Communist bloc, the Chinese leadership could hardly design an autonomous foreign policy of her own—least of all in Europe where Moscow was most active during this period.

It could be argued that even if China had decided to fend for herself in the foreign-policy sector, it was unlikely that it would have been materially different from the Soviet-inspired policy. The colonial character of her past relations with Western Europe, compounded with the fact that Marxist considerations were primordial in overall Chinese political behaviour meant there was little scope for an alternative policy. However, if the broad framework could not be different, China's policy towards Europe—though clearly less important—was more aggressive than even that of the Soviet Union. Consider China's attitude towards a West European economic presence. It was excessively harsh and excessively belligerent. That China was determined to seize all West European economic interests was understandable, since such a policy dovetailed with the type of economic system it wanted to introduce. But what appeared excessive was the treatment meted out to the foreign economic personnel. 'While', wrote one observer on the question, 'nearly all the foreigners who wanted to leave were being kept in China, nearly all those who wanted to stay were being expelled.'[21] Consider, also the Chinese attitude to the establishment of diplomatic relations. With the West European countries, it was particularly harsh and non-cooperative —in any event more than with other areas and other countries. Whereas full diplomatic relations were automatically and promptly established with the Communist countries and even with the non-Communist Asian countries, the West Europeans—wanting to establish relations—were informed that the whole question would have to be negotiated.

Chapter 2

A window to the West

By 1952, China's thinking and strategy regarding foreign policy had begun to change; there were some clear signs of diversifying external relations and of breaking out of a marked diplomatic isolation from the international community. Interest in Western Europe was particularly evident, and some signals to this effect were sent out. Though formally, the new Chinese interest in the non-Communist world was not considered as incompatible with the axiomatic and openly proclaimed policy of 'leaning on one side', it is none the less undeniable that this was a first major departure in foreign policy since the 1949 revolution.

Determinants of new policy

Four major developments had contributed to this change—developments that the Chinese leaders could hardly afford to ignore. Since the 1949 revolution, this was the first time that they had to take into account a series of external and internal factors while designing a new policy; for the initial Chinese decision to 'lean on one side', was a voluntary political act and an unsolicited ideological commitment unrelated to the overall political situation. Presumably, two years of actual learning experience in the diplomatic sector had made the Chinese leadership realize that foreign policy is also a reaction to the actions of other nations.

The first change pertained to the Soviet Union. By 1952, the Chinese evaluation of their relations with their senior partner was not completely positive, even if the formal facade of 'indestructible friendship' was maintained. Doubts had indeed begun to emerge regarding the benefits of a very close and rather exclusive relationship.

At the security level Moscow was disappointing. The protection that China had hoped for did not materialize. All the Soviet military provisions that China had received to fight the Korean war had to be paid back, and at no point during the active phase of the war did Soviet support go beyond verbal rhetoric. If security protection was not invocable to defend Korea—a neighbour of both—what guarantee was there that it would be forthcoming for areas in which China was more interested than the Soviet Union? In this connection, the Vietnam conflict was particularly worrying to the Chinese; for its rapid escalation had resulted in a heavy American commitment to supply arms to the French government. For the Chinese who had just emerged from the costly Korean war, seriously bruised and drained, the prospect of another military encounter with the United States was not reassuring, particularly in view of the fact that China was encircled by a heavy American military presence on her periphery and also that the Vietminh resistance movement 'was on the brink of a collapse'.[1]

At the political level, the Chinese assessment could not have been different. In addition to multiple disappointments—including the Soviet refusal to part with Outer Mongolia—the constrictiveness of Sino-Soviet relations must have become increasingly apparent, that China was exposed only to Soviet views or Soviet pressures on all diplomatic issues and that for the sake of maintaining international Communist solidarity China was invariably obliged to follow its senior partner on most issues on which the CPSU had publicly expressed its views.

The second major development was the emergence of an independent foreign-policy behaviour by some of the non-Communist Asian countries. The refusal of some of them to accept the American position on Korea and their attempts to introduce independent mediatory efforts to resolve the conflict must have been an eye-opener to the Chinese leadership. Undoubtedly, this was a far cry from the fixed perception that China had developed regarding these countries in the immediate aftermath of the Chinese revolution. The diplomatic exchanges that China had with these countries to end the Korean war thus opened wider prospects of greater interaction with the outside world and generated a distinct desire to participate more actively and more autonomously in international affairs.

The third development was Stalin's death in March 1953. Now that the charismatic leader was gone, and there was no one else within the Soviet leadership—locked as it was in the succession battle—to assume his mantle, Mao Zedong probably saw himself as the one most qualified to lead the international Communist movement. This was hardly possible as long as China continued to follow the foreign policy framework established by the CPSU. China had therefore to assert itself within the international system with its own foreign policy and with its own ideas.

The fourth important catalyst was economic. China urgently needed such commodities as rubber, petroleum, iron and steel, non-ferrous metals, medicines, cotton and gunny sacks, all of which were unavailable from the Soviet Union and Eastern Europe. In addition, the over-ambitious and heavy-industry-orientated five-year plan (beginning on 1 January 1953), for which China was gearing up, required a wide degree of items and commodities which the other Communist countries would not be able to meet completely.[2] Thus some degree of economic interaction with Western countries was viewed as vital to meet not only China's immediate needs, but also long-term requirements.

The pattern of new policy

Presentation of the change was made in two ways: through declarations and through participation in four international conferences. Although all the declarations made or articles written or conversations held with non-Chinese made a point of underlining China's 'adherence to one side',[3] all of them, at the same time, announced Chinese willingness to interact with the non-Communist world. Admittedly, Chinese leaders had always shown such willingness previously, but after 1952 the tone was different: it was more repetitive, more moderate, more friendly and more insistent; so much so that the British representative in Beijing,

Humphrey Trevelyan, wrote to the British Foreign Secretary, Anthony Eden, on 31 August 1954:

> it seems to be in Chinese immediate interests not to embark on dangerous foreign adventures during the early period of industrialization and socialization, and not, by an appearance of aggressive intention, to run the risk of losing the confidence of neutralist Asian Governments and those elements in Western Europe and Japan which were inclined to believe in Chinese good faith.[4]

At the four multilateral conferences, held between 1952 and 1956, the new Chinese foreign policy became even more evident. The first such conference in which China decided to participate was the Moscow international economic conference in April 1952.

A large delegation—larger than the Soviet one—was sent to the economic gathering where more than 60 per cent of the 470 participants were businessmen from West European countries. Since this was the first major occasion for China to participate in a conference where so many West European businessmen were present, the Chinese delegation took a number of initiatives. The first was declaratory. On different occasions it made a point of expressing its willingness 'to establish connections and do business with trade, industrial and business interests in all countries that desire to trade with China',[5] at the same time making it quite clear that it had no intention of inveigling businessmen into promising to supply goods that fell under trade restrictions imposed by Western powers. Second, since at the conference 'more and more emphasis was laid on business contacts and trade deals', than on speeches and resolutions the Chinese delegation heavily used the secretariat of the conference to meet different business groups to explore concretely with them items which could really be exchanged without 'dangling a political bait'.[6] Some agreements were in fact concluded that involved 'huge sums of money'.[7] Third, the Chinese organized a fairly large exhibition of their industrial products and handicrafts at the Sovetskaya Hotel where many of the participants were staying.

The Moscow conference was thus important: it was at that gathering that the new Chinese objective of opening up to the outside world commercially emerged very clearly. It was in many ways a sign of the new Chinese realization that they could not build their socialist economy completely on their own or with the help of the Communist bloc countries. The conference thus inaugurated a process that was to be accelerated after the conclusion of the Korean armistice agreement in July 1953.

The second international conference—also non-governmental—in which China participated was the Asian and Pacific Peace Conference that was held in October 1952. Actually, it was hosted by China and held in Beijing. The Chinese behaviour at this international political gathering testified to the changes then taking place in China's foreign policy. At the conference—attended by political personalities generally known for their political moderation—China talked about peace and coexistence in a tone and language that was markedly different from the ones used during the first two years after the revolution.

Following the new Chinese stance, the conference sent a message to the United Nations appealing for measures 'to end the fighting in Vietnam, Malaya and other countries', and declaring that 'countries with different social systems and ways of life can coexist'.[8] Whatever may have been the Chinese motivations for hosting such a conference, the fact is that it was at this gathering that it became increasingly apparent that changes in China's policies were not limited to the commerical sector. New and more political orientations were also injected into China's foreign relations.

The real acceleration of relations with Western Europe began with the 1954 Geneva conference on Korea and Indo-China.[9] Clearly it was more important than the two preceding ones. For one thing, it was a high-powered ministerial level diplomatic gathering that was specially convened to negotiate solutions on two major Asian crises in which China was either directly or indirectly involved. For another, it was the first official meeting where China had to deal with Western countries with whom she either had no or only minimal diplomatic relations. The importance China attached to this meeting can be gauged from the fact that Zhou Enlai personally led a two-hundred-member Chinese delegation. Seizing this first opportunity to be present in an important West European city, the Chinese delegation systematically sought to establish—outside the framework of the conference—contact with West Europeans at the economic as well as at political levels.

That the contacts at the economic level were not accidental is evident from the fact that the vice foreign minister for foreign trade, Lei Jenmin, was attached to the delegation, who soon on arrival began to show interest in what China could buy and sell. Meetings were held with representatives of West European companies, with unofficial commercial delegations and sometimes even with leading political figures who were thought to carry weight in the economic sectors of their countries. Though much of the work was carried out by those in charge of the economic sector in the delegation, Zhou Enlai personally sat in on some of the meetings.

From the experience in Geneva, the Chinese delegation must have returned to Beijing with a great deal of precise information of what was available in Western Europe and what they could reasonably obtain without raising American objections.

Political contacts in Geneva

China's contacts with the West Europeans were not limited only to questions of trade; the Geneva conference also provided an excellent opportunity to develop political contacts. With the British an agreement was even reached on 17 June 1954 to send a Chinese chargé d'affaires to London,[10] undoubtedly an important step on the road to normalization of bilateral relations. It is interesting to note that China no longer insisted on the closing down of the British Consulate in Tamshui in Taiwan, previously a *sine quo non* for the establishment of relations—clearly a major concession. Accords were also reached in Geneva with the representatives of the Netherlands and Norway for the establishment of diplomatic relations.

The Geneva conference also provided an excellent opportunity for the inauguration of Sino-French talks.

The Chinese were apparently eager to maintain regular contact with the
French delegation outside the formalistic framework of the conference. The most
important was the one that took place on 23 June in Berne between Pierre
Mendès-France, newly invested as premier, and Zhou Enlai.

The bilateral Sino-French meetings, however, did not involve any exchanges
on bilateral relations. Zhou's strategy at the time was strictly to avoid any
discussion pertaining to relations between the two countries. Even when the
French foreign minister, Bidault, made some attempts to open talks regarding
technical assistance, Zhou did not follow them up.[11] Similar strategy was
followed with an unofficial French delegation that arrived in Geneva. When
Savary and Lacoste, members of the Socialist party, met Zhou in the middle of
June, he confined the entire discussion to Vietnam.[12]

Why is it that the Chinese shunned all discussions on bilateral political
relations with the French when they were not doing the same with other West
European countries? What weighed heavily in the adoption of such a selective
attitude?

For one thing, heavily involved as China was in the Vietnam war, it was hardly
feasible to discuss bilateral issues before the Vietnam problem was completely
settled to the satisfaction of all the contending parties, including of course the
Vietminh. This was apparently not on the cards at the time, since the convoluted
Geneva negotiations were moving towards a lame compromise whose successful
implementation, at best, was going to be problematic. Second, the Chinese were
not at all sure if France was politically ready to recognize the Beijing government.
Despite some left-wing pressure groups favouring recognition, the country as a
whole was not ready for such a major initiative. Besides, France's dependence on
the United States was indeed too great—more than Britain's—to permit the
French decision-makers to take an independent stand on China. Furthermore,
there was not much to gain on the economic front, since France—among the
major West European countries—was indeed too marginal and was expected to
remain so for some time to come.

In any event, the 1954 Geneva conference is a watershed in Chinese diplomacy
so far as Western Europe is concerned, for it was at that time that China had been
able to do the necessary ground work for establishing significant contacts with the
West Europeans. In many ways, this was perhaps the first major sign that the
Chinese were moving away from their original diplomatic stance of leaving
Western Europe to the Russians. More than three years of diplomatic experience,
principally limited to the socialist bloc, had apparently made them realize the
importance of acting independently even in Soviet spheres. One wonders if the
independent and outgoing diplomatic stance in Geneva was not a sign of a new
Chinese determination to project themselves as an equal of the Soviet Union on
the diplomatic front—particularly now that Stalin was no more, and that the new
Soviet leadership, involved in an intra-mural dispute, was having difficulty in
orchestrating a coherent foreign policy.

China's diplomatic role at Geneva was not at all marginal even though it was
not accepted by the great powers as an equal. If anything, China seemed to be

holding the 'key to peace in Southeast Asia';[13] at least this is what the West Europeans thought. Pierre Mendès-France, the new French prime minister, for example, met Zhou Enlai with the conviction that it was China and not the Soviet Union which was playing a 'decisive role' in the region. Great Britain, too, was on the same wavelength and did not see how a solution could be found to the conflicts in the Far East without an understanding with China. In fact, even at the time of the 1949 Chinese revolution, the British government had recognized the importance of China in the Far East.

It was perhaps this common Anglo–French perception about China and the overall situation in the region that led the two countries to collaborate closely in Geneva in order to find a solution to the Far Eastern impasse. This very important point was precisely stressed in a British weekly:

> One of the most encouraging features of Geneva was the team-work of Mr. Eden and M. Mendès-France. For the first time since 1940, the entente-cordiale is something more than a form of words. On the brink of a disaster, France at last found a leader who matched the hour. But it is fair to say that unless Mr. Eden in the first phase of the conference, had made the initial contacts with Mr Molotov and Mr. Zhou Enlai, and unless he had loyally supported the French Prime Minister last week in his final tussle with Mr. Dulles, the triumph of M. Mendès-France would have been impossible.[14]

Thus despite American efforts to reduce China's role at the conference, the general Anglo–French accord, compounded with the Chinese determination not to be marginalized, kept Beijing right in the centre in Geneva. In fact, Zhou Enlai pointedly expressed views not only on Korea and Vietnam but also on Berlin, and continued to insist that the Geneva conference was a five-power affair in which China was participating as an equal.[15] In any event, one thing is certain: without China there would have been no agreement in Geneva.

The Bandung conference of 1955 was of course very different from the Geneva conference. It was an Afro–Asian affair where all the independent countries of the two continents had clustered together to see if they could not reach some consensus on a wide spectrum of issues, despite the diversity in socio-economic systems and notwithstanding the different foreign policies they may have chosen to follow. Here too—as in Geneva—the Chinese delegation became the centre of attraction, and Zhou Enlai's friendly and remarkably moderate attitude testified to the changes that had been introduced in China's foreign policy.

Bandung must have quelled any lingering suspicions regarding the change in China's diplomatic posture; for even more than in Geneva, Zhou openly assured the conference that his desire was to be conciliatory and that his country wished to seek common ground with Asian countries. Sidestepping the frontal assaults from pro-Western delegations, who publicly attacked new communist imperialism, Zhou patiently worked to gain confidence, to extend the area of contacts with each of the states and to inspire trust in China's peaceful intentions. Even on the controversial question of Taiwan, the Chinese prime minister declared his readiness to enter into bilateral negotiations with the United States.

The four international conferences in which China had participated thus were a landmark in the new ongoing Chinese process of opening up to the outside world.

It had its small beginnings at Moscow where trade was the principal Chinese pre-occupation and finally climaxed into a full-fledged new diplomatic stance in Bandung.

Decisional process behind new policy

The question that one could raise at this point is the manner in which this particular decision to reorientate China's foreign policy was taken. Who made it and at what level? In sum, what was the Chinese decision-making process in the fifties?

Given China's closed and totalitarian system, only very tentative hypotheses can be proposed regarding the functioning of the decisional process. First, it is more than likely that a few years after the revolution most foreign policy decisions—whether 'high' or 'low'—were taken at the very upper echelons of the party leadership. The bureaucracy's role at the time could only have been minimal, since the Chinese hierarchical structures and totalitarian system left very little real leeway for it to voice its views. Second, according to some sources[16] the decision as to whether China should open up or not was a source of factional dispute within the party leadership, given that the operationalization of an outgoing policy would have unavoidably resulted in some degree of disengagement from the Soviet Union—undoubtedly an important decision. Third, the tilt in favour of a more open policy must have taken place only with the accord of Mao Zedong; for it is indeed difficult to imagine that so soon after the revolution such a major volte-face was conceivable without his implicit or explicit accord. Fourth, once the decision had been taken, the task of its implementation was assigned to Zhou Enlai, since China's foreign relations in the fifties were not that complicated or wide-ranging that they could not be handled by one person. Zhou was certainly not the real architect of China's new policy, but he was certainly its proponent who displayed a remarkable capacity for finally operationalizing it with great dexterity and finesse.

The effects of the new policy

China's new stance did have some effect on Sino-West European relations. They finally did open up, first of all in the economic sector—a sector to which China had given primordial attention; and a sector which generated less controversy among the Western powers; in sum, a sector in which the West European countries could afford to take some initiatives without seriously jeopardizing their relations with their transatlantic ally, the United States.

Private West European commercial initiatives

Different West European economic groups, who had conjured up visions of a vast and lucrative China, and who were apprehensive of being left out by their competitors, began to exercise severe pressures on their respective governments to respond promptly to China's new overtures. American opposition notwithstanding, this is what happened. Paradoxically, business groups belonging to West Germany were the first to respond. In most cases, they were 'old China hands' seeking to establish their businesses in the markets with which they had previous experience. Presenting themselves under the name of OSTAG (East inc.) they jointly concluded, during the Moscow conference, a skeleton agreement on 25 June 1952 for commodity trade of DM 150 million.[17]

France was the second to respond. After the initial contact made at the Moscow conference, a trade delegation of sixteen members went to China in June 1953 and concluded on 5 June a trade agreement of FF 10 million (new francs). Under the accord, France agreed to sell machinery, drugs and chemicals, while China undertook to sell agricultural products.[18] Considering that hitherto there was hardly any Sino-French trade to speak of, this was certainly an important development. The French were clearly concerned about competition and did not wish to 'let our rivals' get ahead of them.[19]

A British delegation of nineteen businessmen, including representatives of large and well-known firms, followed suit. Sponsored by the British Council for the Promotion of International Trade, on 6 July 1953 it concluded an important commercial accord that allowed an exchange of goods for £30 million.[20] These agreements, however, never got off the ground, for all of them—concluded unofficially—included items that had been embargoed by the fourteen nations (thirteen NATO members plus Japan) on the Paris Coordinating Committee (COCOM) whose principal responsibility was to formulate and apply a uniform list of items forbidden to the Communist countries, including China. The embargoed items were included in the agreements not so much because the contracting parties wanted to evade the COCOM regulations but out of ignorance of the exact items that were banned.

In any event, the whole process of commercial exchange was accelerated after the 1954 Geneva conference. Now that China had decided to take 'advantage of the contradictions between the various Western countries',[21] and had launched a real campaign to build up relations, almost all the West European governments began to show an interest in developing economic relations with China.

Interestingly enough West Germany—also established in 1949—became China's biggest trading partner in the fifties. Britain and France—despite their political contacts—found themselves in a much more inferior position. (See Table 2.1).

Although West Germany's economic interaction with China went through the same process as France and Great Britain of establishing contacts with the Chinese at Moscow and Geneva, West Germany had some distinct advantages. The first advantage was political. Having just emerged as a new state, and having no relations with Taiwan, the Federal Republic, unlike France and Great Britain, did not have any major political problem with China, certainly a distinct advantage since Beijing, at the time, did seem to attach a great deal of importance to political differences when taking economic decisions.

The second was geographical. China's main commercial mission for Western Europe was located in East Berlin. This made it easier for the Federal Republic to

Table 2.1 Trade between China and West Germany, Great Britain and France
(in US$ million)

	1954	1955	1956
West Germany	57.6	72.0	90.3
Great Britain	44.4	56.6	65.1
France	18.2	19.5	37.4

maintain regular contacts with Chinese officials, and to obtain rapid information regarding Chinese needs. The first direct contact, for example, dates back to the summer of 1952 when the chairman of the West German East Asia Association (founded by German firms interested in Asia) met the chairman of the China National Import and Export Corporation, Lu Xuchang.

The third advantage was institutional. Within the framework of the East Committee of the German Economy, established in October 1952, a 'China Working Party' had been.established in December 1952 which had the exclusive authority for maintaining and developing contact between West Germany and China. That such an institutionalized arrangement was indeed beneficial can be gauged from the fact that the British Council for the Promotion of International Trade, established in 1952, was boycotted by main industrial groups on the grounds that it was a Communist front organization. For almost two years, until the establishment of the official China Association in March 1954, Sino-British trade was seriously affected.

The fourth advantage was the wide network of pressure groups[22] which favoured trade with China—a network which had strong political support in the government as well as outside. The minister of transport in the Adenauer government, Hans Cristoph Seebohm, publicly declared his support for expanding trade with Beijing.[23] The president of the Senate of the city-state of Bremen, Wilhelm Kaisen, was even more outspoken. At a meeting of 700 West German businessmen in Hamburg on 13 March 1954 he underlined the fact that Germans, who had 'for centuries' close ties with the Far East, could contribute much to China's economic development. 'I do believe,' he concluded, 'that we Germans have not finished playing our role in China'.[24]

In any event, even if West Germany was reaping more benefits than other West European countries, the important fact, none the less, is that a fairly generalized Sino-West European interaction had been inaugurated for the first time since the revolution. And China, with this opening to the West, had indeed acquired some degree of autonomy from Soviet control.

American–West European commercial differences

The second major consequence of the new Chinese diplomacy was the emergence of differences between the United States and Europe regarding the commercial policy that the Western countries ought to follow *vis-à-vis* China. A severe embargo had been imposed on the export of strategic items to Communist countries, including China. The Paris Coordinating Committee (COCOM), established to monitor this embargo, substantially expanded the list of items after the declaration of the Korean War.[25] By September 1952, COCOM became even more restrictive on China, and a special committee (Chincom) was established to coordinate this stringent embargo. The disparity between the Soviet–East European list and the China list was known as the 'China differential'.[26]

When the Korean War ended, the trade controversy surfaced. Unlike the United States, the West European countries did not see any point in the continuation of more Draconian restrictions against China than against the other Communist countries. Secretary of State Dulles's argument that the 'Chinese Communist aggressive front extends from Korea in the north to Indo-China in the south' and that free trade would 'build up' China's 'war economy which might later be used against us' did not hold water for the West Europeans.[27] Great Britain was the first to object and was the first to decide unilaterally—after many vain discussions with the Americans—in May 1957 to abandon the differential between Soviet–East European and the Chinese lists.

Most of the West Europeans followed suit. France and West Germany, for example, abandoned the China differential in June 1957. The impact of these decisions was quite striking for notwithstanding John Forster Dulles's predictions against any increase, the trade did increase substantially. West Germany's trade rocketed to $162.3 million in 1958, while the French trade increased to $55.1 million and that of Great Britain to $125 million.[28] It is interesting to note that trade with China was the first major issue on which most West European countries distanced themselves from the United States and took the unilateral decision to drop the 'China differential' from their embargo lists.

The broad West European consensus to deal with China did not stem from the fact that they had identical perceptions regarding China, but was principally dictated by the fear of being left out of the competitive game of penetrating the Chinese market. The decision by the French and other West European governments to drop the China differential from their embargo lists soon after the British initiative was not the result of coordinated action but was probably a sign of concern of being excluded from the Chinese market should there be any delay in rapidly following the British.

American–West European political differences

The third major consequence was political. Differences also emerged between the United States and some West European states regarding their overall appreciation of the Far Eastern situation. While the United States called for a united Western stance to contain Communist 'expansionism' in the area, her two main West European allies, France and Great Britain, were more benign in their assessments.

Notwithstanding the increasing French dependence on the United States to contain the North Vietnamese onslaught on the South, the Mendès-France government had increasingly come to the conclusion that China was holding the 'key to peace'[29] in South-east Asia, and that a political solution for Indo-China was the only viable way out of a difficult situation.[30] Franco–American differences of opinion on Indo-China had become increasingly evident at the Geneva conference. There was hardly any major issue on which they could really agree and, despite American opposition, the final agreement on Indo-China was worked out closely by France and China.[31]

The British position were even more distant from the United States. Differences, in fact, had already emerged when London recognized the Chinese Communist government, when it recommended a more benign attitude towards China and when it finally came out in favour of a political solution in Indo-China. The dimension of Anglo–American differences became evident when Great Britain refused to accept American Secretary of State Dulles's assertions that China was determined to expand in South-east Asia. Although this had become clear even from the carefully phrased British declarations, the British government was more blatant in its confidential utterances. 'We are not greatly impressed', wrote the Foreign Office to the British Embassy in Washington in November 1954, 'by the five examples of China's "aggression" cited by Mr Dulles before the Foreign Relations Committee.'[32] The Foreign Office dispatch then systematically countered the examples Dulles had given to prove Chinese aggression. It did not agree that the 'free Siam movement' inside China was meant to 'stir up' trouble in Thailand, that the Communist forces had been doubled in North Vietnam since the Geneva conference, that two Laotian provinces were dominated by Communists, that 'very substantial military force' was maintained in Yunnan to undermine the non-Communist world, and that Communist activities in Singapore were growing.[33]

The new pattern of Chinese diplomacy had thus contributed in bringing out the differences among Western countries regarding the policies they sought to follow towards China. But it was by no means a breakthrough. Trade with Western Europe did increase, but within limits. Political differences did make their appearance, but they were not that wide. Besides, most of the West European nations, in the fifties, had very little leverage to pursue autonomous policies. In fact, they had none.

The only exception was Great Britain which had demonstrated that it could—Atlantic unity notwithstanding—take a more independent position than other West European countries on a wide spectrum of international issues, including China. For China, this was important. In fact, it was perceived as a very promising situation. Since China was heavily influenced by the Marxist framework, under which inter-state relations among capitalist countries are essentially contradictory, diplomatic initiatives in the direction of the most autonomous of them all could be beneficial.

Focal point—Great Britain

Seizing upon the Anglo–American contradictions within the capitalist world, China began to show a clear intent of focusing her diplomatic attention more on Great Britain than any other West European country. Under the circumstances, this seemed understandable for a number of reasons. First of all, England was the only major West European country that had recognized China, and had actually established a diplomatic presence in Beijing. This was done despite American opposition. Cultivating nations with which some relations already existed was of course much easier for China than for those with which none existed. Second, Britain in the fifties was much more autonomous in her Asian foreign policy than any country on the Continent. The new Federal Republic of Germany, established in 1949, was hardly in a position to formulate a foreign policy that would be different from the United States. The cold war, raging in the heart of Europe, left no leverage for her, least of all regarding the distant Far East about which the United States apparently had very strong views. France, although having some independent foreign policy perceptions, was hardly in a position to take an independent line on China, given its dependence on the United States on Vietnam. There were, of course, some neutral countries with whom China had developed relations, but there was not much to be done with them, considering their limited capacity to meet China's economic and political needs.

Third, Britain not only recognized China, but was favourably disposed towards cultivating Beijing (within limits), partly because of British interests in Hong Kong and partly because of Asian Commonwealth countries' pressures on Britain to adopt a benign line. This was confirmed by a discussion within the Foreign Office. Summarizing the discussion, the Foreign Office official wrote:

> In short our vulnerability in Hong Kong and the importance of keeping the sympathy of the New Commonwealth make it expedient to follow a reasonable conciliatory line in our dealings with China.[34]

The fourth reason was economic. Since 'the century-old myth of a lucrative China market had remained alive' among the British decision makers[35] and since Britain, despite the embargo against China, had 'tacitly allowed its businessmen to do business with China overtly or covertly with Hong Kong as their base',[36] for China it was important to focus attention on Great Britain. One of the very first signs of this special interest was the appearance of a large number of articles, comments and official declarations in the Chinese press in the summer of 1952, stressing the importance of expanding trade with Great Britain—more than with any other West European country. Jack Dribbon, the secretary of the British–China Friendship Association wrote an article to this effect for *People's China* in July 1952. 'China,' he argued, 'offers an ever-expanding market to Britain in trade on a basis of equality and mutual benefit'.[37] This, in his view, was the only viable way out for about 800,000 British men and women who were unemployed at the time. In the next month, an editorial in the same journal was even more categorical. Referring to Vice Foreign Minister Zhang Hanfu's July statement on Sino-British trade, it declared that 'the Chinese Government and people have now reiterated their willingness and readiness to develop trade relations with any British firm or their joint agent on the basis of equality and mutual benefit'.[38]

The proliferation of Chinese declarations in July–August of 1952 was clearly designed to slow down the virtual exodus of British businessmen who were moving out because of rampant restrictions on their activities imposed by the Chinese government on the grounds that business relations were neither equal nor beneficial to China. The Hong Kong and Shanghai Bank, which had a major presence in China, announced, for example, in March 1952 that it had decided to close down its offices in Hong Kong. The British-American Tobacco Company, another important company in China, reached an agreement in April 1952 with the Chinese government which allowed it to close its offices in the country. Many followed suit, particularly a large number of smaller firms. The overall situation had become so serious that the British representative in China informed the Chinese government that British companies had decided, because of the difficulties they faced there, to cease operations and to apply for the closure, custody, transfer or leasing of their businesses.

Most of these difficulties stemmed from the fact that the British companies operating in China were heavily involved in the Chinese economy through investments and through commercial activity that took place within China, whereas the Chinese Communist regime was solely interested in trading with Great Britain and in importing badly needed items.

Having drawn the line and established the broad framework for Sino-British economic relations, the whole process of a Chinese pattern for commercial interaction was accelerated, particularly at the Geneva conference. While the Chinese press became even more reiterative regarding the build-up of Sino-British trade,[39] a new dimension was added to the commercial exchanges—conducting talks with British political and bureaucratic personnel. The Chinese exchanges were not limited to the British businessmen, but were extended to include those who were involved with decision-making at the economic as well as at the political level. This new and more overtly political process was inaugurated at Geneva, where the difficulties that British businessmen faced was discussed in private talks between Zhou Enlai and Anthony Eden in the summer of 1954. A number of important British personalities subsequently arrived in Geneva to continue these discussions. The importance that the Chinese attached to this aspect of their activity in Geneva is evidenced by the fact that Zhou Enlai personally participated in some of the meetings. For example, the Chinese prime minister invited Harold Wilson, ex-president of the Board of Trade in the Attlee government, and Wilson Robson-Brown, a Conservative member of Parliament and well connected in British metallurgical circles. The first meeting was held with the Chinese vice trade minister, but in the second Zhou Enlai was personally present.[40] Another important visit to Geneva was that of Tennant, the overseas director of the Federation of British Industries. Seizing the occasion of this visit, the Chinese presented a detailed list of items that they would be interested in buying from England.

The British visits to Geneva were reciprocated by the arrival of the Chinese Delegation in London (28 June–14 July) led by two deputy directors of the China National Import and Export Corporation. The visit was a success in the sense that the delegation made important contacts, examined different possibilities for enlarging commerce and paved the way for reciprocal visits to China by British merchants and industrialists.

Chinese interest in trade with Britain can be discerned from an article by the Secretary General of the Chinese Committee for the Promotion of International Trade, Qi Zhaoting, who wrote an article entitled 'The Vast Possibilities of

Chinese–British Trade'. In it he reiterated the views expressed by the Chinese Trade Delegation that visited Britain: the trade between the two countries could well reach the figure of £80 million within a period of eighteen months. Listing all that China needed in the way of power plants, railways, construction of buildings etc., he wrote that China 'will be happy to greet the day when shipments of goods begin to flow freely between the two countries, helping to lessen undesirable international tensions and to foster peaceful coexistence among nations'.[41] But these highly ambitious figures were not reached. By 1957, they were only £27 million, roughly the same as in the late forties, but none the less considerably more than before World War II. The lack of any major breakthrough could be attributed to a number of factors. The first was an absence of confidence among major British business groups about dealing with China; having been made by the Beijing government to abandon their pre-revolutionary commercial and manufacturing interests within China. The second constraint was Chinese. The Chinese government did not wish to ask for credits; its policy at that time was to pay 'on the nail' for what they could afford to buy. And since their capacity was indeed very limited, the prospects for rapid and extensive commercial interaction were not considerable. But the most important factor was the strict embargo that had been imposed by the Western powers for trading with China—an embargo Britain had accepted for the sake of avoiding any major tension with her transatlantic partner.

At the diplomatic level, there was some breakthrough in Sino-British relations. The Chinese government, which had hitherto refused to send a representative to London, agreed to do so in Geneva. Huan Xiang, director of the European department of the Chinese Foreign Ministry, was sent as the Chinese chargé d'affaires. Undoubtedly this was a major decision, and clearly an important sign of the new policy that was being designed towards Great Britain. Equally important was the sudden Chinese decision—also after the Geneva conference—finally to accept Humphrey Trevelyan as the British chargé d'affaires in Beijing. The importance of the decision can be gauged from the fact that in July Trevelyan and his staff were issued with diplomatic cards instead of temporary passes.[42]

Another important sign of change in Chinese diplomatic behaviour was the invitation that was extended to the British Labour Party to send a delegation to China—a decision that was also taken after the Geneva conference. The importance of the Chinese change can be discerned from the fact that the Chinese dragged their feet for more than a year before sending the invitation.[43] The arrival in August 1954 of the high-powered delegation, led by Clement Attlee, was 'treated as a major event' with meetings arranged with important Chinese leaders, including Mao Zedong.[44] For the occasion, an editorial appeared in the *People's Daily* underlining that relations had indeed progressed since the Geneva conference and that further improvement was possible provided both countries sincerely observed the principle of peaceful co-existence.[45]

On the occasion of this visit, the Chinese attitude did undergo some change. Though still stressing the importance of expanding trade, there were some signs that China was now willing, albeit prudently, to expand its relations and give a more political content to the relationship. This new trend was confirmed by Zhou who in at least two of his speeches in the presence of the Labour Party delegation declared that it was 'necessary to increase friendship',[46] and that his government was 'ready to take steps to promote peaceful cooperation' between the two countries.[47]

This was undoubtedly a major decision, for there were indications that there was not complete unanimity within the party leadership,[48] and that the tilt in favour of politicalization of relations was probably managed by Mao Zedong. The British Foreign Office had suggested that the pro-Soviet lobby led by Liu Shaoqi opposed going too far with Britain, an important sign of which was Liu's refusal to meet Morgan Phillip, who was the secretary of the Labour Party and who had expressly asked to meet him.[49]

To push Sino-British relations on the non-economic front, Zhou personally took the initiative in proposing in very concrete terms the exchange of technical publications and the exchange of cultural delegations.[50] The British attitude to what was slowly becoming a new Chinese diplomatic stance was very prudent. In fact, it was frankly negative. While generally following a conciliatory line, a decision was taken that Britain must 'beware of carrying professions of friendliness to the point where we misguide our public opinion about our intentions or our pressure on the Americans to the point where they have doubts about where we really stand'. To Zhou's proposal to exchange technical publications and cultural visits—clearly innocuous proposals—the British answer was a clear 'no'. An internal Foreign Office response was that 'Her Majesty's Government should take no initiative to develop the exchange of publications.'[51]

Perhaps the most valid explanation for this reluctance to go beyond minimal relations was the British fear of harsh American reaction. Maintenance of some relations was viewed as important to please the Asian members of the Commonwealth and to maintain Britain's smooth presence in Hong Kong; on the other hand getting too close to the Chinese would displease Washington. So Britain finally chose what could be characterized as a balanced approach—neither too close nor too distant.

If one were to accept the hypothesis that the Chinese leadership was originally divided with regard to the warming up of Sino-British relations, lack of any meaningful headway probably led the CCP to backtrack from such a decision. It is no wonder that by the mid-fifties Chinese attacks on Great Britain were once again resumed in the Chinese press, leading the British representative in Beijing, O'Neil, to predict that, under the circumstances, Britain's relations with China could not 'be other than fundamentally difficult and bad'.[52] In fact this is what appears to have happened. Apart from exploiting the 'contradictions' that appeared to be rampant among the Western nations in the economic sector, China apparently lost all political interest in Western Europe in general and Great Britain in particular.

Conclusion

The Chinese process of opening up to Western Europe in the fifties had failed. Spanning approximately four years, it began in the economic sector and extended itself, lumberingly, to other areas. The Geneva Conference was a real landmark in this process; for the experience gained and contacts established at this high-powered diplomatic conference contributed to the diminution of Chinese 'prejudices and pre-conceptions' *vis-à-vis* the outside world,[53] and to the acceleration of the process in a more political direction. In the words of a British diplomat stationed in Beijing, the Geneva Conference 'came as a startling revelation to them to find that China could behave as a great power at an international conference and that it was possible to make sensible and practical arrangements with Western capitalist countries'.[54]

The failure of this policy can be attributed to two basic causes: since the Chinese leadership was divided on the question, it was really difficult to design a coherent and a clear-cut policy. The messages were not quite clear, the policies were not clearly formulated and uncertainty was rampant in most diplomatic initiatives. Though Zhou Enlai, the real architect of such a policy, clearly signalled China's intentions to develop economic relations with Western Europe, most of his declarations regarding political relations were obscure and contradictory. They invariably fell short of declaring that China wished to establish political relations. The second was the Western response. It was neither prompt nor clear. None of the West European countries were in a position to respond to Chinese overtures, given that the United States was openly against normalization of relations with China. Even Great Britain—the most autonomous of them all and with whom China most wished to interact—found itself constrained by the firm American position. Under such circumstances, the fate of such a policy was sealed. Neither the domestic nor the international situations were really propitious enough to make it work.

The failure of the half-hearted Chinese attempt finally contributed to the placing of the whole policy on the backburner and in the shifting of Chinese attention to Eastern Europe where the growing rumblings of discontent were finally escalating into a full-scale crisis in Hungary and Poland.

Chapter 3
Involvement in Eastern Europe

If the 1954 Geneva conference had permitted China to open a window to Western Europe, the 1956 East European upheavals pushed her 'to intervene decisively in the European theatre'.[1] The hitherto elusive policy of maintaining some distance was apparently no longer possible. In fact, the 1954 international conference and the ensuing East European events in 1956 were major landmarks for Chinese diplomacy, in so far as they had set in train a European connection from which there was no turning back.

A number of factors had contributed to the activation and the consolidation of this new trend. First of all, there was the surfacing of Sino-Soviet differences. A wide array of events in the socialist bloc, following the death of Stalin in 1953, had accentuated Chinese doubts regarding Khruschev's capability for giving a coherent lead to the international communist movement. Most of the initiatives taken by him to accelerate the process of de–Stalinization—dramatically highlighted at the Twentieth Soviet Party Congress—had confounded the international communist movement and had begun, for the first time, seriously to undermine the ideological authority of Moscow. More questions were asked than ever before, and maintenance of the old pattern of centralized socialist authority was becoming increasingly difficult. For the Chinese Communist Party this new trend in favour of the diffusion of power was certainly not in the interest of the movement. Whatever may have been its pretensions regarding its own future role in the international movement, at least in the mid-fifties, the Chinese Party strongly favoured the continuation of Moscow's leadership and the orchestration of a coherent international line.

Second, Khruschev's decision to visit India, Burma and Afghanistan in 1955 was, in Chinese eyes, an implicit abandonment of the original Sino-Soviet understanding of Chinese preponderance in Asia. According to one interpretation, Soviet activation in Asia was 'a demonstration against Chinese pretensions in Asia' and the serving of notice 'on Mao that Russia's interest in Asia was no less than China's and that he was not going to tolerate any division of the world into Communist spheres of influence'.[2]

This new Soviet determination to tamper with an original understanding probably freed the Chinese from any remaining inhibitions that they may have had about designing their own policies towards Europe. If the Soviets could formulate their own policies towards Asia, there was no reason why China could not do the same in Europe.

Third, the Polish crisis of June 1956 resulting in the return of Gomulka, the dissident party leader, probably was the decisive element that finally catalysed the Chinese leadership into taking a stance on Europe. It was one of those fluctuating and explosive situations on which they could not possibly afford to remain silent; they had to react, for any failure to respond promptly to critical situations within their own ideological orbit would have been tantamount to an abdication of responsibilities by a major Communist nation at a time when the whole socialist bloc appeared to be becoming rudderless with the rapid acceleration of de–Stalinization. Besides, responding to the Polish crisis actively was a clear response to the new globalization of Soviet foreign policy, and the continuation of the process of Chinese involvement in the European theatre that had already begun—though timidly—at the Geneva conference.

Chinese thinking in intra-bloc relations

The Chinese response to or involvement in Eastern Europe was at two levels. The first was the adoption of a public position on the broad ongoing debate regarding the emergence of centrifugal forces within the socialist bloc. The second level was the operationalization of the Chinese position *vis-à-vis* developments in Eastern Europe.[3]

The Chinese position was, first of all, publicly aired through an article that appeared in the *People's Daily* on 5 April 1956.[4] Although this article, 'based on discussions of an enlarged meeting of the Political Bureau', was a general response to the Soviet process of de–Stalinization, it also voiced the Chinese position on intra-bloc relations. The Chinese took a middle position on the debate that had surfaced. On one end of the spectrum was Togliatti who condemned Stalinist excesses and who argued for the establishment of 'a polycentric system' that would respect 'the full autonomy of the individual Communist parties and of bilateral relations between them'.[5]

This was an explicit call for the dethronement of the CPSU from the hegemonial position it had held within the international communist movement since the 1917 revolution and for the establishment of new arrangements in which all Communist parties would be equal.

The Soviets were against such a position. While they were apparently prepared to accept exceptionally the formula of 'equality and independence' in the case of Yugoslavia,[6] they were reluctant to extend it to other socialist states. For them there was no justification for any sweeping changes in intra-bloc relations. 'Ideological unanimity and fraternal solidarity of Marxist parties', in their view, was essential for safeguarding their independence.[7]

The Chinese took a middle position. On the one hand, they were reluctant to recognize Togliatti's new pattern of polycentrism, and still considered the CPSU as the centre of the international Communist movement but, on the other hand, they argued for the attribution of greater leeway to local Communist Parties in designing their own domestic policies. This distinction for the Chinese was indeed vital since it permitted Communist Parties themselves to decide what was best for them domestically, while maintaining the much-needed overall unity of the whole bloc internationally.

Such a formula accorded well with past Chinese policies, for this is what the CCP had consistently done during the entire Maoist phase before 1949. While designing its own independent domestic strategy—often in defiance of Moscow's edicts—it had faithfully followed the CPSU line on practically all major international issues. The clear-cut position that fixed limits on what was nationally permissible and internationally disallowed became increasingly evident in 1956 as China got involved in the East European crises.

The Polish crisis

The Polish crisis in the summer of 1956 gave the Chinese the necessary opportunity to apply this general consideration to the specific reality of the area. In fact it was Gomulka's ascendency that provided the appropriate opportunity. Apparently he was on the same wavelength as the PRC. While he professed utmost loyalty to the socialist camp, he demanded large autonomy in building socialism in Poland. Since the developments in Poland accorded with the Chinese formula on intra-bloc relations, the Chinese leadership encouraged the Poles 'to follow an autonomous internal policy and develop their own social system'.[8]

Mao Zedong personally 'showed sympathy for the Polish liberal faction and for Gomulka',[9] by writing a personal letter to the Polish Central Committee expressing his confidence in Gomulka.[10] And in a conversation with the Polish leader, Edward Ochab, during the latter's visit to Beijing in September 1956, he is reported to have declared: 'it seems that China and Poland have been keeping company for some time already without even knowing it. It is a good company and we are glad of it.'[11]

Chinese sympathetic response to Polish developments can also be discerned from the favourable press coverage of the eighth plenum of the Polish United Worker's Party held in October 1956. The very first despatch of *Xinhua* declared that many people in Poland 'spoke enthusiastically about' the event.[12] The *People's Daily* published the full text of Gomulka' speech, delivered at the 8th Plenum, obviously an important indicator of Chinese support of the Polish road to socialism.

The Chinese, however, did not limit their support to the publication of supportive articles about Poland. They apparently went much further in actually influencing the hesitating Soviets. When the crisis reached its zenith with the sudden arrival of Soviet leaders in Warsaw (Khrushchev, Molotov, Mikoyan and Bulganin), and with the parallel movement of Soviet troops, the Chinese reportedly advised Khrushchev against any armed intervention even if the Polish revolution 'got out of hand'.[13]

While most observers generally accept the fact that the Chinese had taken steps to dissuade the Soviets from committing 'the error of great power chauvinism',[14] apparently different versions exist regarding the exact nature of the Chinese intervention. While some suggest that a dissuading letter was handed to the Soviet leaders during their visit to Warsaw[15] by the Chinese embassy staff others seem to argue that Chinese pressures were exercised through Liu Shaoqi who was in Moscow at the time, and who was mandated by his party to express China's categorical opposition 'to the use of force to make the Poles submit'.[16]

In any event one thing is certain: the Soviets abandoned the idea of any intervention. Hesitant and divided as the Soviet leadership was, it informed the Poles that Soviet troops had been ordered to return to their base. Undoubtedly this was the first time that the Soviet leaders had jettisoned their plans of intervention in the face of Chinese intervention.[17]

The Hungarian crisis

If the Chinese dissuaded the Soviets from intervening in Poland, it was the other way round regarding Hungary: they persuaded them to go in. The Chinese, however, did not—as they subsequently suggested—oppose the Hungarian events right from the beginning.[18] At first, their evaluation of the events was analogous to the Polish crisis. They viewed them as renovative, and as an attempt to adapt socialism to Hungarian conditions. In fact, the Chinese ambassador in Budapest assured the Imre Nagy Government of his country's support.[19] According to some indications the Chinese were against the first Soviet intervention that took place during the night of 23–4 October and had abstained from characterizing the Hungarian events as counter-revolutionary. If anything, they had pressed for a Soviet withdrawal.

The favourable attitude towards the Hungarian events was, in fact confirmed through an official declaration made on 31 October. This major attempt to intervene in Eastern Europe (which was in prompt reply to a Soviet declaration of the same day) permitted the Chinese leaders to explain publicly their stance on the developments in the area. While applauding the new Soviet moderation, evident in its declaration, the Chinese seized the opportunity to criticize the Soviets for having neglected 'the principle of equality among nations in their mutual relations',[20] to underline the five principles of co-existence in the determination of relations among socialist countries[21] and to announce openly their support for the Polish and Hungarian demands 'for the strengthening of democracy, for independence and equality, and for the elevation of the standards of living as a result of the development of production'.[22]

But this open and publicly announced Chinese support was suddenly withdrawn. Paradoxically, this happened on the day the Soviets had moderated their attitude towards the events in Eastern Europe, and the day after the Chinese themselves had extended their support for Hungarian and Polish demands for greater autonomy.

The reason clearly was the rapid evolution of the Hungarian political situation over which nobody appeared to have any control. Presumably carried away by the rumblings of discontent, Imre Nagy, on 1 November, abolished one-party rule, formed a coalition government with some of the political parties and proclaimed the neutrality of his country by denouncing all obligations Hungary had under the Warsaw Pact.

For the Chinese, the rapidly changing Hungarian situation was unacceptable. It was no longer comparable to the Polish situation. For them, it was virtually an abandonment of Communist rule and a serious set-back to international Communist unity. Liberalizing Communist regimes and seeking legitimate internal autonomy was one thing, but destroying the hegemony of the Communist party internally, and opting out of the socialist bloc was completely another matter.

The Chinese thus changed rapidly; their evaluation of the Hungarian situation was no more what it had been a few hours earlier. First of all, the Chinese statement of 31 October, welcoming the Hungarian Revolution, was modified in later editions of the Chinese press. The *Xinhua* diffused a correction of its earlier declaration from which the words 'and Hungary' were simply removed. The corrected statement was printed the next day on 1 November.[23] Such an initiative on the part of the Chinese press clearly implied that the Chinese leadership was withdrawing its criticism of Soviet actions in Hungary.

In their subsequent statements, the Chinese made it a point to distinguish clearly between the Polish and Hungarian situations. The two events thereafter were considered 'different in character'.[24] While maintaining support of the Polish party's attempts to attain some degree of autonomy within the socialist system, China denounced Imre Nagy's decision to extricate Hungary from the socialist bloc. A Chinese publication of some importance underlined this point. 'The Polish and Hungarian events are following different paths. In Poland, the mass movement since the beginning is under the firm control of the party, the government and the revolutionary people. The imperialist conspiracy and counter-revolutionary elements cannot therefore manifest themselves. In Hungary, they could find an opportunity to stage a revolutionary "coup d'état"'.[25] In line with this new evaluation, the Chinese then took a series of informal diplomatic initiatives to persuade the Russians to take all 'necessary measures to smash the counter-revolutionary rebellion in Hungary'.[26]

The most important initiative was that of sending Liu Shaoqi to Moscow in a demonstration of active support of the Soviet Union to crush the Hungarian revolt. Presumably, he is the one who pushed the divided and hesitating Soviet leadership to intervene. When the Soviet troops finally quelled the Hungarian uprising on 4 November, the Chinese applauded the Soviet intervention as a 'brotherly help' and asserted that the Soviet Union had 'respected the territorial integrity and the sovereignty of the Hungarian People's Republic'.[27] The Soviet intervention, furthermore, was characterized as a 'glorious manifestation of proleterian internationalism. The importance of the great friendship of the Soviet Union for the peoples of the socialist countries of Eastern Europe has been gloriously proved once more in the Hungarian events'.[28] Zhou Enlai personally sent a 'message of congratulations' to Janos Kadar and announced China's 'material and financial aid of 30,000,000 roubles to Hungary'.[29] Mao Zedong too made a reference to Hungary. At the eleventh session of the Supreme State Conference he declared:

> deceived by domestic and foreign counter-revolutionaries, a section of people in Hungary made the mistake of resorting to acts of violence against the People's Government with the result that both the State and the people suffered. The damage done to the country's economy in a few weeks of rioting will take a long time to repair.[30]

The Chinese role in Eastern Europe

But were these actions—Soviet non-intervention in Poland and intervention in Hungary— really the result of Chinese firmness and behind-the-scene Chinese pressures? Was it through their efforts and their decisiveness that 'the prestige of the CPSU'—wobbling at the time—was finally safeguarded?[31] Or was it—as Soviet writers suggested—that during the Hungarian events the Chinese themselves were hesitant[32] or that they 'gambled on the difficulties within the international communist movement . . . in an effort to undermine the prestige of the CPSU and portray themselves as guardians of revolutionary traditions'.[33]

From the mountain of official writings that appeared after the explosion of the Sino-Soviet dispute, it is not possible to single out even the approximate truth. The multitude of explanations given by each side regarding the 1956 events and regarding their mutual relations at the time are too numerous, too contradictory and too vitriolic to permit an exact evaluation of the Chinese role in 1956.

However, some of the writings that have appeared in the West concerning the 1956 events do permit the advancement of some broad conclusions so far as China's role is concerned. But they are only hypothetical, since most of them are based on evidence that does not have the certitude of the archive material.

First, China was fairly consistent during 1956 events. Through their writings, declarations and reported conversations, they had designed a new and coherent framework for intra-bloc relations. To put it simply, they were in favour of the development of wide autonomy on domestic affairs, but were vehemently opposed to any action or initiative that would jeopardize the unity of the international Communist movement. Much damage, in the Chinese view, had already been caused to the movement by the hasty, uncoordinated and almost anarchical process of de–Stalinization inaugurated by the post-Stalinist Soviet leadership. Such initiatives, argued the Chinese, must be avoided in the interest of socialist unity.

Following this line of thinking, the Chinese leaders, therefore, favoured the enlargement of Polish autonomy, but came out against the Hungarian model of autonomy, once it became clear that it was jeopardizing the unity of the socialist bloc and the international Communist movement.

Second, by adopting such a clear line, China had enhanced her image and influence among East European countries. In fact, the Chinese position had elicited a general euphoria. Mao's pronouncements regarding non-antagonistic contradictions, and the general developments within China were given a large coverage by the East European media. According to one observer of the Polish press, 'since the time of the physiocrats no European country had displayed so much interest in Chinese affairs'.[34]

The Polish press particularly highlighted the democratic process that was developing in China and the vital importance of its emulation by other socialist countries.[35] In Hungary, the impact was even more palpable: Chinese revisionism actually strengthened the hands of anti-Stalinist intellectuals 'more than any other single influence'.[36]

Third, China's influence on the Soviet decisional process regarding the 1956 events was probably crucial. From all indications, it would seem that it was

Chinese pressures that contributed to dissuading the Soviet troops from intervening in Poland at the height of the Polish crisis on 19 October, and in
persuading the Soviets to withdraw their troops after the first intervention
in Hungary during the night of 23–4 October, and finally in pushing them to
intervene again on 3 November. The principal reason for this weighty Chinese
impact on the Soviet decisional process at the time can be attributed to the overall
situation within the Soviet and Chinese parties. While the CPSU in 1956 was still
plagued by succession problems, fratricidal disputes and dithering collective
leadership, the Chinese party at the time had none of these problems. Mao
Zedong, still at the helm, knew what he wanted and was able to carry the party
with him. Under such circumstances the Chinese party was able to have effective
sway over the CPSU, especially when one takes into account the important fact
that the Soviet party—at least at the time—was eager to consult the Chinese
party on most important issues pertaining to the international Communist
movement.[37]

Whatever may have been the nature and effectiveness of behind-the-scenes'
Chinese pressures, the indisputable fact is that the 1956 events impelled them to
appear forcefully on the European scene, and to play, for the first time, a major
role in East European affairs. And it was this role that probably emboldened the
party leadership to envisage an even greater participation in European affairs.
The editorial, published in the *People's Daily* on 29 December 1956, was the first
major sign of Chinese intention to intervene ideologically in the European
Communist movement after the twentieth Soviet party congress and after the
Hungarian and Polish crises. In this balanced and moderate declaration an
attempt was made to defend Stalin without papering over his excesses, to stretch
out a friendly hand to Yugoslavia without accepting its interpretation of the
Hungarian events and to appeal solemnly to the entire international communist
movement 'to strengthen international proleterian solidarity with the Soviet
Union as its centre' without forgetting to advise the Soviets 'to respect national
interest and sentiments of other socialist countries'.[38]

Zhou Enlai's visit to Moscow, Warsaw, Budapest and again Moscow in
January 1957 was the second major manifestation of the growing Chinese interest
in Eastern Europe.[39] The importance and the urgency of the visit can be gauged
from the fact that Zhou interrupted the Asian visit. The same balance between
international Communist solidarity under Soviet leadership and national interest
of socialist countries was reiterated throughout the trip. While stressing in
Moscow the importance of 'international proleterianism' and the meritorious role
played by the Russians in Hungary,[40] the Chinese prime minister made a point of
stressing in Warsaw that intra-bloc relations 'must be founded on the principle
of the respect of their sovereignty, non-interference in their internal affairs,
equality and mutual benefit'.[41] In Hungary, while condemning the 'reactionary
imperialist forces' and 'counter-revolutionary' elements 'who had exploited the
Hungarian situation', Zhou took account of the 'legitimate discontent of
the working masses and of the Hungarian youth due to the serious mistakes
of the former leaders'.[42]

The Polish Prime Minister Cyrankiewicz's visit to Beijing in April 1957 was
the third major manifestation of the ongoing Sino-East European interaction.

The joint communiqué, issued at the end of the visit, declared that the two parties 'are determined to continue their efforts to strengthen further the solidarity of the countries in the socialist camp based on Marxist–Leninist principles of proleterian internationalism and equality among nations'.[43]

China abandons her balanced policy

However, if a balance was studiously maintained between broad domestic leverages and international solidarity in Chinese declarations and policies, there were already in 1957, none the less, some signs of a tilt for an even greater centralist approach to bloc unity. Principal leaders were apparently getting increasingly concerned with growing signs of resurgent nationalism and revision-ism in Eastern Europe and even in the Soviet Union. The orthodox Communist leadership in the area was having difficulties in containing this expanding trend. The conservative lid was off and there was no way of putting it back. The Poles, under Gomulka's leadership, whom the Chinese had so far protected from Soviet onslaughts, were apparently getting out of hand. Despite all the friendliness they were showing, and all the gratitude they were manifesting for the Chinese, they were refusing any more to fall in line with the Chinese formula of maintaining a balance between domestic autonomy and international Communist solidarity under Soviet leadership. Though this was already discernible from Gomulka's different declarations, it became clearly evident during Zhou Enlai's Warsaw visit in January 1957. While the Chinese prime minister harped on Soviet primacy in the socialist bloc, the Poles highlighted the vital importance of local diversity; while he invariably ended his speeches with such set phrases as 'long live the unity of the socialist countries with USSR at their head', the Polish leaders made it a point to counter them by highlighting the different roads to socialism and by stressing equality of rights and friendship with all socialist countries.[44] The Chinese fear of dissident Polish behaviour was confirmed during Prime Minister Cyrankiewicz's April 1957 visit to Beijing, for he refused to accept the Chinese formula of Soviet leadership of the socialist camp.[45] Even behind-the-scenes' Chinese pressures were apparently useless in persuading Gomulka to fall in line. Attempts were also made by the Stalinist faction within the Polish party to invoke the Chinese objections to Gomulka's dissident behaviour.[46] But this too was of no avail, since Gomulka was apparently determined not to give in on the question.

The Chinese were indeed getting concerned about Gomulka's note of dissent, as they feared that it might have a spillover effect in other Eastern European countries. Mao Zedong personally gave vent to his irritation at Gomulka's apparent determination to go it alone. In a telephone conversation with Zhou in January 1957, who at the time was in Moscow, he stated:

to be a first secretary [of a Communist Party] is some kind of material gain which is liable to swell one's head. When a man's head gets swelled we have to give a good bawling out one way or the other. But we did not come straight to the point on every question. We did not play all our cards but kept some up our sleeves.[47]

Speaking about Khrushchev and Gomulka, Mao also stated 'we have had an eventful year in 1956. Internationally it was a year in which Khrushchev stirred up storms. It is still eventful now'.[48]

On the other hand, Gomulka, the Chinese realized, was a good ally. For it was he—much more than any other East European leader—who had often publicly hailed the Chinese leaders for their 'understanding', their 'support' and for their 'great boldness' in 'developing creative teachings of Marxism–Leninism'.[49] 'An expression of the great strength of the Communist Party of China and its close unity with the nation,' he declared at the ninth plenum of the Central Committee of the Polish United Worker's Party, 'is the introduction in this country of new methods in solving non-antagonistic contradictions. Similarly, the thesis about the hundred blossoming flowers is a bold step forward, so far unknown in the practice of socialist construction in other countries.'[50] Besides it was also Gomulka who often made it a point to persuade his East European counterparts to cite in joint communiqués Chinese successes on the same footing as that of the Soviet Union. At least in one case he was successful.[51]

The Chinese were thus faced with a searing dilemma: should they push a reluctant Gomulka to fall in line with their well-known formula of maintaining a balance between domestic autonomy for socialist countries and international Communist solidarity under Soviet leadership; or should they, in the face of the Polish opposition, jettison the principle for the sake of maintaining friendly relations with Poland—their principal friend in Eastern Europe at the time? The Chinese decided not to push Gomulka, and apparently satisfied themselves—at least in early 1957—with the more limited objective of persuading him to 'reserve the differences' he had with the Russians and to 'uphold our solidarity'.[52]

The Chinese were also increasingly getting concerned with Yugoslavia and the nature of her dissidence. This too contributed to the Chinese tilt in favour of more international Communist solidarity. The post-Stalinist Soviet attempts at normalization of relations with Yugoslavia in the mid-fifties, ran the Chinese argument, did not bring the Yugoslavs back into the Communist fold. If anything, it confirmed them in their conviction of the rightness of their independent policies. For, after all, was it not the successful Yugoslav defiance of Moscow that had led the Soviet leaders to accept the equal validity of Yugoslav susceptibilities on a wide array of international issues, including Eastern Europe?

Independent Yugoslav policies had thus paid off, and there was no rational reason for her to backtrack from such a position. Besides, in her search for allies and friends, Yugoslavia was, at the time, in the process of designing a prestigious policy of non-alignment; and any initiative on her part to move closer to the socialist bloc would have been counterproductive.

Though the Chinese had welcomed Soviet–Yugoslav *rapprochement*, they were none the less becoming concerned about the advantages Tito was reaping from such a position and the liberties he had begun to take to assert even more forcefully his independence from the socialist bloc.

Tito's speech at Pula (11 November 1956), for the CCP, was a case in point. On this occasion, he had severely attacked 'those hard bitten Stalinist elements' who were maintaining themselves in 'their posts in Eastern Europe'.[53] Edward Kardelj had gone even further: he had specifically attacked the Kadar Government (7 December 1956) for having dissolved the Workers' Council in Budapest and elsewhere in Hungary, instead of seeking to cooperate with it.[54]

The pattern of Chinese reaction to the persistence of Yugoslav dissidence was initially cautious. At first, the *People's Daily* reproduced important passages of Tito's Pula speech.[55] At the same time and in the same issue it published hostile reactions of other Communist parties to this speech, and summarized the Yugoslav journal, *Borba*'s rebuttal of these attacks.[56]

This technique of faithfully reproducing texts or their summaries of opposite viewpoints without any comment was the Chinese way of being objective. But, on the other hand, the publication of myriad negative reactions to Yugoslav declarations was the Chinese way of highlighting the weaknesses in Yugoslav thinking.

The general surge of revisionism within the East European ruling parties was the third important reason for the Chinese decision to opt for a more strict line in intra-bloc policy. Internal party discipline had become lax, demands for greater autonomy from Moscow became more persistent, and a process of lively exchange of views took place among East European Marxist intellectuals in the course of which even the tenets of Marxism–Leninism were questioned. Leszek Kolakowski, for example, a former Stalinist ideologue and a gifted young scholar of philosophy, attacked the dogmatization of Marxism and demanded that the party abstain from interfering in scientific and intellectual pursuits. Wolfgang Harich, an East German philosopher, expressed concern over the inability of Marxism to adapt itself to specific national conditions.

To China's alarm even the Soviet leaders had begun to reconcile themselves to the idea of a political let-up, and to the introduction of some degree of autonomy, with a greater reliance on the community of economic relations, in order to maintain unity within the Communist bloc. Leading members of the conservative 'anti- party' group favouring a more strict line, were summarily removed in the Soviet Union.

Compounded with all this was the rapidly changing political situation within China. The 'blooming and contending movement', officially authorized in May 1956 under the influence of the twentieth Soviet Party Congress, generated a multi-dimensional process of open beration of the Chinese leaders, the CCP and the socialist system itself. Though much of the discontent was the manifestation of domestic pent up forces—a phenomenon rampant in most authoritarian societies—the parallel East European explosion must have contributed to the aggravation of the events in China. The spillover effect of the Polish and Hungarian events was unavoidable since the Chinese leaders themselves had approved of the Polish upheaval, and since the Chinese press had blown the lid off the events in the two countries.[57] The measure of the impact can be gauged by the establishment of the so-called 'Petofi clubs'—modelled after the Hungarian associations for free discussion—in a number of Chinese universities.[58] Strikes too were staged by workers and students 'in certain places'.[59] Mao is personally reported to have admitted in 1959 the close connection that existed between developments in Eastern Europe and China in 1956–7.[60]

It was these rumblings of discontent within the country, and the difficult economic situation China was facing that generated a debate at the upper echelons of the party. What should China do in the light of the growing economic and political difficulties? And where did things go wrong? And who is responsible?

It is now generally established that it was this internal debate that finally brought out all the grievances that the conservative wing of the party had regarding the liberal policies pursued in China.[61] The blame was laid squarely on the shoulders of those Chinese leaders who had liberalized the internal political system, and who—being at the helm of affairs—had introduced pragmatic policies in the economic sector which had slowed down the pace of economic development. The left wing of the party came out the winner of the debate in the summer and autumn of 1957. It was the combination of all these elements (external and domestic)—including the return of the left wing to the helm—that finally resulted in the review of Chinese domestic and external policies.

Internally, the 'blooming and contending movement' was abruptly ended. Dissident elements within and outside the party were not only severely reprimanded in the press, but were summarily deprived of their positions. In the economic sector, it was decided 'to hasten the tempo of construction by adopting a policy of industry and thrift in order to move it forward with gigantic and rapid strides'.[62]

Externally the delicate balance establishing support for the autonomy of Socialist countries and the collateral maintenance of socialist bloc unity under Soviet leadership was abandoned. From then on, it was only international solidarity that really counted for the Chinese. Although, signs of this tilt, as we have seen above, were already evident in Beijing, the new policy was really inaugurated with Mao's arrival in Moscow to attend the fortieth anniversary of the Bolshevik revolution to attend a meeting of the Communist countries—a meeting, according to one source, that was originally proposed by the Chinese.[63] The occasion was ideal for the proclamation of such a policy, since all the chiefs of the international Communist movement were present.

Three components of China's policy

There were three broad components of the new Chinese line so far as Eastern Europe was concerned. The first was to isolate Yugoslavia which had refused to fall in line with the heavily Chinese-influenced proposal that the socialist bloc unity, under the circumstances, was more important and more urgent than all attempts to recognize the autonomous power of each socialist country. Since Yugoslavia had refused to sign the 1957 Moscow declaration, which embodied this thinking, for the Chinese it was essential to isolate the Yugoslavs in order to limit the contagion of dissidence and revisionism. First of all they withdrew their ambassador in September 1958. They then abandoned their policy of holding back on attacking Yugoslavia, or using restraint in their criticisms. In a series of widely diffused articles, the CCP publicly denounced the Yugoslavs for having refused to sign the 1957 declaration of the representatives of the Communist and workers' party, and for 'venomously' attacking 'the proleterian dictatorship in the Soviet Union and other socialist countries'.[64]

The main thrust of the Chinese attacks was, however, on the link that Yugoslavia had developed with 'imperialist reactionaries'. This was a telling argument, for nothing, at the time, was more damaging to the prestige and image of a communist party than the argument that it had gone over to the other camp. And this is what the Chinese tried to to—destroy Yugoslavia's credibility in the international sector.

Typical of this line of argument, for example, was the resolution adopted on 23 May 1958 by the CCP's second session at the eighth national congress. 'The leading group of the league of Communists of Yugoslavia', it declared, 'claim to be standing outside the socialist camp and the imperialist camp. In fact this is not so; they have always directed the spearhead of their attack against the socialist camp headed by the Soviet Union, but have not cared to touch U.S. imperialism in the least.' 'If anything', argued the resolution, Yugoslavia 'caters to the policy of the imperialists headed by the United States against Communism, against the Soviet Union and the socialist camp. That is why it is applauded and rewarded by the U.S. imperialists'.[65]

Every occasion thereafter was used to discredit the Yugoslav Communist League. The dimension of the venomous campaign can be gauged from the fact that by the end of 1958, as many as 175 anti-Yugoslav articles and speeches appeared in the Chinese press.[66]

The second component of the new policy was to persuade the other revisionists in Eastern Europe to fall in line with the Chinese argument that socialist bloc unity must be maintained. Paradoxically, the Polish party under Gomulka was perhaps most resistent to this idea. The CCP, therefore, abandoned its policy of mildly trying to persuade the Poles to 'resolve their differences' with the Russians,[67] and began to push Gomulka to accept the new line. Apparently they tried everything: informal arm-twisting directly on Gomulka,[68] covert encouragement of Stalinists to question Gomulka's policies at high-level party meetings[69] and finally even direct and open denunciation of Gomulka and his supporters for their 'softness towards Titoist revisionists'.[70]

The third component of this policy was the Chinese decision increasingly to interact directly with East European countries. In many ways, this contradicted the Chinese insistence that only Moscow was the leader of the socialist bloc; for designing their own autonomous policy—howsoever pro-Soviet it might have been—in an area directly under Soviet influence was an implicit indication that the Chinese wanted to have their own policy towards Eastern Europe.

The East Europeans were not against such a line, since it gave them a larger leeway *vis-à-vis* the Russians. Furthermore, most of the East European leaders still were Stalinist in orientation, and considered direct Sino-East European interaction as one sure way of protecting themselves against any Soviet attempt to de-throne them. A large consensus, thus, existed on both sides to expand Sino-East European relations.

Chinese breakthrough in 1958

The Chinese finally did succeed in making a significant breakthrough in Eastern Europe. Independently of Moscow, they were able to establish a wide spectrum of interaction and exchanges; at the same time they were able to generate considerable interest in China's foreign policy and in China's developmental model among the East Europeans.

The number of Sino-East European exchanges—always a good barometer— had increased significantly. In 1958, 150 delegations from Poland, Czechoslovakia, Bulgaria, Hungary and Albania visited China, while 105 Chinese delegations went to Eastern Europe.[71] Trade also increased significantly. In fact, it reached the $670 million mark in 1958—the highest figure China had ever reached since the revolution and which remained the peak for years afterwards (see Table 3.1). The number of non-political accords that China had concluded with East European countries in 1958 and the first half of 1959 in cultural, technical and economic sectors had also reached its optimal point.[72]

Table 3.1 China's trade with East European countries (minus Yugoslavia) 1950–60 (in US$ million)

Year	Total	China's imports	China's exports
1950	20	5	15
1951	205	65	140
1952	320	155	165
1953	340	190	150
1954	370	240	130
1955	435	235	200
1956	465	265	200
1957	500	275	225
1958	670	410	260
1959	655	325	330
1960	640	340	300

Source: Joint Economic Committee, *An Economic Profile of Mainland China*, Vol 2, Washington, February 1967, p. 594.

In the foreign policy sector, too, Eastern Europe followed China on a wide spectrum of issues. The press and the party leadership supported Beijing in its criticism of Yugoslavia, expressed their prudent reservations about Khrushchev's proposal for a summit meeting on the Middle East (Soviet Union, the United States, Great Britain, France and India) without China, and openly supported China on Quemoy in 1958, despite Soviet reservations regarding the way the Chinese were handling the crisis.[73]

However, by far the most significant facet of the new budding relationship was the favourable East European reaction to Mao's Great Leap Forward. The East

European press published many stories about the wonders of the Chinese communes, and about the importance of emulating them in Eastern Europe.[74] Even the Bulgarian Communists—traditionally close to Moscow—were carried away by this euphoria for China. Fifteen collective farms were in fact merged on the lines of the Chinese communes, and the Bulgarian Communist Party organ, *Robotnichesko Delo*, proclaimed that 'in our country collective farms would be amalgamated on the Chinese model'.[75] Volko Chervenkov, the deputy prime minister, went even further and praised the communes as an 'example' for all countries 'for quick transition to Communism'.[76] Todor Zhivkov, first secretary of the Bulgarian party, officially announced that his country would follow in the Chinese footsteps and fulfil Bulgaria's Third Five-Year Plan 'in three to four years' and that Bulgaria would make a 'Great Leap Forward' in which every year would be equivalent to several years of development.[77]

Similar eulogies of the Chinese model of development were also discernible in the press of other East European countries. The Hungarian newspaper *Nepszabadsag* wrote that 'since the socialist camp has come into existence, the world has seen an unprecedented development in the history of mankind. But China's development surpasses our dream'.[78] The Polish newspaper *Trybuna Ludu* published a speech delivered by Stefan Jedrychowski, a member of the Politburo of the United Worker's Party, praising the Chinese communes. It quoted him as saying:

> the Chinese People's Republic can be proud of its glorious achievements in the field of production increase. The decisive importance of these successes was the process of rapid socialization of China's agriculture . . . which led to the establishment of 740,000 production collectives which were, in turn, transformed into a new type of social ownership—26,000 people's communes.[79]

Similar uncritical adulations were also discernible in East Germany and Czechoslovakia.[80]

Soviet reaction

The Soviet Union became concerned with this direct Chinese intrusion in Eastern Europe and the generally favourable reaction in the area to internal Chinese developments. The Soviet leaders began to wonder if it was in their interest to allow the Chinese to develop unabated their own independent influence in the Soviet backyard and if the continuation of this trend would not finally prove disastrous for Soviet foreign policy.

The first sign of this concern was the hesitations that became increasingly discernible among Soviet leaders regarding their own policy towards Yugoslavia. They began to wonder if they really did the right thing in following the Chinese in criticising the Yugoslavs, and if it were not, in the final analysis, counter-productive to Soviet interests. For one thing, this policy had really not paid off; Yugoslavia was not isolated. If anything, her relations with the outside world had continued to grow. For another, a continuation of such an attitude of harassment, the Soviets feared, might well undermine the new outgoing Soviet policy towards the non-aligned world, since Yugoslavia was part of this group and had successfully established firm bridges with India, Indonesia and Egypt—the very countries with whom Moscow was developing relations.

The Chinese intrusion was also worrying the Soviets since many of the East European countries had—as we have seen—begun to look up to the Chinese. Particularly worrisome, of course, was the implicit rejection of the Soviet model of socialism. The 'last straw', in the words of Khrushchev, was the positive Bulgarian reaction to the Chinese model.[81]

The Soviets decided to counter the Chinese. They could not possibly afford to have the chasm between them and the Yugoslavs grow any wider, nor could they possibly permit the Chinese to develop a significant political and ideological presence in what was clearly perceived as a Soviet backyard. The Chinese policies and even pressures regarding Eastern Europe during the earlier period (1956 and 1957) were acceptable to the Soviets, since they were being 'more royalist than the king' in so far as they were insisting that Moscow was the leader of the international communist movement. But, after 1958, it was different. China had begun to show clear signs of fending for herself and of having her own policies independent of the Soviet Union.

For Khrushchev, it was possible to counter the Chinese in 1958 since the orthodox Stalinist faction within the Soviet party had been effectively isolated, with most of the leaders out of power by June 1957.

A new policy was activated whose first component was the introduction of some moderation in Soviet policy towards Yugoslavia. This became evident in June 1958 at the fifth congress of the Socialist Unity Party of the German Democratic Republic where Khrushchev took a more benign attitude towards the Yugoslavs. The contrast between the vitriolic attacks by the Chinese and the low-key criticisms by the Soviets was indeed very striking. While being critical of Yugoslav policies, Khrushchev rejected the Chinese denunciation of Tito as a 'traitor and imperialist agent' and referred to the Yugoslav leader as 'comrade Tito'. He also declared that it would be 'wrong' to exaggerate the present differences between the Yugoslav and Soviet parties.[82] This party congress thus was the starting point of a new Soviet attempt once again to promote Soviet–Yugoslav reconciliation—a reconciliation under which Yugoslav non-alignment and Yugoslav specificity was finally accepted, never to be challenged again.

At the same time, Moscow also initiated a campaign to counter the Chinese attempts to influence Eastern Europe ideologically. This was done at two levels. The first was at the bilateral level through discussions with East European leaders. They were informed that the Chinese 'method of organization of agriculture was ill-suited' to their countries.[83] Parallel to this bilateral approach, the Soviet leaders—for the first time—began openly to express critical views regarding the Chinese people's communes. The first specific criticism of the Chinese communes was made by Khrushchev on 1 December 1958 when he told the American senator, Hubert Humphrey, that the egalitarian aspect of the commune would not work.[84] Thereafter, the criticism became more pointed and the attacks more specific. In fact, soon after the meeting with Humphrey, Khrushchev simply called the communes 'old fashioned' and 'reactionary'.[85]

Eastern Europe follows Moscow

In the face of the new Soviet determination to contain China, the East European client states were left with no option but to follow Moscow. Some degree of leverage and some degree of autonomous thinking was possible as long as the Soviets themselves were hesitating, and as long as—which was the case in the mid-fifties—China had some influence over the Soviet leaders. After 1958, this was no longer the case. The so-called 'anti-party' group had been removed from power, and the Soviet leadership had begun to show clear signs of concern about the increasing Chinese impact on Eastern Europe.

The situation in Eastern Europe was itself changing. Political control by the Stalinists was declining, and the emerging revisionist groups were apparently not enchanted with the Chinese pressures to radicalize domestic and international politics. Whereas, the 1956 Chinese call for greater diversity and greater equality responded to the aspirations of the small socialist states, the fiery 1958 declarations, favouring a general tightening up of the socialist bloc, were not only tantamount to abandoning the process of increasing autonomy already underway in Eastern Europe, but were a direct contradiction of the East European objective of greater autonomy and greater liberalization.

In effect, China was swimming against the rising tide of revisionism; and as she had neither the military clout nor the economic power to neutralize the disadvantage of preaching unpopular causes, the goodwill she had built up in Eastern Europe in 1956 was seriously eroded by 1959. Eastern Europe then began to follow the Soviet lead. The press, for example, became highly critical of Stalin, and began to muffle criticism of Yugoslavia. Also it gave wide publicity to China's agricultural débâcle.[86]

Albania and Romania were the exceptions to this fairly generalized East European submission. For different reasons, and in different ways, both of them successfully defied Moscow, though one more openly (Albania) than the other. Albania blatantly refused to fall in line with the new Soviet determination to call the shots, and to weed out the growing Chinese influence in the area. And the Soviet decision once again to bury the hatchet with Belgrade made Tirana even more defiant. Though Moscow–Tirana tensions were already building up after the Soviet inauguration of a new and more liberal ideological line at the twentieth Soviet party congress, they took a serious turn with Khrushchev's Albanian visit in May 1959, and finally burst out in the open at the Romanian party congress in June 1960 where Albania refused to side with Moscow and the East European parties against Beijing.

For Albania, China, under the circumstances, appeared to be the only Communist country with whom close ties could be forged. For one thing, the CCP increasingly appeared to be on the same ideological wavelength and had the same rigid bipolar view regarding the configuration of international forces as Albania. For another—and this too was important—China had become the most ferocious opponent of Yugoslav 'revisionism' among the Communist countries. But, it would be an exaggeration to suggest that already in the late fifties, Sino-Albania relations had suddenly become warm or mutual understanding had rapidly been reached on a wide spectrum of issues. The process of Sino-Albanian *entente* had just begun, and it really took off only a few years later in the early sixties with the explosion of the Sino-Soviet dispute.

Romania was the other exception. A traditional Russophobia, compounded with irredentist longing for the recovery of Bessarabia, had generated a Romanian desideratum to become as autonomous from Moscow as was possible geopolitically. A slow process had already begun after Stalin's death with the mounting pressures for Soviet troop withdrawal, with obvious Romanian reluctance, to accept Khrushchev's idea of accelerated economic integration through CMEA and finally with the Romanian decision to avoid taking sides in the rapidly developing Sino-Soviet dispute. Signs of all this were already evident in 1954, but became more notable after the Soviet troop withdrawal in 1958. But the pattern of Sino-Romanian relations was very different from that of Albania. Whereas, with Albania they were ideologically tinged, with Romania they were more diplomatic, though the ideological dimension was not totally absent.

Thus China's first major and autonomous intrusion in Eastern Europe ended in dismal failure. Although, by 1959 her isolation from the area was significant, it became very generalized after the 1960 Moscow conference of Communist parties, and after the 1962 Bulgarian, Hungarian, Czechoslovak and Italian Communist party congresses.

Internal struggle for power

This growing isolation from Eastern Europe coincided with dramatic internal developments. For the first time since the revolution, Mao's authority had been seriously challenged. The so called 'struggle between the two lines' had finally resulted in his being ousted from the post of president of the Republic and the emergence of Liu Shaoqi and Deng Xiaoping as the new frontline leaders. But this important domestic change did not generate any corresponding change in China's external policies. No attempt even was made by those who were now formally at the helm to reverse the process that had isolated China from Eastern Europe and was pushing her towards a head-on collision with Moscow.

The reversal of such a policy would have brought the new frontline leaders into open conflict with Mao, who was the principal architect of China's foreign policy, and who was apparently determined to continue in the same direction so far as Eastern Europe and the Soviet Union were concerned. This the new leaders wished to avoid at any cost, given Mao's stature, charisma and even power within the country.

In fact, it is interesting to note that the Chinese leaders had prudently avoided direct confrontation even when they were changing domestic policies. Both Liu and Deng were indeed very careful to avoid the mistake Peng Dehuai had made earlier—the mistake of openly throwing down the gauntlet at Mao and finally paying for it dearly. Liu and Deng were discreet. While designing new liberal agricultural policies to remedy the damage that Maoist policies had inflicted on Chinese agriculture, they carefully acted—unlike Peng—within the norms so as not to give the impression that the whole agricultural policy was being changed. In fact, the changes that were announced did not contain even a hint of criticism of Mao Zedong, the architect of rejected policy. On the contrary, they hailed his new demonstrated wisdom. The general epithet 'the king is dead, long live the king' that underlined continuity was rephrased in China to 'Mao has failed, long live Mao'.

In the foreign-policy sector, the frontline leaders had to be doubly careful. The risks of a real confrontation were even greater. First, Mao apparently had very firm views regarding the broad direction that China should take with foreign policy; and any note of dissent on the subject would have brought them on a collision course with Mao—a prospect none of them wished to entertain. Prudently defying him in economic matters was one thing, since Mao himself was prepared to admit his errors, but challenging him on international issues was another matter since Mao had firmly and irrevocably decided to defy the Soviet Union. Besides, the Soviet Union was a sensitive issue on which the country had already been rallied; and any expression of dissenting opinion could make them easy targets of attack. The tragic fate of Peng Dehuai was too fresh in their minds. Although his opposition to Maoist agricultural policy may have contributed to his downfall, the decisive element probably was the charge of pro-Sovietism with which he was tagged.

Second, since China had already gone pretty far in her defiance of Moscow, it was indeed very difficult to retreat from that well-established position, short of giving in to the Soviet Union which no one—not even the opposition—was prepared to do. It was, therefore, not worthwhile to make an issue out of the existing state of Sino-Soviet relations. In this connection, it is important to note that when the importance of maintaining unity on international affairs was invoked, even Peng Dehuai began to have second thoughts regarding his own position in Lushan. In his memoirs he wrote:

> I also took the fact that our Central Committee was boldly speaking out against imperialism and modern revisionism and actively supported the democratic and national liberation movements in the international arena. And if the authority of the CPC Central Committee, headed by Mao Zedong, were damaged, that would do even greater harm to the international proletarian movement. Having thought that over I began to doubt my earlier line in insisting on my point of view.[87]

Third, it is not even clear if—with the exception of Peng—there was any division within the Chinese leadership regarding Mao's policy towards the Soviet Union and Eastern Europe. Without the archival material, it is indeed very difficult to advance this hypothesis with any certainty. There was probably none or, if any, very little. In any event, Mao had a free hand with China's foreign policy. No one was willing to cross swords with him on a policy that had already been designed and implemented, the code word of which was 'anti-Sovietism'.

Conclusions

The year 1956 was thus a major landmark in China's European policy. The Hungarian and Polish upheavals had catapulted China on to the East European political scene. For the first time since 1949, China was no longer a spectator or a distant friend passively watching developments, but was sucked into the East European maelstrom in different successive roles.

Initially China appeared as a friendly mediator, then as a leader wanting to give direction to a region that was increasingly becoming rudderless, thereafter as a struggling helmsman striving to maintain influence, and finally as an ideological purist combating 'revisionism', but slowly losing out to the Soviet Union.

The rise and fall of Chinese influence in the short span of three years can be attributed to two causes: the first was the Soviet factor. The Chinese developed meaningful influence only when the Soviet leadership was dithering, and only when it tolerated a Chinese presence; but when the Soviet leadership became more coherent and more determined to assert itself, Beijing could hardly maintain any influence in the area. It was condemned to decline. The primordial Soviet influence was hardly challengeable.

The second factor was the different political options taken by China and Eastern Europe. In fact, by the late fifties, they were moving in opposite directions. As China was moving more and more to the left, radicalizing her policies, Eastern Europe was moving in the opposite direction—towards greater liberalization and more openness. The common ground that had brought the two closer to each other had disappeared. The return of Liu Shaoqi and Deng Xiaoping at the helm of Chinese affairs in the early sixties could have halted this widening gap, but this was hardly feasible since the Liu–Deng leadership had decided to focus mainly on internal affairs and to avoid any challenge to the apparent Maoist determination to collide with the Soviet Union.

Thus, with the exception of Sino-Albanian relations that maintained an upbeat rhythm and the Sino-Romanian relations that continued to advance on an even keel, China became isolated from Eastern Europe by the early sixties. All the influence and all the goodwill that had been carefully established with effect from 1956 had evaporated by the early sixties.

Chapter 4
The process of perceptual change

China's failure in Eastern Europe slackened her interest in the area. Although the Chinese press was awash with denunciatory articles or declarations against the five CMEA countries (plus Yugoslavia) in the first half of the sixties, in real operational terms she had lost all interest. There was no policy, no real strategy and no real goal to speak of. Everything had been reduced to ideologically flavoured declarations against all of them.

The Chinese leaders had probably realized that there was not much they could do in the area. Moscow had re-asserted its authority, and it was indeed pointless to take any major diplomatic initiatives. The only way out would have been the formulation of a pragmatic and an ideologically free policy, but this was hardly feasible at the time when Beijing was increasingly getting locked in an ideological battle with Moscow. It could hardly berate the Soviet leaders for being revisionist, while glossing over the revisionism of East European countries.

Loss of interest in Eastern Europe resulted in an increase of interest in Western Europe—an interest that had already emerged in 1954, but put aside when China became involved in Eastern Europe in 1956. Initially it grew slowly and discreetly, but finally it flowered into something really significant. Interestingly enough, China did not allow this new interest to be hamstrung by ideological considerations. Despite the generally avowed role of ideological factors in China's formal foreign-policy declarations, there was a remarkable flexibility which took into account a wide spectrum of factors such as balance of power, national interest, economic motivations, etc. The contrast was indeed striking: a highly ideological beration of Eastern Europe, and a pragmatic policy towards Western Europe. Before the open operationalization of such a policy—discussed in the following chapter—the movement in the direction of Western Europe was slow and hesitant. This may be attributable to the important character of the change and the hesitations or even disagreements this may have generated within the party hierarchy, but it was also because the Sino–Soviet dispute had not completely surfaced in 1959, making a prompt and rapid shift rather difficult. Chinese policy towards Western Europe was thus showing all the signs of hesitation in 1959—of wanting to go ahead with a revised policy and yet remaining prudent.

Consider the Chinese reaction to the establishment of the European Economic Community (EEC)—which illustrates this state of mind and this initial state of hesitation. Formally in the late fifties the Chinese press took a highly critical view of the EEC, but informally, at the decisional level, the Chinese leaders adopted a more benign attitude to the development.

The press, for example, strongly criticized regional groupings in Western Europe (the EEC and the European Free Trade Area). They were perceived as a concrete expression of the 'intensification of contradictions among capitalist countries',[1] and a reflection of the 'disintegration of the Western World'.[2] The general crisis of capitalism in Western Europe was expected 'to become even more unstable with the crisis of overproduction occurring ever more frequently'.[3] The Common Market, viewed as 'an internal cartel organised by monopolistic groups of the six West European countries . . . to ease the contradictions among themselves' did not really, in the then prevailing Chinese view, constitute a threat to the United States; 'on the contrary the latter could use the Common Market to expand her own economic influence and prop up West German militarism'.[4]

However if the formal reaction was critical, the pattern of internal thinking at the decisional level was neither that categorical nor that critical. The few Chinese missions that operated from Western Europe—particularly the one in London—were following the Community events rather closely and were sending out reports back to Beijing that were not critical. In fact, some of them had clearly expressed the view that the establishment of the EEC was undoubtedly a major event that China must watch closely, since its eventual growth could have major ramifications on the configuration of international forces.[5] In sum, many of these reports—accepted by the Chinese leadership in Beijing—[6] projected a different perception and a different evaluation from what appeared in the press. The Chinese media thus did not really represent the internal official thinking at the party and the governmental levels. And yet the media was allowed to voice critical views about the EEC—views that represented the official Soviet line.

The question then is: why was such a state of affairs allowed to prevail in 1959? Was it a sign of discord among leaders, or was it that those airing such views in the media or journals were unaware of the decision-makers hesitations and doubts and were ignorant of the precious information that was specially accessible to those who had the responsibility of power?

Permitting the development of such a situation is not a standard Chinese practice. But in 1959 it was allowed to develop. Chinese leaders probably did not see any point in letting the media present the benign internal perception because a number of considerations restrained them from coming out formally in favour of the Common Market.

First, the Chinese decision-makers did not see any palpable diplomatic advantage in reacting favourably to the Common Market; China had diplomatic relations with only two of the six founders of the Community; and given the existing international situation at the time it was virtually impossible for the other four members to interact with China. The leadership, therefore, calculated that such an initiative on their part would have been a gratuitous act with no beneficial fall-out.

Second, Moscow's official denunciation of the European Community,[7] intellectually backed by the arguments advanced by the Institute of World Economy,[8] and politically supported by six Communist parties of the member states[9] hardly left any room for manoeuvre by the Chinese leaders. Any attempt on China's part, however subtle, to adopt a benign attitude would have been tantamount to a public defiance of Moscow, a situation hardly entertainable at the time, since Sino–Soviet relations had not yet deteriorated to such a pitch as to justify open dissent with Moscow. The time, as some Chinese argued, thus was not ripe. Besides, the issue was not perceived crucial enough to Chinese interests to warrant a dissenting role.[10] The risks were indeed too great and the benefits—if any—too small to justify any separate initiative.

Domestic constraints were no less weighty. Having pushed the country to the left in 1958 with considerable fanfare, the Maoist leadership could hardly afford a benign attitude towards new developments in capitalist Europe. Clearly, China had become a prisoner of her own rhetoric from which it was not easy to extricate itself, at least not at the time. The constraints, at the time of the establishment of the EEC, were thus considerable. Despite realization of its evident importance to long-term Chinese interests, the Chinese just could not afford to take a favourable attitude.

But this did not last. Open signs of change became rapidly apparent in the early sixties. Beijing began to manifest a more open interest and more unequivocal determination to give a new direction to its foreign policy, a policy that was more outgoing in character, at least so far as Western Europe was concerned.

A number of rapidly changing factors pushed China in this direction, factors which had not matured in 1959. The main element, of course, was the explosion of the Sino–Soviet dispute. After a few years of behind-the-scenes' wranglings— of which one knows more today than at the time—the disagreements between the two giants had surfaced in August 1960 with the dramatic withdrawal of Soviet technicians from China. The fact that such a drastic step was taken publicly was an indication that the long-suspected Sino–Soviet differences had irreversibly escalated into a dispute which could no longer be concealed. The lid was off, and it was only a matter of time before it assumed a more sulphurous character. The original Chinese concern to avoid any action that would displease the Russians was thus no longer relevant. The public surfacing of the dispute now made it possible for them to go their own way more freely than previously.

Parallel with this development was the drifting apart of India and China. From a warm bilateral interaction that was based on friendship and peaceful co-existence, relations had soured after the Tibetan revolt of 1959 and had finally degenerated into a real border conflict in 1962. Without going into the respective merits of the actors involved in these two confrontations, China undeniably faced a major diplomatic isolation and serious economic problems. In addition to the already existing isolation from the Western world—with whom relations at the time were indeed minimal—China was now on a collision course with Moscow and New Delhi, two major neighbours and two major centres that claimed to represent the socialist and the non-aligned worlds respectively.

It is true that, during the sixties, China had established diplomatic relations with twenty countries, seventeen of which were the newly independent African states; but this was hardly a consolation, since none of them were in a position to help China in facing some of her specific problems of national security or economic destabilization. If anything, this new connection was probably counter-productive in so far as it pushed Mao and his supporters to intensify their campaign of proselytization in the Third World, and in so far as it galvanized China into giving six times more aid to the developing countries than before the 'great leap forward'. In 1961, for example, while in the depths of economic depression, China gave $163 million to Ghana, Mali, Burma, Indonesia and Nepal.[11]

The economic ramifications of the Sino–Soviet dispute were even more catastrophic. The sudden withdrawal of Soviet aid was felt all the more since it was playing a crucial role in the development of the Chinese economy. As many as 291 major industrial plants were being assisted by the Soviet Union; and with this and East European support between 1952–9 China was able to expand production of her heavy industry by about 25 per cent. The flow of equipment and technical assistance had had a vital effect on the quality of China's industrialization, enabling production of such prestige items as jet aircraft, submarines, large generating equipment, metal-cutting tools, tractors, trucks and electronic equipment.[12]

The sudden Soviet decision to stop aid and withdraw technicians created an economic stasis. The transport system came to a grinding halt because of the lack of oil. Factories remained uncompleted because of Soviet non-cooperation. Equipment and machinery remained unused because of the absence of technicians and the paucity of spare parts. The unilateral Soviet action, in the words of a Chinese economic planner, was like 'taking away all the dishes when you have eaten only half the meal'.[13]

China's economic difficulties were further aggravated by the fact that at the time she was facing 'the worst series of natural disasters since the 19th century'.[14] In 1959, the total area afflicted by drought was 13.13 million hectares; in 1960, it went up to 24.66 million hectares.[15] Besides, grain production had dropped from 195.05 million tons to 143.5 million tons, and overall agricultural production had plummeted with the output of cotton and oil-bearing crops dropping by as much as 35.2 per cent and 54.8 per cent respectively. Compounded with all this were the growing difficulties among the national minorities. Already in 1958, the Chinese were talking about 'Islamic reactionary circles' in Gansu and Xinjiang. More serious was the March 1959 revolt in Tibet which resulted in the departure of the Dalai Lama to India. For the first time since the revolution, China was faced with serious internal and external crises. Internally everything seemed uncertain. Different factions were jockeying for power. Although Liu Shaoqi had arrived at the helm of internal affairs, it was not at all certain how long he would last. New policies of 'readjusting, consolidating, filling out and raising standards' had been agreed upon[16] by the party central committee, but it was not clear for how long they would be implemented.

Dualistic foreign policy

In external affairs, the nature of the crisis, however, was different. It was not internal within the party, but rather in the fact that China had become increasingly isolated. Mao was still in charge of foreign affairs, and after the fall of Peng Dehuai, there was indeed no one who was either able or willing to challenge him in this sector.

To risk a generalization, it could be argued that the post- 'great leap forward' foreign policy was rather dualistic in character: one side was revolutionary, while the other was more traditional, more diplomatic and more power orientated; one was clamorous, the other was low keyed; the one had the imprint of Mao, while the other had the diplomatic finesse of Zhou Enlai. On the face of it, such diplomatic behaviour may seem paradoxical, but in fact it was not since the two apparently contradictory policies were directed at two different regions.

In fact, the two policies had one thing in common: both of them were directed against the Soviet Union. While the one wanted to outdo the Soviets in revolutionary fervour in an area where this was possible, the other was designed towards the area that had the potential power of effectively countering Soviet influence and which had the economic power for coming to the aid of hard-pressed China.

The revolutionary foreign policy was directed at the Third World. After 1959, there was a vigorous upswing in China's contact with emerging nations, with a particular focus on people-to-people relations, on the wars of liberation and on economic and technical assistance to these countries.

On the other hand, policies towards Western Europe were different. They were more discreet and more traditional. What is more they were, in the beginning, more economico-political rather than diplomatic. The Chinese decision-makers must have been well aware that there were real obstacles to the establishment of any solid political bridges in the direction of Western Europe, which was still not in a position to strike out diplomatically on its own, given its continuing dependence on the United States. On the economic front, according to Chinese thinking and calculations, there was, however, some hope of interaction. Economic contradictions, ran the Chinese argument, among the developed countries invariably become so great that many of them are pushed to fend for themselves within a broad framework of their established political unity. Such behaviour, according to the Chinese, was already established in the late forties and early fifties, when Western Europe, despite its even greater dependence and its greater incapacity to act independently of the United States, defied Washington on the question of foreign trade. If it could do it during the height of Cold War when imperatives for unity were much greater, why could Europe not do the same in the early sixties when the atlantic alliance had evolved with the emergence of de Gaulle?

The economic factor was another weighty factor that had galvanized China into action. The highly adventuristic policies connected with the 'great leap forward', compounded with the sudden Soviet withdrawal had placed China in a very difficult economic situation. There were shortages of everything including foodstuffs; and there were clear and marked signs of economic stasis. China literally had no choice but to seek out non-Soviet sources for much-needed foodstuffs and for extricating the Chinese economy from economic stagnation.

While it is difficult to document the Chinese decisional process or the personalities involved in it, it would seem that China's foreign policy—at least in the early sixties—was dualistic in character with a heavy stress on ideology *vis-à-vis* the Third World and with economic considerations holding sway over all other considerations with regard to Western Europe.

Different foreign policies could thus be pursued, at the same time, in different regions without their having any impact on each other. They were indeed heavily compartmentalized; the source was the same, but the pattern of behaviour was different.

A new perception of Western Europe

Signs of change towards Western Europe became apparent from the Chinese press. If the Chinese press in 1959 was allowed to criticize the EEC, despite the fact that the Chinese leaders were not against the new alliance, the constraint was no longer there after 1960. The press was now used to announce the change. The number of news items and favourable commentaries increased considerably. The *Xinhua News Bulletin* in 1962 and 1963, for example, gave extensive coverage of British negotiations to join the EEC and of the rapidly evolving United States-EEC relations.[17] Similar interest was also discernible in the *People's Daily*[18] and in *Hongqi*, where the focus was on the emergence of new power centre, and in the *Beijing Review*, where a close and a regular analysis was made of the new political developments in Western Europe.[19] Even more noteworthy was the publication of a manual on international organizations which dealt thoroughly with European organizations, including the Organization for European Cooperation, the European Economic Community and the European Free Trade Association, etc.—information was provided regarding their origins, their institutional framework and their general policies.[20] The commentaries on Western Europe were even more striking for their favourable evaluation. They had certainly increased in comparison to what had existed before (see Table 4.1).

Table 4.1 Europe as seen by the *People's Daily*: 1960 and 1963

	Total	Unfavourably	Favourably	Other
1960	997	818	176	27
1963	721	359	363	10

Source: Stephen Kux, *The Chinese Perception of Western Europe 1960–81*, op. cit.

While not papering over difficulties and differences among the West Europeans themselves, the principal focus was on the growing contradictions between the United States and Western Europe. To a large measure, this ideological and political focus on contradictions between the United States and Western Europe, rather than among the West Europeans themselves, is very much impregnated with the Maoist strategy of focusing on 'principal contradictions' and on isolating the 'chief enemy'. The Chinese had repeatedly analysed this aspect of their strategy. A party article to this effect declared in 1959:

> Our experience teaches us that the main blow of the revolution should be directed at the chief enemy to isolate him, while as for the middle forces, a policy of both uniting with them and struggling against them should be adopted, so that they are at least neutralised; and, as circumstances permit, efforts should be made to shift them from their position of neutrality to one of alliance with us, for the purpose of facilitating the revolution.[21]

The articles that appeared in the Chinese press, during the first four years of the sixties, were clearly influenced by this mode of analysis. In fact, it had become the linchpin of most of Chinese writings on Western Europe. The European countries certainly, ran the Chinese argument, had their own contradictions, but they were less important than the one they had with the United States. 'The main contradictions', argued an articles, 'that characterize the Common Market is not with the socialist countries but with Great Britain and the United States'.[23]

What was the content of this analysis on Western Europe? What was the substance of the new thinking? Where was the focus? Are there any broad and conceptualized themes that one can extract from the mass of articles that were published in the Chinese media in the early sixties?

Four basic themes are perceptible. The first theme pertained to the growing strength of Europe. The Chinese leaders had come to the conclusion that Western Europe had undergone a very profound change and that its economic development was 'nearly on a par with the United States'. In fact, argued the Chinese, the economic development of Western Europe was much greater than that of the United States, making her 'a countervailing power to 'Great Britain and the United States'.[24]

Second, as a result of this new economic resurgence, their level of contradictions increased, and their capacity for political resistance became much greater.[25] This increasing but unavoidable phenomenon of contradictions was evidenced by the fact that Common Market countries 'are erecting high tariffs and are steadily becoming formidable rivals to the United States in the capitalist market'.[26] The political ramifications of this West European economic resurgence were also becoming evident, particularly in nuclear weapons' control where the West Europeans 'do not want to be simple U.S. cannon fodder' and 'want their own independent nuclear armament'.[27] 'The United States', declared one article, 'has lost its nuclear monopoly and its political and economic positions in the world have been weakened, while the West European nations, West Germany in particular, have grown stronger. The United States is less and less able to boss Western Europe'.[28] Another commentary, focusing on de Gaulle's France characterized the Common Market as the 'third force', and predicted that it 'would not only seriously harm traditionally important British influences, but would also end the post-war US control of the Western world'.[29] Yet another article — also on de Gaulle's France — went even further and argued that 'a unified Europe in de Gaulle's mind is an independent political, economic and military bloc under the leadership of France and is the third force playing the role of arbitrator between the Soviet and the US–British camp.'[30]

The new thinking finally received a well-publicized and a highly dramatic endorsement in January 1964 in an editorial in the *People's Daily* on Mao's intermediate-zone theory. Originally advanced in 1946, it resurfaced with an additional argument that the whole of Western Europe had developed sufficient common economic interests and purpose to be characterized as the 'second intermediate zone', trying its 'best to free itself' from American control.[31]

The third main theme was the establishment of transnational groupings among capitalist countries (EEC, EFTA and Alliance for Progress). Though this development was considered as a 'temporary truce' before the inevitable onset of the political storm,[32] or as 'reactionary' in character, the EEC was singled out for a closer scrutiny and for a more objective analysis. It was, for example, perceived as 'a countervailing power'[33] which had increased its economic clout and had thus 'become a force that is capable of confronting the United States and Great Britain'.[34] It was even admitted that the establishment of the Common Market had played 'a certain role' in bringing about an economic upswing in the six countries.[35]

The fourth major theme was regarding Great Britain, the quintessence of which was a volatile attack on her policies, and on the close ties she had established with the United States. Most of the writings on Great Britain—and there were many—were principally focused on British attempts to join the EEC.[36] Having arrived at the conclusion that Britain was too close and too dependent on the United States, China approved de Gaulle's determination to keep Britain out of the Common Market. In justification of the French action, a Chinese commentator wrote:

> If de Gaulle ignored all these acts of hostility, and if he took no counteraction, France would be completely isolated when the West European countries, enticed by US nuclear·weapons, allowed Britain to gatecrash the Common Market. By then France would not only be unable to stand as an equal with the United States and Britain, but would find it impossible to maintain her present status. If in the face of US and British onslaughts, France failed to take the bull by the horns, her position would become critical and she would be at the mercy of Washington and London. That is why de Gaulle decided to act promptly, shut the door of the Common Market with a bang, and turn down the US proposal for the establishment of a multilateral nuclear force.[37]

Where did China place herself in this new and broad picture of the changing configuration of international forces? What was the Chinese view of their own role in the international system in which Western Europe had been identified as an autonomous unit, and as an important component of the so called 'intermediate zone'?

An answer to these questions to some extent had already been given in the *People's Daily* editorial of January 1964 that revived the concept of the 'intermediate zone'. In this important statement, emphasis were laid on the eventual link up between all political forces, other than the United States. For the first time, the CCP had expressed interest in the establishment of some degree of cooperation between Western Europe, 'the socialist countries and the people of various countries'.[38]

But it was perhaps in a number of conversations that Mao Zedong had with different foreign delegations that China's role emerged more concretely. Interestingly, in all these statements—which were verbal and which were reported by foreign delegations—Mao presents China's role in practical and power terms bereft of all ideological frills.

To the French parliamentary delegation visiting China in January 1964, he talked about a 'third force' of which China was a part. 'It is necessary', he declared, 'to create a third force and bring Great Britain in it. We should include Great Britain because she will separate herself from the US. This would be a good thing: a London–Paris–Peking–Tokyo axis'.[39] To the Japanese socialists he declared: 'France, Germany, Great Britain—provided she does not act as a broker for the US–Japan and ourselves. This is the third force'.[40] In yet another statement he includes Italy in the third force: 'France, West Germany, Italy, Great Britain, Japan and the US. This is the third force, the intermediate zone.'[41]

A new Chinese perception of the international system had thus emerged—a perception that had clearly shifted away from the unity of the imperialist camp to that of its growing disintegration. And within this broad perception, China had apparently assigned to herself the task of working closely with all those who would contribute to this disintegration. Western Europe obviously was given the pride of place in this new strategy.

Conclusions

The increase and the final focalization of Chinese interest in Western Europe surfaced when Beijing became isolated from its socialist allies. The decision to build new bridges in the early sixties was in response to a given situation and was not the result of any spontaneous, inherent and general urge to diversify relations. The urge was there and it had often been translated in the past—as in Geneva in 1954 and in Bandung in 1955. But China's decision to take other options in foreign relations in 1960 had a very specific purpose—to break out of a situation of isolation. Paying particularly close attention to Albania and Romania was a part of this policy, but the principal focus had undoubtedly shifted to Western Europe.

The second major element that catalysed China to take new diplomatic initiatives was economic. The closing off of close ties with socialist countries, compounded with a difficult economic situation—attributed to climatic reasons—had created a serious situation in which China needed help. Once a decision had been taken, considerable efforts were then deployed by the CCP to inspire the publication of articles in the Chinese press, highlighting the emergence of Western Europe as an autonomous unit. The purpose of such a concerted exercise was to prepare the ideological ground for a major shift in China's policy towards Western Europe. This is obviously an important precursor in any Communist society for any change, since it gives the appropriate legitimacy to the action.

In this connection, it is particularly important to emphasize that editorials and articles signed by 'commentators'—cited here—are not a daily occurrence in Chinese papers, but are written on instructions from above and are published only after clearance by one or more members of the Politburo. A major editorial 'must be read with the same attention one would give to a speech by a President of the United States'.[42]

Chapter 5
Attempts at diplomatic breakthroughs

From the raft of documentation available on the subject, one can discern the emergence of a three-pronged policy towards Western Europe in the sixties. The first was a public relations operation, the second pertained to the economic domain, while the third was in the realm of diplomacy.

Public relations

There was indeed a marked decline in China's international image, or at least that is how it was perceived by the Chinese leadership.[1] The taciturnity that shrouded the country, plus the natural disasters of the early sixties — characterized by Zhou Enlai as 'the worst series of disasters since the 19th century'[2] — had fuelled considerable international speculation regarding the situation in the country. The Western press was awash with news, articles, commentaries etc., highlighting China's economic difficulties. Some of these articles had presented mind-boggling versions of mass starvation brought about not only by natural disasters, but also by the highly adventurous policies pursued by the Chinese leadership. A significantly increased exodus into Hong Kong and the appearance of news items on 2 and 6 February 1961 regarding the Canadian sale of 40 million bushels of grain and the Australian sale of 1,050,000 tons to China (plus 40,000 tons of flour) aggravated media speculations even further. Though the actual quantities involved were small from the standpoint of Chinese consumption,[3] the Canadian and Australian revelations of the agreements only further fuelled speculations regarding the state of the Chinese economy.

There was apparently a great deal of concern within the top Chinese leadership regarding what was appearing in the Western Press.[4] It was feared that all this might generate discussions regarding the wisdom of Chinese policies and prove detrimental to the newly designed Chinese policy of making overtures towards Europe.

A public relations job was viewed as vital to counter this increasingly rampant impression.[5] While the publication of informative articles on agriculture in the Chinese press was considered necessary, inviting West European public figures to visit was singled out as the most efficacious way of rectifying a negative impression. Moreover, calculated the Chinese leadership, this public-relations operation ought to help to advance China's new goal of establishing links with Western Europe.[6]

Two categories of personalities were selected: one consisted of 'journalist writers', the other was composed of public figures. Among the 'journalist writers' invited were Edger Snow (American citizen but residing in Switzerland) in 1960, Felix Greene (British), also in 1960, Jules Roy (French) in 1964 and K.S. Karol

(French) in 1965. The selection was prudent, in fact too prudent for all of them were favourably disposed towards China (some more than the others), but were none the less politically independent enough to form a judgment of their own. All four of them, who were well received and given widely publicized interviews with important Chinese leaders, finally published books which had varying degrees of impact on Western readers.[7]

The list of public figures was, however, longer and more diverse (see Table 5.1). They were all well received. Some of them were given real 'red carpet' treatment. Consider, for example, Field Marshall Montgomery's trip. He was allowed to travel extensively, and 'was warmly welcomed wherever he went'.[8] He was also received by leading personalities, including Mao Zedong, Zhou Enlai and Liu Shaoqi. Both in China as well as outside, he made a number of statements to the effect that his visit enabled him 'to correct the wrong impressions of the New China which are generally held in the Western world'.[9] In addition, he declared that 'the statements being made in the Western world that the people of China are starving and mutinous and the country is on the decline are totally untrue'.[10] 'There are', in his view, 'great misconceptions in the Western world about the New China, particularly in the United States.'[11]

Consider also the views expressed by Hewlett Johnson, the Dean of Canterbury, after his visit to China. He went even further then Montgomery and stated that Chinese deeds were compatible with Christianity: 'China I feel', he wrote, 'is performing an essentially religious act, entirely parallel with the Christian abhorrence of covetousness freeing them from the bondage of acquisitive instinct and paving the way for a new organization on a higher level of existence'.[12]

François Mitterrand, however, was less euphoric and perhaps more objective in his assessment of China. But he too was carried away by the positive aspects of the Chinese revolution and by the well-organized institutions and structures that had been established after 1949, 'Compared with the past', he wrote, 'China's political and economic anarchy has given place to a system that is meticulous, irksome, tedious, but none the less adapted for that for which it was conceived. From Beijing, the Central Government controls all the cogs of the wheel. The experts are consulted. The party's politburo commands; and immediately thousands of militants formed by long discipline start acting . . .'[13]

Economic initiatives

The second prong in China's foreign policy was in the economic sector. An interest in Western Europe became increasingly evident. The unilateral Soviet and East European decisions to slow down their economic interaction with China generated severe problems for the Chinese economy. Under the circumstances, turning to Western Europe and Japan were the only options left in order to obtain some relief for China's immediate economic difficulties, and to enable the country to continue the process of modernization. Japan, of course, was the most convenient economic partner because of her geographical proximity, cultural similarity and remarkable economic dynamism. But historical experience, compounded with the new Chinese realization of the disadvantages of an excessive

Table 5.1 West European personalities visiting China, 1960–5

Name	Year
Field Marshall Montgomery	1961
Hewlett Johnson (Dean of Canterbury)	1961
Queen Elizabeth (Grandmother of the Belgian King)	1961
François Mitterrand (member of French National Assembly)	1961
J.A. Del Vayo (Foreign Minister during Republican Spain)	1961
Philip Noel-Baker (British Labour MP)	1962
Ralph B. Schoenman (Bertrand Russell's Secretary)	1963
Patrick B. Pottle (Bertrand Russell's Secretary)	1963
Raymond Scheyven (Belgian Deputy)	1963
Edgar Faure (member of French Parliament)	1963
François Bernard (Leader of French Parliamentary Delegation)	1964
Paolo Battiono Vittorelli (Senator Italian Parliament)	1964
William Worbey (British Labour MP)	1965
André Malraux (French cultural minister)	1965

economic reliance on only one partner, made them highly prudent about making the same error. A real diversification of China's economic relations was evidently viewed as the only viable solution that would avoid past errors.

The implementation of such a policy, however, proved difficult. Natural disasters had compelled China to expend most of her financial resources on the importation of much needed food from Australia and Canada. With a wilting economy, there wasn't much left. In fact, the overall trade with Western Europe declined in 1961 and 1962 (see Table 5.2).

By 1963 things began to change. In fact, it was a turning point in Sino–Western economic relations. Things began to look up. Economic interaction became accelerated, and trade was on the upswing. The first important sign was a four-week visit to Western Europe by Lu Xuchang, Chinese vice-minister for trade. Accompanied by some leading members of import-export corporations plus a professor (Lu Huanchang) of the Beijing Institute of Chemical Technology, he visited industries and met officials in Great Britain, the Netherlands and Switzerland.[14] The ostensible goal of this goodwill mission was to find out about the latest technology in the chemical, petroleum, energy and transport sectors, but the visit was also 'a political demonstration' of the new Chinese interest in Western Europe.[15] In fact, the Chinese decision to send a high-powered delegation was both a sign and a signal—a sign that internal Chinese hesitations about turning to Western Europe were over and a signal that an option in the direction of Western Europe had been taken.

The second important sign was the general upsurge in economic activity and initiatives. The number of visits, meetings etc. increased considerably from 1963. A Chinese purchasing mission, for example, arrived in France in March 1963. This was followed in May by an important meeting in Switzerland between Lu Xuchang and a number of French personalities from the economic sector. This,

Table 5.2 Western Europe's trade with China
(US$ million)

Year	Exports	Imports
1959	413.6	178.1
1960	378.3	248.4*
1961	177.9	196.6*
1962	148.7	175.5*
1963	172.5	181.0

Sources: U.S. Mutual Defense Assistance Control Act Administrator; *Reports to Congress* of various years; United Nations, *Yearbook of International Trade Statistics for 1961 and 1963.*

* Includes silver.

in turn, was followed in September–October by a series of visits by French industrialists to China.[16] The pace was even more accelerated in 1964 and thereafter.

With West Germany too, steps were taken to accelerate economic interaction. In July 1962, the Chinese ambassador to Switzerland, Li Jingzuan, proposed expansion of Sino-West German trade to Otto Wolf von Amerongen (in charge of commercial negotiations with Communist countries).[17] But the process of real interaction began in 1963. In the middle of that year, the PRC initiated discussions with individual German traders in Hong Kong and Beijing. The Chinese Council for the Promotion of International Trade invited a member of Bonn's consulate in Hong Kong to Beijing and to the Canton Trade Fair. The general secretary of the Canton Trade Fair—who was also a department head in the Ministry of Foreign Trade—informed a German delegation to the Fair of the Chinese wish to conclude an official trade agreement and to establish a trade mission in Bonn[18] In fact, from then on, during the rest of the year, the Chinese began to press for relations between the two countries to become more official and that the 1957 'unofficial trade agreement be renegotiated'.[19] At the beginning of 1964, Beijing also informed the German authorities, through journalists and industrialists, of their wish to develop trade relations.[20]

All this rippled through the economic sector; when it became unmistakably apparent that China was really serious, pressures began to build up on the German government to respond positively. A number of German businessmen publicly came out in favour of the relaxation of credit restrictions and of an increase in commerce. In February 1964, one German industrialist, who had just returned from China, urged the German government to examine seriously the possibilities of establishing a trade mission in Beijing.[21] The director of Demag also supported this trend for greater economic relations, and expressed his fear that West Germany would be left behind other nations in the exploitation of the Chinese market.[22]

Relations were developed with Italy in 1963–4, including the visit of successive Italian delegations to Beijing,[23] and a large Chinese presence at the Italian exhibition held in Hong Kong in March 1963.[24] An agreement was also concluded on 30 November 1964 regarding the establishment of non-governmental commercial offices in Beijing and Rome in order to accelerate economic and trade development between the two countries.

Notwithstanding the emergence of a general economic interest in Western Europe, during the first half of the sixties China's principal interest was in Great Britain. For one thing, Britain, at the time, was the only major West European country with whom China had diplomatic relations, clearly a basic precondition for any sustained economic interaction. Britain was also the only West European country that was in a position to meet Chinese needs. Her urgent need in the aviation sector, for example, could only be met by Britain. In fact, in 1963 the largest British exports to China were aircraft and spare parts for aircraft.[25] Finally, London was perhaps the only capital that was able to resist most American pressures against trade with China.

The importance China attached to Britain can be gauged from the fact that the Chinese commercial counsellor's office in London—which was separate from the diplomatic mission—was expanded to a staff of twenty officials. Zhou Enlai, furthermore, was quite forthright in personally declaring to the president of the Board of Trade, Douglas Jay, that China was prepared 'to clear away all obstacles to expansion of Sino–British trade'.[26]

The third important sign of the rapidly growing economic activity was a marked West European presence at the Canton Trade Fairs. This was particularly striking during 1963 and 1964.[27] Even more significant was the increase in West European industrial exhibitions in China which displayed their latest technological items, and which were sold to the Chinese at reduced prices at the end of the exhibition (see Table 5.3).

A fourth important sign of this opening up was the Chinese purchase of whole plants from Western Europe. This process also began in 1963. Six agreements

Table 5.3 West European exhibitions in China, 1963–4

1963		
29 July – 2 August	British exhibition held by ICI, Formica and Morgan Crucible Group	Beijing
September	Danish exhibition of optical and electrical goods	Shanghai, Beijing
1964		
15 – 25 April	British Scientific Instrument Manufacturers Association	Beijing
4 – 14 June	British mining and construction equipment	Beijing
5 – 25 September	French industrial exhibition of measurement control and automobile equipment	Beijing
2 – 14 November	British agricultural and mining equipment	Beijing

Table 5.4 Sale of whole plants to China, August 1963 – December 1965
(in US$ million)

Plant	Country of origin	Value	Date of contract
Urea	Netherlands	6.0	September 1963
Synthetic ammonia	United Kingdom	7.0	October 1963
Petroleum refinery	Italy	5.0	December 1963
Ammonia nitrate	Italy	14.2	December 1963
Synthetic ammonia	Italy	3.6	December 1963
Industrial alcohols	France	3.0	January 1964
Palm-oil processing	Netherlands	2.0	May 1964
Crude-oil cracking and olefins	West Germany	12.5	July 1964
Synthetic fibre (nylon)	West Germany	1.5	July 1964
Polyethylene	United Kingdom	12.6	September 1964
Porous silica	Sweden	1.8	December 1964
Acrylon	West Germany	4.6	May 1965
Glass	West Germany	3.5	mid-1965
Polyester resin	United Kingdom	0.1	July 1965
Acrylic fibre	United Kingdom	8.4	August 1965
Air liquefaction	West Germany	3.3	August 1965
Tube expansion	Italy	3.0	1965
Instruments	United Kingdom	1.0	1965
Cellulose	Finland	*	1965
Bleach	Finland	*	1965
L–D steel	Austria	12.0	1965
Cold-strip steel	West Germany	17.0	1965

Sources: Robert L. Price, 'Investment Trade of Communist China, 1950–1965' in *An Economic Profile of Mainland China*; studies prepared for the Joint Economic Committee of the United States Congress, February 1967, vol. 2, p. 603, Table 16.

were concluded during that year. They increased to eight in 1964 and eleven in 1965 (see Table 5.4). It is important to note that the range of installations chosen in 1963 and in subsequent years had a dual purpose: they represented areas of technology in which Soviet processes and design would not have satisfied Chinese demands; and they included extraction, processing and exploitation of fuel oil— an indication of a new direction that China was taking.[28]

The most important indicator of change was the trade sector. Here too, 1963 was a landmark, for it was during this year that the trend towards decline in Sino–West European relations was reversed; and reached the unprecedented figure of $897.1 million in 1966 (see Table 5.5). The importance of 1963 in the inauguration of accelerated Sino–West European trade was confirmed by Lin Haiyun, China's vice-minister for trade.

> Since the second half of 1963, we have held trade talks with manufacturers and firms in various Western Countries, including France, Sweden, Holland, and the United Kingdom, Italy and West Germany, and have purchased a number of complete industrial plants from them—a fact that has aroused interest and attention in industrial and commercial centers in many Western countries.[29]

Table 5.5 China's trade with West Europe, 1960–6 (in US$ million)

Country	1960	1961	1962	1963	1964	1965	1966
Austria	28.7	5.6	4.7	4.3	3.9	6.6	13.9
Belgium and							
Luxembourg	54.5	13.6	12.8	17.7	21.0	31.2	35.7
Denmark	19.1	17.7	13.1	7.3	12.0	12.6	14.2
Finland	11.1	8.6	7.2	8.7	13.4	14.0	18.7
France	75.5	5.3	60.2	79.5	80.4	103.8	146.0
Greece	0.1	0.1	0.1	0.1	0.1	0.1	0.5
Ireland	1.4	0.9	0.6	0.9	0.1	1.2	2.0
Italy	63.8	42.0	33.4	38.4	42.3	94.8	119.2
Netherlands	28.3	19.3	17.5	28.7	25.9	44.4	46.3
Norway	7.2	6.7	2.4	5.3	9.1	10.0	10.2
Portugal	0.6	0.4	0.2	0.4	0.4	0.2	0.2
Spain	0.8	*	0.2	1.5	0.2	1.7	3.6
Sweden	19.1	11.9	10.0	12.4	26.2	28.8	39.1
Switzerland	16.9	14.9	15.5	14.1	21.4	30.9	37.2
United Kingdom	159.5	122.0	89.0	89.1	118.4	155.5	188.3
West Germany	164.9	70.2	70.5	56.1	77.1	151.7	221.9

Sources: US Department of State, *Battle Act Reports* up to 1965; data for 1966 from US Department of Commerce, *Preliminary Reports.*

* Less than $50,000.

Among the West European countries, Great Britain was China's most important partner during 1963, 1964 and 1965, but in 1966 West Germany overtook Great Britain, and thereafter never ceded her leading position to anyone else in Western Europe.

Political interaction

On the political–diplomatic front too, the level of Chinese interest in Western Europe had increased by the early sixties. Their analysis of the overall situation in the region was driving them to the conclusion that Europe was becoming more powerful economically and more resistant politically to the policies of their transatlantic partner. All this new evolution, ran the Chinese argument, was in its very initial stages, but it was only a question of time before the growing and inevitable 'capitalist contradictions' would push the West Europeans to fend for themselves.

It was possibly this reading of the political situation that contributed to the restoration of the Maoist theory of intermediate zones. Once again, it made its appearance in the *People's Daily* on 21 January 1964.[30] Thereafter with a metronomic regularity, it usually found a conspicuous place in authoritative articles by leading Chinese political figures[31] in polemical declarations again the Italian Communist Party[32] and the Soviet Communist Party,[33] and in apparently authorised editorials in important Chinese newspapers etc.[34]

This rather sudden and widespread appearance of the concept was a reflection of the new political line that was emerging—a line that stressed the revolutionary importance of the Third World and the diplomatic significance of Western Europe in the international system. Within the broad framework of this perception, it was France that was increasingly singled out as the country that would distance itself from the United States and would carry the other West European countries along with it to establish a countervailing power to the United States and the Soviet Union.

It is interesting to note that France had often been a source of considerable attraction to the Chinese intellectuals, even those who were Marxist orientated. Among all the Western European countries, it was usually France that was given the pride of place as a centre of new political thinking, as a historical model for revolutions and as a culture centre whose writings 'give much comfort and stimulation to our workers'.[35]

Why was this? Was it because France had been a major centre of revolution in the past? Or was it because some of the important Chinese leaders had lived in France and had been grounded in Marxism there? It was, one could argue, both. France's revolutionary past dovetailed with the Marxist theory of revolution. Marxists all over the world were inspired by the 1789 French Revolution, and were deeply influenced by the subsequent pattern of political developments which took place there. In the case of the Chinese Marxists it was even more so since many of them had actually lived there.

In any event, China's diplomatic interest in France was evident even before de Gaulle came to power in 1958. In 1956, when France was still heavily involved against the Algerian nationalist movement, and when she had pursued rather an adventurist policy against Nasser during the same year, Mao Zedong declared to Edgar Faure that 'France can again play a role of *rapproachment*, of mediation'. 'France,' said Mao, 'has a glorious history. She must surmount her present difficulties. She is more qualified than China of playing such a role and this role comes to her more than to us'.[36]

However, the real and publicized interest in France became much more evident after de Gaulle returned to power in 1958 and after the establishment of the fifth French Republic. This was discernible at two levels. The first was at the level of press analysis. With the exception of Algeria, where France did come in for some criticism,[37] the Chinese commentators, even before recognition, studiously avoided singling out France as a target of attack. This conspicuous abstention was all the more striking when one takes into account the contrasting fact that the other major West European countries were not spared for pursuing 'reactionary' or pro-American policies.

The second level of interest was diplomatic. At practically all the meetings that Chinese leaders had with West European leaders, they invariably made it a point to convey their friendliness towards France or to underline the commonality of their views with that of France on a wide spectrum of international issues. Field Marshall Montgomery's outburst against American policies—in a meeting with Mao—for example, reportedly resulted in the latter advising him to discuss the whole matter with de Gaulle.[38] Again to François Mitterrand—also in 1960— Mao Zedong deliberately stressed that 'we have no conflicts with France', and emphasized that China would not contest the rights granted to France by the Geneva agreements of 1954.[39]

The Chinese first raised the question of recognition in July 1962 during the conference on Laos in Geneva and subsequently, at different meetings with a high-powered French mission that came to Beijing in September 1963, high Chinese officials openly expressed the hope that France would recognize China.[40]

Despite China's growing interest in France, there were two major constraints to the actual establishment of relations. The first was French colonialism. It was hardly possible for Beijing to establish formal relations with France as long as the Algerian problem was not settled. The Chinese foreign minister Chen Yi had made this clear.[41] Having publicly proclaimed an interest in Third World revolutions, and having, in fact, made the Third World the focal point of her foreign policy, a Sino–French *détente* would have been difficult to explain, particularly in the early sixties when violent Algerian revolution had acquired the status of a major symbol for the Third World in general and the Arab world in particular. Besides, the Soviet Union would have capitalized on such a happening, particularly if one takes into account that the Third World had become a major issue of Sino–Soviet dispute. Hypothetically, it could be argued that it would have been embarrassingly difficult for the Chinese to take any such decision, had such an eventuality presented itself in the late fifties or early sixties. Happily for the Chinese this did not happen owing to the second major constraint—which was France herself. De Gaulle was apparently not ready to make such a move at the beginning of his mandate. Although the broad contours of his new and increasingly independent foreign policy were apparent soon after his ascension to power in 1958, he was too bogged down with the task of stabilizing his own domestic position and too involved in settling the intractable Algerian problem to operationalize his new foreign policy—at least so far as China was concerned.

The two obstacles were finally removed by the early sixties. The Algerian issue was resolved with the conclusion of the Franco–Algerian agreement in March 1962, and his domestic position was considerably improved after his proposal that the French president be elected directly by the French population was accepted in the October 1963 referendum.

In addition, there were ostensibly three international developments in 1963 that facilitated the implementation of his decision to formalize relations with China and actually setting in motion the French bureaucratic machinery to reach this objective. The first was the conclusion of the partial Nuclear Test Ban Treaty on 5 August 1963 between the Soviet Union, the United States and Great Britain. For de Gaulle, this had seriously compromised his foreign-policy strategy, the linchpin of which was a *rapprochement* with Moscow. By signing the first major agreement with the United States and Great Britain, the Soviet Union, in the eyes of de Gaulle, had in effect rejected his vision of establishing a 'Europe from the Atlantic to the Urals'. Additionally the privileges of big powers had been reinforced,[42] and had jeopardized French plans for also becoming a nuclear power. As China—equally determined to go nuclear—had also rejected the Test Ban Treaty, de Gaulle decided that development of relations with China were clearly in the interest of France—and the sooner, the better.

The American military intervention in Vietnam in August 1963 was the second factor that weighed heavily in the French decision to recognize the People's Republic. In fact, it reinforced de Gaulle's original thinking that the neutralization of the Indo-Chinese peninsula—to be negotiated with China—was the only viable and lasting solution for the whole area. Since Great Britain and Canada tended to go along with American policies in Vietnam, de Gaulle considered that the rapid development of relations with China had become urgent in order to define a common and a different position in South-east Asia.

The third factor was the aggravation of the Sino–Soviet dispute. Its consummation by the summer of 1963 and the consequent isolation of China convinced de Gaulle of the importance of seeking Chinese support for the effective implementation of his strategy.[43]

Edgar Faure goes to Beijing

The Gaullist policy of seeking out China was thus set in motion in 1963. The first step that was taken was to entrust Edgar Faure with the task of sounding out the Chinese on the question and unofficially to discuss with them the modalities of establishing diplomatic relations. Faure was clearly an ideal person for this difficult and delicate assignment. He had known the Chinese leaders well, and had had the occasion in 1957 of informally discussing the question with the Chinese authorities, including Zhou Enlai.[44] Besides, he had also met Mao during his last visit. Also—and this was important—the Chinese authorities apparently had confidence in him. There was some commonality of views on numerous international issues, and, furthermore, during his brief tenure of premiership in 1955, he had taken the unusual step of receiving a Chinese youth delegation in Hotel Matignon.

Edgar Faure arrived in China on 21 October 1963 and stayed there until 2 November. Needless to say, he was well received. 'Mr. Faure', declared his host at a banquet given on the day after his arrival, 'has always stood for the recognition of the People's Republic of China and the restoration of China's seat in the United Nations . . . We appreciate and value highly Mr. Faure's efforts to promote Sino-French friendship'.[45]

The negotiations were difficult, indeed very difficult. Before the establishment of relations, an accord had to be reached on Taiwan, and on China's membership of the United Nations. Since France had a diplomatic presence in Taiwan, this was the most difficult question—all the more so since Faure had a strict mandate not to accept any Chinese preconditions and not to commit France regarding Taiwan's future status. In line with their policy, the Chinese insisted on the break with Taiwan as a precondition for any recognition—a precondition that Edgar Faure was instructed not to accept. Faure attempted to find a solution to this intractable problem 'by going around the obstacle rather than eliminating it'.[46] That is to say that France would recognize the People's Republic without taking the initiative of actually breaking with Taiwan. This, according to Faure's line of reasoning, would then drive Taiwan into initiating the break, since the latter was committed to a very strict policy of automatically breaking with all governments that recognized Beijing. The French emissary also made it clear that France would not take any position regarding China's claim over Taiwan, while assuring the Chinese, at the same time, that France was not proposing a two-Chinas' formula.[47]

For the Chinese, who had hitherto always been intransigent on the question, accepting Faure's formula was indeed very risky; for what if Chiang Kai-Shek decided not to break with governments recognizing Beijing? And what, furthermore, would be the consequence of accepting the French decision that it would not make a formal statement accepting Chinese sovereignty over Taiwan?

This was a unique situation that China was faced with. In the past, there were no risks involved since China had always seen to it that governments recognizing Beijing (a) had formally undertaken to break with Taiwan, and (b) had recognized—also officially—that Taiwan was a part of China. The Faure formula was very different, since it left the onus of breaking with France on the Taiwan government, and since it remained silent over the status of Taiwan.

The rumours circulating at the time did not help matters. The grapevine telegraph was on in the French press with reports that the French, like the Americans, were striving to create a two-Chinas' situation, and that they were going to recommend to Chiang not to break diplomatic relations in order to test the mainland's behaviour. Finally, China accepted Faure's formula. The advantages accruing from French recognition were far greater than the risk China would be taking. By itself, this was a major breakthrough and could—even more importantly—incite other West European countries to follow suit, a perspective which could change the overall political situation.

The third issue—French support to China's admission to the United Nations—was less important; but the Chinese, on this point too, insisted on obtaining firm assurances from the French; their past rather unpleasant experience with some West European governments which were not forthright in their support of Chinese membership of the UN—despite their recognition—was not very reassuring.

Edgar Faure's response on this question was clear. His government, he declared, would openly back the PRC's admission to the international organization. His argument—which juridically made sense—was as follows: 'China is a signatory of the UN Charter. She is a member of the Security Council. If the Peking government is China, then it is for that government to enjoy this prerogative . . . It is therefore evident', continued Faure's argument, 'that if France recognized the People's Republic she would have no reason to refuse her a seat in the UN. France will therefore support the replacement of the Chiang Kai-Shek delegation to the General Assembly and the Security Council by that of the People's Republic'.[48] The Sino–French agreement, finally announced on 27 January 1964, through a two-lined joint communiqué, simply declared that the two governments 'have decided through common accord to establish diplomatic relations and to designate ambassadors within three months'.[49]

To avoid any speculations that the laconic joint communiqué might have generated regarding the mainland's policy towards Taiwan, and to nip in the bud any rumours regarding the PRC's attitude to two Chinas, the Chinese Ministry of Foreign Affairs issued a statement a day after the communiqué. In it, it was made clear that 'recognition of the new government naturally implies ceasing to recognize the old ruling group overthrown by the people of the country', and it was with 'this understanding (*dans cet ésprit*) that the government of the People's Republic reached agreement with the government of the French Republic on the establishment of diplomatic relations and the exchange of ambassadors between China and France'.[50] This point was reiterated by Zhou Enlai personally while travelling in Africa.[51]

The French handled their break with Taiwan gently. De Gaulle despatched General Peshkoff, French Ambassador to China during World War II, to inform Chiang Kai-Shek of the new agreement.[52] Almost at the same time, de Gaulle, in his typical Gaullian style, made a farewell gesture to Chiang by paying homage to his 'worth, patriotism and nobility of spirit'.[53]

It is important to note that the French authorities had taken the decision not to initiate the rupture. These were apparently de Gaulle's injunctions—who had envisaged the perspective of maintaining consular relations modelled after the British.[54] But this was not to be, since Chiang—after some hesitation—took the decision himself to break off diplomatic relations with France on 1 February, much to the relief of the People's Republic, and many French leaders—at least those who had been involved in the negotiations.

What would have happened if Chiang had decided not to initiate the breakup? What would have France done in such circumstances, since de Gaulle personally had taken the firm decision not to take the lead to break with Taipei? And how would have the People's Republic have reacted in the absence of a Franco–Taipei rupture? All these are of course hypothetical questions on which one can only speculate.

Chiang Kai-Shek could have continued his ties with France. There were no major obstacles. The United States was pressing Chiang to relent from his decision of breaking with Paris.[55] Presumably, Washington wanted to create a two-Chinas' situation, and had considered the new situation as a litmus test. Besides—and this is important too—Chiang had subsequently rallied to the idea of not automatically staging a break with a government that recognized Beijing. A statement to this effect was made by Chiang's spokesman on 4 July 1971.[56] This was of course a little too late for the Sino–French situation, but could have happened earlier. A decision by Chiang Kai-Shek to maintain ties with France would have made it very difficult for the latter, considering de Gaulle's proverbial stubbornness about not abandoning principled positions.

The Chinese, however, had taken their own precautions. Not only had they made it verbally clear that a breakup with Taipei was a *sine qua non*, they had also repeatedly confirmed this in writing shortly after the publication of the laconic Sino-French communiqué. Furthermore—another precautionary step—in the unlikely event of no diplomatic break between Paris and Taipei, the PRC would not send her ambassador to France, since the joint communiqué stipulated that the designation of ambassadors could be done within a three month period. The Chinese thus had sufficient time to extricate themselves were it to become necessary. In any event, one thing is certain: China would have never allowed herself to be trapped in the two-Chinas' situation—at least not in 1964.

It is important at this point, to raise questions about France's interaction with her allies regarding her recognition of China. Did France consult or at least inform its allies of the decision? Were there any preliminary discussions and were there any reactions to the question? In the absence of the availability of archival documentation, it is of course impossible to delve into the subject with any certainty. But from the information that has filtered into the press, it is possible to make a tentative analysis of the subject. It is highly unlikely—with de Gaulle at the helm— that the French government would have consulted its allies. Consultation implies seeking a response before actually taking a decision. This in the France of de Gaulle—particularly in the sixties—was improbable, since recognition of China had become a linchpin of Gaullist Asian policy about which France wished to maintain her sovereign rights. Besides, consulting, particularly the United States, would not have made any sense in view of the generally known American opposition to any such action by her allies. Some American sources have apparently claimed that France had given an 'assurance' to Washington towards the end of 1963 that it did not envisage a recognition 'in the immediate future'.[57] This is most unlikely, since a decision in the autumn of 1963 had already been taken, and Edgar Faure had already returned to Paris after having successfully found—in cooperation with the Chinese—an appropriate formula for recognition. Besides, the American statement was never confirmed from the French side.[58]

On the other hand, it is more than likely that France had informed its allies of the decision, and there were some discussions. An observer has reported about the NATO ministerial meetings in Paris where the subject was brought up, and about the meetings between de Gaulle and Dean Rusk, and between de Gaulle and the American Ambasador, Bohlen, where the matter was presumably discussed.[59] The West Europeans, on the other hand, were given short shrift. They were neither consulted nor directly informed, undoubtedly a paradoxical situation with regard to West Germany in view of the fact that interacting with West Germany was a cornerstone of Gaullist foreign policy.

The reaction of both the United States and Western Europe was negative. A spokesman for the American State Department made it know that 'the US regrets the French decision' and considers that it came at a time when 'Communist China is actively encouraging aggression and subversion in Southeast Asia and elsewhere'.[60] The British made it clear that a 'wrong moment was chosen to act in a scattered manner in Asia'.[61] And the Germans were unanimous in expressing concern at the French initiative at a time when they thought that the Western powers 'could act only in harmony with Washington'.[62]

What was the impact of this recognition on Sino–French relations? Did they surge ahead? Did levels of interaction in the political and economic sectors increase? Can one discern any concrete advantages to the two countries? What about the recognition's impact internationally? Did it have a ripple effect? Did it push the other countries to turn to China?

The institutionalization of bilateral relations did have some effect. Only the establishment of embassies[63] and the exchange of high-level ambassadors[64] permitted the two countries to maintain a constant contact, exchange views and have relatively easy access to their respective top leadership. This in itself was a major advantage, since interaction between the two of them prior to the recognition had had to be channelled through Berne, obviously a long and tedious process. Sino-French trade also increased. From $80 million in 1964 it increased to $103.8 million in 1965 and to $146 million in 1966.[65]

By far the most important diplomatic windfall was the emergence of Chinese caution *vis-à-vis* France. Although the Chinese were already reining in their critical observations before recognition, they became even more circumspect after January 1964: so much so that they prudently abstained from making any critical remarks about French foreign policy. Even when the French intervened in Gabon in 1964—an act that would have been normally denounced as imperialistic—the Chinese were totally silent; if anything the level of Chinese public eulogization of French foreign policy increased, and on issues of direct concern to China (Vietnam, Laos, Kampuchea), the Chinese leadership increasingly welcomed French initiatives.

The increasing Sino-French 'convergence of international interests' has also been attributed to recognition.[66] Though this phenomenon would have continued even without recognition, the 'common reflex' of the two middle powers on a wide spectrum of international issues, including the Nuclear Test Ban Treaty, superpower hegemony, the Congo crisis and military alliances may well have been accelerated after the French recognition.

The international consequences were perhaps even more striking, even if they were not, on the face of it, palpable. First of all, the Sino-French *rapprochement* raised the prestige of de Gaulle's France among the Third World countries. This was not so much because France had recognized China, but because it had defied the United States—a pattern of behaviour that went down very well with the underdeveloped world at the time. De Gaulle received plaudits from many non-aligned leaders, including Ben Bella, Fidel Castro and Tito. Also, he received invitations from many Third World countries, including some in Latin America.

The granting of independence to Algeria and recognition of China are undoubtedly two important acts that have greatly contributed in generating a new international image of France which she still enjoys unlike any other country with a colonial past.

French recognition also had some impact on the African continent; for during the same year the Congo (Brazzaville), the Central African Republic, Zambia and Benin recognized China. That this too was of significant international consequence is evident from the fact that the balance between those who favoured China's admission to the UN and those who were against began slowly to shift in favour of the former.[67]

The ripple effect of French recognition of China on Western Europe was interesting. While most of the major countries had bemoaned the lack of unity in the Western world and had even criticized the French initiative, Sino-French *rapprochement* catalysed economic pressure groups to push their governments who had not recognised China, to do something. They apparently feared that the new French recognition would give France an economic edge over them.

The West European governments were quite aware of the situation, and of the dangers of being left out from the economic fall-out that might occur from the French political initiative. But there was precious little they could do. Their political leverage was very constricted. They were either unable or unwilling to take the political decision of following France in the foreign-policy sector. The American pressures against normalization were much too great to permit them to follow France. The majority of them, in fact, continued to support Washington in its Asian policy and in its policy of keeping China out of the United Nations.

Sino-German negotiations

West Germany was perhaps the only country which tried to find a solution to this searing dilemma of maintaining close political ties with the United States and of seeking some economic understanding with China. Economic pressures were indeed building up within the country that the government could not possibly afford to ignore. The international political situation too was evolving. First of all, as China's major West European economic partner the Federal Republic feared some economic ostracism after the French recognition, should this development be ignored. Mindful of this disadvantageous situation, economic groups had in fact accelerated their pressures on the government to do something. In February 1964 a German industrialist, who just returned from China, urged the government to examine the possibilities of establishing a trade mission in Beijing.[68] Another recently returned visitor, the director of Demag, added his voice to the general call for an improvement in relations, and declared that other nations were a step ahead in exploiting the Chinese market.[69]

The political situation too was changing. The Chinese position on the German question, for example, was showing some signs of evolution. At the time of the commencement of the Sino-Soviet dispute, China had perceived East Germany as a potential ally, on the grounds that the new outgoing Soviet policy towards Western Europe in general, and the Federal Republic in particular, would inevitably generate Soviet-East German tensions. This to quite an extent was confirmed in the late fifties when East Germany did show signs of some political disenchantment with Moscow, and of considerable ideological interest in China.[70] The whole weight of Chinese diplomacy was, therefore, directed at supporting East Germany for all that she represented and of denouncing the policies of the Federal Republic.[71]

The purpose of this political exercise clearly was to accelerate the pro-Chinese orientations of East Germany, which in geopolitical terms had become increasingly important. Nothing indeed in the whole of Eastern and even Western Europe could have been a greater success for Chinese diplomacy than to have a faithful and a powerful ally in the heart of Europe. It cannot be excluded that—attracted as always by geopolitics—the Chinese began to conjure up such visions.

East Germany's importance was all the greater not only because it was in the heart of Europe, but because it was geographically located at the other tip of the socialist bloc—undoubtedly a strategic location that could have opened possibilities for the two countries together to erode Soviet influence in Eastern Europe and, at the same time, to prevent it from expanding in other regions.

The Chinese leadership, which had often shown considerable realism in understanding the outside world and in clearly defining its foreign-policy interests, have also, at times, shown a marked tendency towards becoming totally unrealistic, to the extent of becoming incapable of distinguishing what is realistically achievable and what is not.

Visions about East Germany belonged to the Walter Mitty pattern of Chinese thinking and behaviour. Correct as they were in their perfectly understandable vision of seeking out East Germany, they overlooked or ignored the brutal fact that East Germany was a part of the Soviet bloc, that she had very little leverage for extricating herself from Soviet domination and that if there were signs of pro-Beijing policies in East Germany—as in other socialist bloc countries—it was in all probability because the post-Stalinist Soviet leadership was either divided or uncertain regarding its objectives. When the Soviets decided to blow the whistle on the ideological meanderings of Eastern Europe, all the Soviet allies fell in line. This was equally true of East Germany. Like other Soviets allies in the area, the East German Communist Party at its sixth congress in January 1963 criticized China openly and in very firm terms. Even more striking was Walter Ulbricht's discourse. It was more vitriolic in its denunciation of the Chinese than any other speech made by party leaders on this or other occasions.

Walter Ulbricht's anti-Chinese performance in January 1963 is probably the real cut-off point for the slow inauguration of a new policy towards the two Germanies. As the Chinese press is the 'voice of authority as it could never be in a democracy',[72] the first contours of the change were discernible from the press. Practically all the Xinhua News Agency coverage of the abortive negotiations regarding Britain's admission to the EEC during the winter of 1963 (January and February) projected—implicitly of course—an image of West Germany that was different from before.

West Germany's role was no longer condemned out of hand and was no longer projected as representing the American voice. The Xinhua despatches from Brussels and from elsewhere in Europe, on the contrary, highlighted the West German dilemma of maintaining ties with the United States while striving to establish coherent European Community policies.[73] A commentary on the talks, written by a Xinhua correspondent in London, went even further. He wrote:

> De Gaulle's action has put West Germany's Adenauer in a great dilemma. On the one hand the power and influence of France and West Germany rest with their cooperation with each other. On the other, heavy US pressure has been brought to bear on Adenauer that he should persuade de Gaulle to withdraw his objection to Britain's entry . . . But for Adenauer, Paris–Bonn reconciliation takes precedence over all else. A treaty of Franco–West German cooperation was signed during his visit to Paris as a further confirmation of a Paris–Bonn axis.[74]

West Germany thus was no longer viewed as sold to the United States, but as an ally of de Gaulle who, according to the Chinese press, was creating the 'third force in Europe'.[75]

Attacks on West German militarism also suddenly stopped by the summer of 1963. This is indeed very striking, since only a year before West Germany had been singled out for repeated attacks for its militarist ambitions. Such a volte-face is all the more significant since it coincided with the American move to give West

Germany some access to nuclear weapons through the formation of NATO 'multinuclear forces'. Although this plan never got off the ground owing to French opposition and British indifference, it can be wondered whether Chinese silence might not be attributed to the new policy of not criticizing West Germany, or whether it was a sign of new Chinese interest in the actual resurgence of West Germany as a major military factor to counteract Soviet expansion in the heart of Europe. In any event, whatever may have been the Chinese reasons for adopting a low-keyed attitude on the proposed West German rearmament, such a stance did not go unnoticed.

Sudden interest in West Germany was evident not only from the conspicuous change in the tone of the Chinese press; it was also discernible from the apparently stray, but none the less well-orchestrated remarks by the Chinese leaders themselves. The intermediate-zones theory, long ignored or forgotten, suddenly resurged in the Chinese press by the beginning of 1964. The CCP made a point of highlighting not only the first intermediate zone but also the second—undoubtedly a new framework for cooperation with Western Europe.

In line with this new thinking, it is more important to note that the first authoritative definition of the scope of the second intermediate zone was made by Mao Zedong personally during a visit of the French Parliamentary delegation in January 1964. In his comments, he specifically mentioned West Germany as being a part of that zone.[76]

The most important initiative, however, was taken by the Chinese foreign minister, Chen Yi. At a specially convened informal press conference for West European journalists—where West Germans were present—he declared that the PRC hoped that the two 'parts' of Germany would be 'united peacefully'. This was certainly an important statement, since the word 'state' was conspicuously absent from his remarks about the two Germanies. Even more important was that he said nothing about Berlin—very unusual indeed, since all Chinese statements on Germany until then had contained remarks about Berlin that were supportive of the East German position.[77]

The remarks and the timing of the press conference were well chosen. They came when West Germany was actively seeking recognition of her claim to West Berlin. The remarks did not go unnoticed, since Bonn 'acted promptly with feelers' that finally resulted in the opening of confidential bilateral talks between the West German and the Chinese governments in Berne.[78]

The two delegations met four times between 25 May and 23 November in 1964. For the Chinese, the talks were a major breakthrough. Coming soon after French recognition, they were obviously very eager to have some fruitful results; for any *modus vivendi* with West Germany would give them an additional presence in Western Europe. In fact, China would then have had representatives in the three most economically powerful countries in Western Europe— undoubtedly a major feather in the Chinese diplomatic cap and this at a time when China was moving away from the socialist bloc.

At the same time, Beijing was realistic enough to recognize that diplomatic recognition *à la française* was not on the cards. The Federal Republic was too dependent on the United States, and did not have, at the time, any great vision or even an idea—however vague—of its own role in international affairs.

Furthermore, within the West German leadership, there was no one at the helm who could give a new political lead to the country. Besides the proponents of the Atlantic Alliance were still stronger than the group that advocated an emulation of the Gaullist model for West German foreign policy. But then, even if there were a de Gaulle, would it have been politically feasible for West Germany in the middle sixties? Was it not a little too early?

Aware of this situation, the Chinese had come to the negotiating table with a limited objective: to persuade West Germany to conclude an official trade agreement; the West Germans, on the other hand, had come to the meeting with a different objective: to persuade China to accept the Berlin Clause. Since the West Germans had strong views on the question, and since they had apparently made acceptance of the Berlin Clause a major objective of their diplomacy, the Chinese negotiating tactics were not to give their counterparts the impression that they had already made up their minds. So, questions on the Berlin Clause were asked, but no firm views were expressed. Everything was left open.

At the same time, the Chinese brought out from their own diplomatic bag the proposal for the conclusion of an official trade agreement. The Chinese diplomatic tactics were clear. they had implicitly tied the Berlin Clause question to their own objective of concluding a trade agreement. It soon became apparent to the Chinese that the Germans were not interested in concluding an official trade agreement, but merely in signing a commodity agreement (*Warenabkommen*)—an agreement in which they wanted an inclusion of the Berlin Clause. Chancellor Erhard's visit to the United States that took place between the first and the second Sino-West German sessions did not help matters. For there, under American pressure, he publicly made it clear that the Federal Republic had no intention of recognizing the People's Republic, nor had it any intention of concluding an official trade agreement.[79] However, while ceding to the United States on these points, the Germans vehemently resisted all American pressure to abandon the talks. This, to them, was their sovereign right, and, besides— asserted the Germans—it was in their national interest.

The Chinese were sold on the idea of a trade agreement. Clearly, this was their major diplomatic goal. In fact, they had even decided on the person they wanted to send as their trade representative.[80] Therefore, when it became increasingly evident that the negotiations were at an impasse, they withdrew any idea of eventually accepting the Berlin Clause. They then denounced what they called Erhard's 'hostile attitude' towards China and made it clear in their last meeting that they could not give in 'on the fundamental principle' of Berlin, since Berlin was not a part of West Germany. China then lost all interest in continuing the talks and showed no eagerness to meet the Germans when the latter attempted to contact the Chinese mission in London.

West Germans attributed the breakdown to the ousting of Khrushchev. Since, ran the German interpretation, the Chinese began to hope that better understanding with the Russians might ensue, now that Khrushchev was no longer in power, a concession to West Germany on Berlin, therefore, would have been a wrong move.[81]

Khrushchev's ousting may well be one of the factors, but not the only one, since it is also evident that the Federal Republic had very little leverage in the talks[82] and was not able to make any concession on the trade agreement—an issue on which China, albeit naïvely, had maintained great hopes. Clearly, they did not see any point in making a concession themselves when the West German government was not prepared to make a concession on trade agreement. The commodity agreement (*Warenabkommen*), in their view, was a poor substitute for what they really wanted from West Germany.[83]

The failure of parallel negotiations between such industrial giants as Demag and Mannesmann and Chinese corporations for the sale of complete plants confirmed the Chinese leaders in their doubts that the Federal Republic was unable to take independent decisions that were unacceptable to the United States.[84]

After the first announcement was made that an agreement had been reached in late 1964, and the Erhard government had decided in principle to provide credits for five years for the export of plants to China, American pressures against such a deal began to build up. Secretary of State Dean Rusk criticized it,[85] Deputy Assistant Secretary of State for Far Eastern Affairs William Bundy expressed 'our concern'[86] and American Economic Counsellor Edward Moline was despatched to Bonn to state the American position vigorously. What is more, the Senate passed a resolution condemning the deal.[87]

Though the talks formally had commenced, in 1966 the Chinese were already becoming sceptical regarding the future of the deal. Who lost interest and at what point? What really happened? Was it the Germans or was it the Chinese who disengaged themselves from the negotiations? No two persons fully agree on what happened.[88] While some attribute the failure to the advent of the Cultural Revolution, others seem to suggest that Bonn had secretly rescinded its guarantee, still others put the blame on 'unreconcilable differences over prices'.[89] Though all of these factors may have contributed to the final breakdown of the negotiations in May 1968, the prolonged nature of the negotiations, the continuous West German efforts to assure the United States that no new policy was being inaugurated,[90] and high-level American pressure convinced the Chinese government at an early date that Bonn was not ready to fend for itself on any issue on which Washington had a clear-cut and firm policy.

China thus lost all political interest in the Federal Republic. In fact, it resumed its previous critical stance with the same suddenness that had been adopted in January 1963 to criticize East Germany. The first major indication of this new trend was Chen Yi's statement of 4 January, 1965, that China could not establish any relations with Bonn as long as it continued with its plans of integrating East Germany with the Federal Republic.[91] And slowly with the passage of time, and the course of the same year, Chinese statements and articles became more and more polemical.

Commenting on West German criticism of an Egyptian invitation to Walter Ulbricht, a Chinese 'commentator' had this to say:

What right have the Bonn authorities to interfere with such arrogance. The West German government is resorting to the threats of cutting its aid to the United Arab Republic in order to force her to cancel the invitation to Ulbricht. This only proves with what impudence the West German militarists are trying to interfere in the internal affairs of other countries.[92]

What is interesting about this articles is not so much the attacks on West Germany, as the sudden support extended to East Germany. The article continued:

> The GDR is a member of the socialist camp. The Chinese people are resolutely opposed to the West German militarist plots to isolate and annex her. The Chinese people are firmly supporting the people of GDR in their just struggle against West German militarists and revenge seekers on the orders of the US and against the too well-know 'Hallstein Doctrine' and defense of its national sovereignty.[93]

Another major critical comment on West Germany appeared in the *People's Daily* on 9 April 1965 in the form of an editorial—also an indicator of the authoritative nature of the comment. The occasion was the convening of the plenary session of the Federal Republic's Bundestag in West Berlin. Apart from supporting East Germany and opposing the Hallstein Doctrine, it came out against 'the rabid provocations of West German militarism'. The editorial declared:

> With the support of US imperialism, the West German militarists have become ever more arrogant and aggressive. Not along ago, the Bonn government, at US instigation, openly proposed the laying of an atomic-mine belt along the frontiers of GDR and Czechoslovakia, the adoption of a 'forward strategy' against the socialist countries and the waging of a 'hidden war' against the GDR. It tried to get hold of nuclear weapons through the US 'multilateral nuclear force' plan and has repeatedly demanded the recovery of the 'Sudetanland' and the restoration of the 1937 borders . . . These criminal activities of West German militarism not only gravely menace the security of the GDR but also threaten European and world peace.[94]

China was back to square one so far as her political relations with the Federal Republic were concerned. Although China was realistic enough to set its sights on the limited goal of concluding a trade agreement, even this was too much for West Germany; for the latter was really not ready to conclude any accord that smacked of politics—however remote; and the Chinese initiative did smack of politics, since there was really no need for an official trade agreement to forge economic ties, and since West Germany was already China's most important European trade partner.

Where did China go wrong? Why wasn't it realized that the Federal Republic was really not ready to branch out politically? Can one attribute this miscalculation to lack of information on the actual state of affairs? There were probably a number of considerations that may have enticed China to attempt Sino-West German *rapprochement*. The first and obviously the most important was the French recognition. The 1964 Sino-French normalization did generate some anxiety and some fear among West German business groups of being left out of what they considered the vast Chinese market. The second probably was that the Federal Republic was showing signs of some autonomous thinking on Western Europe. Without being—unlike the French—against British entry into the Common Market, West Germany was indeed showing some signs of resistance to

American pressures to get Britain into the Market. For the Federal Republic Franco-German relations were becoming the focal point of a West German foreign policy in which Great Britain did not have an equal role. The Chinese certainly grasped this new West German desire to become more independent, but went wrong in transposing this trend to such burning issues that concerned China. Going along with the French to build an integrated Western Europe was one thing, but pursuing an independent line on China was a totally different matter. Also, one wonders if China was not ideologically carried away by the Marxist theory of increasing economic and political contradictions within the capitalist world without taking into account the counter argument that there are indeed limits beyond which capitalist nations politically may not go, even when economic contradictions surface among them.

No political change towards Britain

Towards Britain there was no material political change in the sixties. Notwith-standing the improvement in Sino-British economic relations, no attempts were really made to reinforce Sino-British political relations. And no signs were discernible of a real Chinese let up regarding the development of political relations with London. If anything, an opposite trend—a trend towards greater rigidity—was becoming evident.

The Chinese government showed no interest in the British proposal that diplomatic relations between the two countries be upgraded through the exchange of ambassadors, as happened with France.[95] China even refused to receive a special British representative through whom London wanted to explain its position on Vietnam.[96] At the same time, China once again publicly approved de Gaulle's refusal to allow Britain to enter the Common Market. The Chinese were apparently convinced that Britain was too tied up with the United States and that it was impossible to envisage her becoming autonomous like France. If they had some hope or illusion—however naïve—of creating a dent in American-West German relations, they had none so far as Britain was concerned. Besides, if London did have its policies separate from Washington, they were no less in conflict with China.

While the Chinese were reinforcing their ties with France, and establishing political contact with the West Germans, they systematically denounced British initiatives of June 1965 on Vietnam,[97] charged the government of complicity with Taiwan,[98] warned it, through an authoritative article penned by a *People's Daily* 'commentator' against abusing the name of the co-chairman of the Geneva conference on Laos and against playing 'its double dealing tactics' of helping in the consolidation and stabilization of the 'fascist rule of the racist Smith regime'.[99]

But more than anything, it was the British attitude on the admission of China to the United Nations that irritated the Chinese government, for while consistently voting for China's admission whenever a resolution to this effect was tabled, it backed—also consistently—the 1961 American resolution that a change in China's representation was an 'important question; and as such required a two-thirds' majority. However deft the British arguments may have been to explain their position, for the Chinese this was an unfriendly act.[100] Even before this issued had become a key element, Zhou Enlai had made this clear. In an interview to Felix Greene in 1961 he had declared:

> During the last year, Sino-British relations have not ameliorated as they should have. The responsibility for this lies with the British Cabinet which on the one hand recognises that the PRC is alone qualified to represent China, while on the other hand it supports the US in its defense of the Chiang Kai-Shek clique in the UN. If this obstacle is removed, Sino–British relations will ameliorate immediately and cultural relations between the two countries will also develop.[101]

Other West European countries

With other Western European countries, China made even less political headway. They were simply not ready to follow the French lead, principally because pressures from Washington were indeed too great to permit any of them to take autonomous political initiatives, notably *vis-à-vis* China.

In January 1964, the Italian foreign minister, Giuseppe Saragat, frankly told the Chamber of Deputies' Foreign Affairs Committee that the government was opposed to the recognition of China at that moment since it would cause an increase in world tension.[102] However, despite such a categorical statement, domestic political pressures did begin to build up for recognition.[103] But this was virtually impossible. Since the United States was firmly opposed to it, the Italian government, as it was constituted at that time, apparently did not have the political capacity to resist transatlantic pressures. But none the less—presumably owing to domestic pressures and its desires to prove its credentials of independence—it introduced a new proposal on China at the twenty-first session of the General Assembly in 1966. The Italian representative, Piccioni, proposed the establishment of an *ad-hoc* committee composed of 'persons of the greatest eminence and of long international experience'[104] to sound out Beijing regarding its representation in the United Nations and to ascertain if it was in a position to comply with the UN Charter.

The Italian proposal did not go very far since the issue was considered an 'important question' and, as such, needed a two-thirds' majority—impossible at that time. The Belgian government, to take another example, was even more categorically against recognition. Its deputy foreign minister declared in a radio broadcast on 29 January 1964 that the Chinese policies and actions on different international issues (Korea, Vietnam, India) made it difficult for Belgium to recognize China.[105]

Focus on de Gaulle

But of all the bilateral political interactions that China inaugurated during the first half of the sixties, the one with France was incomparably the most important and most fruitful. Most important because of the number of exchanges and most fruitful because of the establishment of full diplomatic relations. The sameness of view on a wide spectrum of major international issues was also very striking—in any event much more so than with any other West European country. For China, this was indeed a windfall. She naturally tried to reap maximum benefit from this favourable situation by developing its carefully calculated policy of cultivating France—again much more than any other country of the region, big or small.

In this connection, it is important to note that the Chinese leaders made it a point to highlight the crucial role that de Gaulle played in giving France a more autonomous political identity and laying the foundations for institutionalized Sino–French relations. Among the Chinese leaders, there was some degree of fascination with the French leader, with his vision of the world and with his charismatic leadership. In fact, the Chinese leaders 'glossed over their ideological differences to honour him as a leader'.[106] And practically all of them in their informal conversations with French public figures made it a point to underline the esteem they had for the French leader.[107]

This very high opinion of de Gaulle can be gauged from the fact that he was invited to visit China when he was no longer in power; and from the public and repeated expressions of Chinese unhappiness that this could not be realized because of his death. It can also be ascertained from the condolence message that Mao sent to Mme de Gaulle—a message in which he declared that de Gaulle's death was 'a bereavement for the whole of China'.[108]

Abortive initiatives

None of the three policies directed towards Western Europe and analysed in this chapter were much of a success. Despite considerable Chinese effort, the palpable results were indeed few. The campaign to invite West European personalities came to nothing. China was seriously handicapped in this campaign simply because of the absence of any diplomatic ties with most of the West European nations. A systematic organization of invitations was indeed very difficult. With few exceptions, the choice was limited essentially to Great Britain and France. Even those invited had limited impact in shaking the lacklustre image of China that generally prevailed in Europe at the time—the image of a nation with serious problems.

The political impact of these visits was even less striking; for none of those invited appeared to carry much political clout in their respective countries. China could have done better with those who represented the media. Doors could have been opened wide to journalists, since their impact—reporting from a closed country—would have been greater. But here the Chinese authorities were prudent; for invitations were sent out or visas were issued only to those who were sympathetic to China. Presumably, China did not wish to take any risks, given the fact that there was serious economic disarray and was well aware that nothing is worse for a country's image than news about drought, shortage of food and rampant signs of malnutrition.

Not much headway was made in the economic sector either. In fact, total trade with Western Europe declined in the early sixties, and the increase that began to be registered after 1964 was certainly not very significant. China's capacity to trade with Western Europe was limited. The foreign currency needed for such transactions was scarce; and whatever was then available had to be utilized for importing much needed wheat from Australia and Canada for the people who were threatened with malnutrition and even famine in some areas. China's capacity to pay for imports through exports was severely restricted because many exportable items had to be channelled to the Soviet Union to whom there was an obligation to repay loans. Finally, the Chinese acquisition of turn-key plants from Western Europe had further exhausted trading capacity since China had to make down payments varying from 10 to 25 per cent on each of these plants.

Acquisition of additional credits could have removed this major hurdle, but this, under the circumstances, was hardly feasible on a large scale because of the Chinese leadership's publicly proclaimed policy of strict self-reliance. It was scarcely possible to jettison this policy formally during the politically charged atmosphere of the early sixties, for this would have given an additional opportunity for the ideologically orientated orthodox faction in the party to criticize the leadership of Liu Shaoqi and Deng Xiaoping. Besides, it is not certain that China would have been able to raise large credits in the international financial market, given its economic difficulties. China attempted to get over this hurdle by exporting sizeable amounts of silver in 1960, 1961, and 1962 to Western Europe. But this too was becoming difficult since in 1961 and 1962, China had used silver for as much as 27 per cent of her imports.

There were no major diplomatic breakthroughs either. The establishment of diplomatic relations with France could have opened such a prospect. But this was not the case. Dependent as most of Western Europe was on the United States, it was hardly possible to defy its transatlantic partner—least of all on an issue such as China on which the United States held very firm views. Even de Gaulle's interest in China was limited. Despite his declarations regarding the importance of China,[109] the focal point of his new foreign policy was the European Communist world. Beijing, in de Gaulle's strategy, was important, but not as much as Moscow. Beijing could be useful for the eventual neutralization of south east Asia, but *détente* in Europe was a major French priority; and for this, *entente* with the Soviet Union was paramount.

China, thus did not make much headway in the sixties. The three-pronged policy did not bear much fruit. Western Europeans were not ready to respond to Chinese overtures. Clearly, they had not attained the degree of autonomy necessary to act independently in foreign affairs.

The Chinese leadership—at least the one that had advanced the theory that contradictions abounded in the 'imperialist camp'—was thus proved wrong. Western Europe still did not have the necessary clout to fend for itself, and it had been a mistake to have exaggerated Western European capacity for functioning autonomously.

Yet, can one really argue that this was a conceptual mistake? That the Chinese leadership had gone a little too far in its Marxist analysis? That it had too mechanically transposed its theory of contradictions to a political situation that was more subtle and more complex? Or is it not conceivable that the new Chinese perception of Western Europe was a theoretical afterthought to justify diplomatic initiatives that had already been decided upon, and that the Chinese were prompted by more mundane and practical exigencies such as diplomatic isolation than anything else. In other words, could not one argue that theoretical considerations were marginal in Chinese decision-making at the diplomatic level, and that they are taken into account only after a political option has been selected. Also it may well have been that the long and theoretical discussions within the CCP were really an instrument to legitimize change, which, in effect, was introduced for other reasons.

Whatever may be the validity of this line of reasoning, it would be difficult to deny its relevance in regard to Chinese decisions about Europe in the early sixties. What about the Chinese domestic scene? Did it not contribute to the Chinese failure in Western Europe? For, after all, was the CCP not in the middle of battling out an intramural dispute among its leaders with Peng Dehuai challenging Mao, and with Liu Shaoqi—having replaced Mao as head of the state—implementing a new policy? And did all this not contribute in generating hesitations among party leaders regarding the wisdom of Chinese policy towards Western Europe?

Though anything is possible, that reading seems unlikely. For Mao, from all indications, was well in command—along with Zhou—of designing and conducting foreign policy; and there really were no serious reservations regarding the broad options China had taken in the early sixties. It was basically and principally the general hold that the United States exercised over her West European allies, which was really responsible for the lack of any major Chinese breakthrough in Western Europe.

Ideological isolation

China's failure was not only in the diplomatic domain; it was also in the ideological sector, for her isolation from West European communism became equally marked. If the lack of any headway on the diplomatic-economic front was due to West European inability or unwillingness to build bridges with China, the isolation from West European communism was due to Chinese refusal to accept the winds of change that were sweeping West European communist parties.

The changed environment in their own region, compounded with the new thinking that emanated from the twentieth Soviet party congress, plus the tumultuous destalinization in Eastern Europe, had pushed the European communist parties in the 'revisionist' direction. Many of them had come to the conclusion that conditions in Western Europe had undergone a sea change, that a constellation of socio-economic forces within their own societies had envolved, that violent seizure of power was no longer possible, that an understanding with other left-wing forces had become necessary to give new direction to capitalistic societies and that pluralism, an integral part of the West European political system, could no longer be rejected out of hand. The Italian Communist Party, for example, long influenced by Antonio Gramschi's idea of a 'national collective will' that could ignite socialism, invoked in 1965 'the possibility of the conquest of positions of power as a bourgeois state'.[110] The French communists—but much later than their Italian counterparts—accepted the need for a multi-party system not only during the transitional period but even after the establishment of the socialist system.[111]

This new attraction to evolutionary change was not only confined to big communist parties of southern Europe, though they were undoubtedly the principal catalysts. Impelled by the winds of 'revisionism' that were blowing all over Western Europe, the British, Belgian, Swiss and Scandinavian parties were also moving in the same direction.

Opening up to the Western world diplomatically was one thing, but accepting new 'revisionist' thinking in the ideological sector was another matter since it might have a deleterious influence on the international communist movement including the Third World parties—a perspective China was not prepared to accept at the time. All this was anathema to the CCP. Therefore, despite the fact that most of the European communist parties were partially disengaging from Moscow, China simply refused to accept new patterns of thinking; the revisionist character of the change was more dangerous than even the growing political disengagement of eurocommunist parties from Moscow. The priority, in the Chinese line of thinking at the time, was to combat 'revisionism'.

After an initial attempt at polite polemical exchanges with 'Comrades' Thorez and Togliatti in 1963,[112] the Chinese leaders concluded that most of the European parties had become 'new types of social democratic parties'[113] and the 'main bulwark of revisionism of the most rabid type'.[114]

The ideological gap had become unbridgeable, making it futile to deploy any further efforts to seek an understanding with West European parties. This had become clear at the Moscow consultative conference of March 1965 when, despite Chinese opposition, nineteen communist parties had assembled to discuss the international situation,[115] and it had became glaringly evident at the Karlovy Vary Conference of European communist parties in April 1967[116], when a new global perception was adopted.

Casting their prudence aside, the Chinese now came out openly against European Communists. As the *People's Daily* wrote:

The Karlovy Vary Conference was a meeting serving US interests . . . The meeting usurped the name of the communist and worker's party. What kind of Communists are they? The participants: the Brezhnev Kosygin crowd from the Soviet Union, the Ulbricht crowd from East Germany, the Rochet crowd from France, the Longo crowd from Italy, the Gollan crowd from Britain, the Ibarruri crowd from Spain, etc. . . . all are renegades to Marxism–Leninism, working class scabs and enemies of the revolutionary Communist parties. The meeting at Karlovy Vary was a meeting of representatives of the privileged stratum of the Soviet Union and East European countries and the agents of the bourgeoisie of some capitalist countries in Europe. It was a meeting at which new social democratic parties took a further step in colluding with the old social democratic parties. The new social democratic parties and the old social democratic parties have become a [conservative club] to keep all reactionary forces going a bit longer.[117]

With this ferocious attack, China had come to the point of no return so far as the European communists were concerned. All hopes of any understanding or even of patching up had been destroyed.

Conclusion

The first half of the sixties generated two types of parallel policies that were pursued simultaneously. One, directed at the governments, was designed to activate China's relations with Western Europe—relations that hardly existed at the time. The underlying reason behind such a major initiative was the Soviet decision to break with China, and the ensuing difficulties or isolation that China had to face in the economic and diplomatic sectors.

The main objectives of the Chinese initiatives were to break out of their diplomatic isolation and to seek succour in the face of pressing economic difficulties generated by Soviet withdrawal and the serious drought that China was facing at the time. The whole pattern of China's diplomatic behaviour to expand her West European connection was in the best tradition of classical diplomacy in which the balance-of-power strategy was very important.

France clearly was the focal point of this new diplomatic campaign of the sixties, for this was the only major European country with whom full diplomatic relations had been successfully established. Besides, they were on the same wavelength on a wide spectrum of international issues—undoubtedly a factor which weighed heavily in China's decision to give France such importance during the first half of the sixties. That this was not particularly successful was not so much due to a lack of Chinese interest or an inadequacy of Chinese efforts, but rather to a corresponding lack of French enthusiasm coupled with West European inability, regarding China, to strike out independently of the United States. The Chinese had clearly erred in their assessment of the West European configuration of forces, and had miscalculated their capacity to exploit 'contradictions' among capitalist states.

The second policy—directed at West European Communism—was just the opposite of China's benign diplomatic behaviour. It was aggressive, belligerent and ideologically induced. The CCP must have been in a searing dilemma while opting for such a line. Supporting West European 'revisionism' could have opened prospects for accelerating the disengagement of West European parties from Moscow—a goal that would have been identical to what China was seeking in the diplomatic sector. But, China's support of the new Eurocommunism would have been in contradiction to the Marxist orthodoxy that China was defending among Third World parties. Defending ideological orthodoxy was apparently viewed as primary in the light of the importance that China attached to revolutions in the Third World. Besides, the balance within the CCP was rapidly shifting in favour of the ideological purists who were not prepared to have any truck with the 'revisionists' even if it were to lead to the isolation of the Soviet Union.

China's failure among European communists was thus unavoidable. For the West European parties, the new revisionist thinking represented a more effective and a more relevant response to the rapidly changing European situation than what the Chinese were suggesting. The new thesis favouring the liberalization of Communist regimes, accepting different roads to socialism and improving living standards of socialist regimes dovetailed more closely with eurocommunist aspirations than the highly intransigent Chinese line of thinking which the European communists had successfully followed in the past, but which, in the light of the changed situation, they were eager to cast aside.

During the first half of the sixties, China was able to keep her diplomatic policies separate from her ideological policies, and was fairly successful in maintaining a balance between these two different and contradictory patterns of foreign policy. But as subsequent developments were to show, this was an uneasy equilibrium which was destroyed with the onset of the Cultural Revolution, when ideological belligerency spilled over to the diplomatic sector.

Chapter 6
The turmoils of the Cultural Revolution

The uncertainties of the early sixties in Chinese domestic politics were replaced with the certainties of the Cultural Revolution, with the rabid proselytization of Mao's radicalized thinking and with his unchallenged reassertion within the party. With this lurch to the left, the gladiatorial combat was over—at least provisionally—with clear options taken in favour of accelerating internal revolution. Mao's principal adversary, Liu Shaoqi, the favorite of the party pragmatists, had thrown in the towel and had publicly confessed his 'grave mistake of right opportunism'.[1]

However, if Liu was out, Mao was not completely in. It was one of those uncertain situations in turbulent China where real power, at the upper echelons, was diffused among disparate groups all of whom were projecting themselves as Mao's supporters, and where, at the lower echelons, a mass of unruly people had been let loose over whom control was becoming increasingly difficult. The uniqueness of the situation can be gauged from the all-directional, escalating internal crisis and the unprecedented popularity of Mao.

The turmoil was so rampageous, the confusion so widespread, and the determination to 'make revolution' so vehement that even the leaders who had originally unleashed all this had serious difficulties in reining in the unruly Red Guards. Mao's popularity furthermore had reached unprecedented heights. Both at the top as well as at the bottom everybody involved in the turmoil was proclaiming that they were acting in the name and on behalf of Mao Zedong. What he stood for and what he represented had become such 'a new standard of legitimacy and correctness',[2] in the country that no-one could stand up to him. The few real or imaginary challenges that occurred were cut down to size by his political acumen or by his well-tried tactics of 'divide and rule', and of taking his adversaries 'one at a time'—Luo Riuqing in December 1965, then Peng Zhen in April 1966 and finally Deng Xiaoping in July 1966 and Liu Shaoqi in August of the same year.

Under such difficult circumstances, the external ramifications of what was essentially a 'domestic turmoil'[3] were unavoidable. The disorder was indeed too great and too widespread to be contained from spilling over to foreign affairs. Generally in the past this was not the case. China's foreign relations had continued at their own pace and rhythm, pursuing well-defined external goals regardless of the internal situation. The designing of foreign policy was the 'domain réservé' of the top party leadership, particularly that of Mao Zedong,[4] from which the rest of the population was excluded, except of course during periods of crisis when the leaders themselves felt the need for general mass mobilization.

During the height of the Cultural Revolution it was different. The dynamics of the crisis, compounded with the confusion that was rife at the time, made it difficult to contain its expansion. The spillover was unavoidable.

Consequences affecting foreign affairs

The ramifications were not so much on the substance but on the form. They did not so much impinge on the basic foreign policy decisions taken before the Cultural Revolution but on the pattern of Chinese behaviour and on the Chinese way of implementing those decisions.

The first major ramification was situational. There was a general inattentiveness to foreign affairs. The Chinese political leaders were so totally overwhelmed or bogged down by revolutionary euphoria that they hardly had any time to look after foreign policy, except on unavoidable issues that were forced upon them by the international situation.[5] It is indeed difficult to imagine a scenario of Chinese leaders indulging in the luxury of holding meetings to discuss China's foreign policy strategy in the midst of all the political turbulence over which control was becoming increasingly difficult.

The second was institutional. The Cultural Revolution had generated confusion and fear within the Ministry of Foreign Affairs which was briefly occupied by the Red Guards with Yao Dengshen at the helm as the 'four-day foreign minister'. Welcomed as a hero on his return to Beijing, after having been expelled from Indonesia for disorderly conduct, he had managed to exercise control over the ministry. While he was in charge, many embassies were attacked, including those of Burma, India, Great Britain, the Soviet Union and Mongolia. Many foreign diplomatic personnel were physically attacked or harassed, including the French ambassador who was the target of an abusive shouting match, and the British chargé d'affaires who was physically assaulted within the premises of the embassy. The total state of confusion in the ministry can be reasoned from the difficulties the Foreign Minister, Chen Yi, had himself personally to hear which included open subjection to continuous Red Guard criticism for over a year and an ostentatious parading through the streets of Beijing wearing a dunce's cap.[6]

Despite support and protection extended to him by Zhou Enlai and even Mao Zedong, he was charged with having strenuously promoted the reactionary diplomatic line of 'three capitulations and one extinction' (capitulation to imperialism, revisionism and reactionaries from all countries and the extinction of the fire of people's revolution.)[7] It is difficult to imagine the efficacious conduct of foreign affairs when the minister-in-charge was being constantly attacked for what he had done and what he represented.

The personnel in the ministry as well as abroad also became victims of strong attacks 'for bringing about capitalist restoration,[8] thus paralyzing their own diplomats. All the Chinese ambassadors, with the exception of Huang Hua in Cairo, were withdrawn. Some were subjected to questioning and harassment by the Red Guards the moment they got off the plane. One of them, Liu Xiao, one-time vice-minister of foreign affairs, was even imprisoned without trial or investigation, Chen Yi's protests notwithstanding.[9] A campaign of harassment was also inaugurated by partisans of the Cultural Revolution against the pragmatists within the missions abroad. It is interesting to note that invariably it was the clerical or lower diplomatic staff that were involved in this frenetic activity both inside and outside the embassies.[10]

The third ramification pertained to the broad framework of China's foreign policy—as it was defined before the Cultural Revolution. Though the broad contours of China's foreign policy basically remained the same, the patterns of diplomatic operation became tumultuous, extremist and adversial. In sum, if foreign policy remained the same, the manner of implementing it was radically changed. If reactions to international events followed the earlier patterns, they were none the less much more disproportionate to the events than previously.

Policies towards Europe

China's policy towards Europe had all the imprints of the Cultural Revolution. The internal tumult did ṡpill over to foreign affairs, with Chinese activities centring principally on making disproportionate responses to any untoward incidents that took place in foreign countries or on encouraging the establishment of pro-Maoist groups wherever possible.

All this nevertheless did not stop the Chinese diplomatic machine from continuing the routine practices of sending greetings to the host country over whose territory a Chinese leader was flying, or despatching laconic messages to countries celebrating their national days or even giving banquets to visiting delegations whose leaders were being berated in the Chinese press or signing trade agreements or continuing commercial relations etc. All these activities were continued, but the substantive aspects of China's foreign relations were focused on retaliatory diplomatic incidents or helping in the establishment of pro-Maoist groups. This is what Chinese diplomacy was reduced to.

Eastern Europe

Though Eastern Europe was not ignored, it was by no means the centre of Chinese attention, with the exception of course of Albania and to some extent Romania. Chinese embassies, having cut themselves off from the day-to-day political life of the host country, were either carrying out routine diplomatic tasks or indulging in ferocious protestations against some untoward incident—against, for example, the Yugoslavs for having destroyed the news display case in front of the embassy showing Mao's photos,[11] or against the Bulgarians or the Czechs who had declared the Chinese students as *personae non gratae* ,[12] or in Poland where the Chinese embassy was reportedly showing Polish visitors a documentary that highlighted Soviet complicity in the Katyn forest massacres during World War II.[13]

The minimal interest shown towards the Soviet client states was also evident from the absence of any declaratory activity. Very little fiery rhetoric was unleashed against Eastern-bloc countries, the principal focus being the Soviet

Union. Presumably, this glossing over of Eastern Europe was based on the Chinese conviction that most of Eastern Europe was hopelessly tied to the Soviet Union and consequently it was perhaps pointless to indulge in any great rhetoric against them. Besides, the Chinese also realized that they could not actively do much since the authoritarian political system left little scope for any real activity. It has also been argued that Chinese silence on developments in Eastern Europe may also be attributable to the heavy withdrawal of diplomats from Chinese embassies, thus depriving Beijing of some of its experienced observers of the East European scene.[14]

The Soviet client states, on the other hand, were much more active against China. Almost unanimously and regularly they denounced China for her Cultural Revolution. They characterized it as a 'design' to break up the international communist movement and strongly criticized the Red Guard 'terror tactics' and the 'colossal revival of the cult of personality of Mao Zedong'.[15] Some of them even considered using the Cultural Revolution as 'a pretext' to come to terms with the United States.[16]

Eastern Europe's open denunciation of China cannot be explained purely in terms of the satellite character of these regimes, though this is certainly important, for many of them could have either glossed over the events in China, or could have directed only routine and minimal attacks against China. The open and systematic denunciation was also because of very serious East European reservations regarding the Cultural Revolution. Particularly worrying and even distasteful to them was the growing personality cult in China. Having just emerged from such an experience themselves, they could hardly approve what was happening in China.

The Chinese refusal—despite pleas from many Communist parties—to forge a common front with the Soviet Union for a united and well-concerted action in Vietnam was probably the third reason that generated East European criticism. The East European parties were really incensed at the Chinese refusal. Many of them made it a point to highlight the non-cooperative aspect of the CCP, and openly condemned what they viewed as a deliberate attempt to further disrupt the international communist movement. Even Gomulka, generally known for his pro-Beijing views, denounced the Chinese in April 1967 for having 'violated the unity of the anti-imperialist front of socialist states'.[17] The Czechoslovak party went even further. In its party organ, Rude Pravo, it alluded to a secret understanding between China and the United States which consisted of China's assurances that she would not intervene in the Vietnam conflict unless directly invaded, in return for Washington's agreement to hold Chiang Kai-Shek on a leash while the Cultural Revolution was on.[18]

There is perhaps a fourth explanation: the open Chinese support of Stalinist groups in Eastern Europe. Though accentuated during the Cultural Revolution, the Chinese were apparently involved in such activity even during the period preceding the tumultuous events. Beijing, apparently, made attempts in the sixties to overthrow or destabilize regimes in Hungary, Bulgaria, Czechoslovakia, Poland and East Germany. At least charges to this effect were made by the established governments. The Hungarian government, for example, reported in March 1964 that a Chinese-inspired plot, led by Sandor Nagy, a rabid Stalinist, had been suppressed.[19] *Nepszabadsag*, the Hungarian party organ, condemned pro-Chinese elements in the country 'who had become confused by the pseudo-revolutionary slogans of the Chinese leaders and by those rightist elements, and who try to justify their revisionist views through debate with the Chinese leaders',[20] A coup, according to some reports, was also planned for April 1964 in Bulgaria, but was discovered by Soviet intelligence in time. The main accomplices were known to support Mao Zedong.[21] In East Germany, a pro-China cell was discovered whose intentions, according to official reports, was to topple the leadership. In the words of Erich Mueckenberger, first secretary of the Frankfurt-on-Oder Communist Party, they 'have been booted out of the party for encouraging a plot against our country'.[22] In Poland, the government arrested a group of six Stalinists distributing a pamphlet whose title was 'Polish version of Chinese Ideology'.[23] And in the case of Czechoslovakia, Chinese complicity, according to official reports, was even more evident. They had apparently sent a secret letter to Czech diplomats abroad accusing the Czechoslovak leadership of 'succumbing to the pressures of Khrushchev and company and allowing itself into acts which are incompatible with Marxism–Leninism'.[24]

All these Chinese manoeuvrings in 1964 to bring the Stalinists back to power boomeranged in Eastern Europe. Opposition to China stiffened even more. And with the onset of the Cultural Revolution the level of East European vituperation reached new heights, isolating China even further.

China's reaction to the Soviet invasion of Czechoslovakia on 21 August 1968 isolated the country even further from most of Eastern Europe. Practically everybody in the area was attacked: those who favoured the invasion and those who were against it. The first comments that appeared (22 August) on these events were a torrent of invective against not only the Soviet Union but also the victims. The Soviet invasion was characterized as 'savage, hideous, despicable, grisly and fascist', but at the same time Alexander Dubcek was characterized as a 'revisionist', who had opened Czechoslovakia even more to 'capitalism in all sectors internally and externally'.[25] Zhou Enlai did the same. At a reception in Beijing, he berated Moscow but also severely criticized the Czech government.

The CCP had thus become a prisoner of its own rhetoric. Having severely criticized all 'modern revisionism', it was hardly possible for it to support Dubcek—the most 'revisionist' of them all, least of all at a time when the Cultural Revolution was in full swing.

Exceptions to the rule

Albania and Romania were two exceptions to the general degeneration of Sino-East European relations; the former more than the latter. Albania, in fact, had become the focal point of Chinese interest, since its perception of the outside world was identical to China's and since both followed the same ideology. Their bilateral relations were governed by frequent consultations between high-level officials, by delegation exchanges at the ministerial level and by very regular consultations between special economic, military and trade groups.[26]

Purely from a security angle, the relations were hardly of any use to Albania for they did not provide any credible shield against attack from its neighbours. The only hope was that the close Sino-Albanian interaction might in itself deter any potential aggressor. On the other hand, it is more than probable that a military pact would have destablized the situation in the area and would have triggered off greater tension and firmer reactions on the part of Albania's neighbours.

On the economic front, there were, however, palpable advantages. Beijing was in a position to bail out Albania from a precarious economic position. In fact, it was remarkably generous, considering the fact that China itself was in economic doldrums. In June 1965, Tirana and Beijing signed an agreement for a Chinese loan backing Albania's five-year plan (1966–70).[27] No details were disclosed, but it has been estimated that the loan amounted to $214 million.[28] Another important loan was granted in October 1966 for the development of Albania's petroleum industry.[29] The importance of the bilateral economic relations can be gauged from the fact that between 1965 and 1970, Albania commissioned, with Chinese assistance, forty-one important projects, twenty-four of which were in heavy industry.[30]

What concrete benefits did China reap from such a relationship? What was really wanted from a very small and vulnerable country, so far away, so isolated and so much in the heart of Eastern Europe, geopolitically surrounded by adversaries? No palpable advantages are discernible. Apart from having the satisfaction of friendly diplomatic relations at a time when China was isolated, it is difficult to locate any specific benefits that may have accrued to China from this unequal relationship. Much has been written about all the contacts that were established or the aid that was given to pro-Maoist movements in Western Europe by Albania, but did all this really help China effectively to promote its revolutionary model in Western Europe? Such a thesis does not stand up under scrutiny; for the impact was indeed marginal.

In any event one thing is certain: Albania, during the Cultural Revolution, was the only country with which there was 'revolutionary' interaction. But this too was not especially prompt for at first the Albanians were puzzled about what was happening in China,[31] and were even critical of the cult of personality, of the emergence of the army as the main force in Chinese politics, of the Chinese decision to send back Albanian students and of the Red Guards. 'This Cultural Revolution in China', wrote Enver Hoxa on 20 August 1966 'did not begin in a way a serious, down-to-earth party should have started. This revolution was kindled by the army, then by Beijing University and the flames then were spread out everywhere. Chinese propaganda presented it as a revolution that was started from below by revolutionary masses and that developed "spontaneously", whereas in reality it was organized'.[32] After some initial hesitation and some criticism, the Albanians publicly endorsed the Cultural Revolution and the Red Guard movement in 1967. A well-orchestrated media campaign in support of Beijing's internal and external policies was launched. High level Albanian party and government delegations were despatched to the PRC to campaign for Mao. Editorials in party newspapers and journals hailed the Cultural Revolution as a 'valuable contribution' to the theory and practice of scientific socialism. Enver Hoxa's confidant, Kapo, and his defence minister, Balluku, paid extended visits to the PRC beginning in January and February 1967 respectively. It was perhaps Mehmet Shebu's (Chief of the General Staff) visit in October 1967 that was most significant. At the end of that visit a joint communiqué was issued in which, for the first time, the Albanians accepted Mao not only as 'a great Marxist–Leninist', but 'a worthy successor and heir' to Marx, Engels, Lenin and Stalin.[33]

With Romania relations, though friendly, were more restrained.[34] There was none of the Albanian revolutionary interaction and there was hardly any identity of views regarding the broad sweep of the international system. In fact the Romanian perception was in no way different from that of most other nations, whereas the Chinese had swung in a radical direction in the aftermath of the sixties. Though this was already evident after the explosion of the Sino-Soviet dispute, it became even clearer and sharper with the onset of the Cultural Revolution. The factors that brought them together were different. While the Chinese had had hopes of establishing an Albanian-like partnership with Romania, the Romanians had a very limited objective—to acquire some degree of autonomy from Moscow. A neutral attitude in the Sino-Soviet dispute, in Romanian calculations, was perceived as an act of independence, without bringing their relations with the Russians to a breaking point. Therefore, when the Chinese did try to push them to join their anti-Soviet crusade, they refused to go along. In fact, when Zhou, during his eight-day visit to Romania in June 1966, made anti-Soviet declarations from Bucharest, the Romanian government was incensed. According to some reports, it made it clear to the Chinese prime minister that his denunciation of the Soviet Union 'cannot be accepted or supported by the Rumanian leaders'.[35] The Romanian fear of China going off the rails was so great that they took a number of precautions.

First, *Scinteai*, the organ of the Romanian Communist Party, simply deleted the anti-Soviet passages from Zhou's banquet speech. Second, the Romanians made it clear that they were not prepared to grant the Chinese unlimited liberty on their territoy to engage in open polemics against another socialist country. Ceauşescu personally informed Zhou that Romania would not tolerate any immoderate utterances against Moscow; and the Sino–Romanian rally where Zhou was planning to denounce the Soviets on the eve of his departure was delayed by two hours. Finally, when the two leaders arrived they spoke briefly, with the Chinese prime minister focusing on the bonds of friendship that united the two countries. In fact, although rallies were normally interminable, this one lasted for only forty-five minutes.[36]

The Soviet occupation of Czechoslovakia in August did create some concern among the Romanian leaders, since Brezhnev had warned that it could be repeated in other socialist countries, should they drift too far away from the socialist line. In the wake of Czech events, the Chinese once again attempted to push Romania to become more independent of Moscow, and less neutral in the Sino-Soviet dispute. Zhou even promised China's support in case of Soviet intervention.[37] Romania responded to Chinese overtures by praising Beijing for its friendly attitude and 'expressed the hope of increased cooperation with the CCP', but did not go any further.[38] It could hardly do so, since the risks of Soviet intervention in Romania would have increased had the Romanians gone the Albanian way of forging very close ties with Beijing.

It should also be mentioned that if Romania was resisting Chinese pleas to join them, it also went on record as not being a party to the other similar Soviet attempts. Whether it was the Warsaw Council meeting (March 1969) or the meeting of Communist parties (June 1969), Romania refused to join in condemning China.

Thus Chinese influence in Eastern Europe was further diluted during the Cultural Revolution. Although China had lost considerable leverage by the early sixties, the situation worsened during the Cultural Revolution in so far as all the Soviet-dominated countries began openly to denounce China. The development of close relations with Albania was hardly a consolation since it turned most of the East European countries even further away from Beijing. Besides, even the Albanians were becoming increasingly reserved regarding China after the Soviet invasion of Czechoslovakia. In October 1968, Enver Hoxa, for example, criticized Zhou Enlai's pressure on Albanian to seek an alliance with Yugoslavia, expressed his puzzlement at the absence of any real Chinese foreign policy, berated the Zhou-Kosygin meeting of September 1969 and even charged that the Chinese were already taking a moderate attitude towards the pro-Soviet East European bloc.[39]

Western Europe

Western Europe too was not spared during the Cultural Revolution whose turmoil also influenced China's policy towards this area. If ideological radicalization of the Cultural Revolution had further aggravated the already existing Sino–East European tensions, there was no reason for the same thing to happen in the West since there were no real disputes with any of the West European countries where China had a diplomatic presence. And yet it did happen. Most of the tension, disputes and diplomatic incidents occurred only during the height of the Cultural Revolution, thereby confirming the general thesis that domestic radicalization had spilled over to foreign policy, and internal tensions were transposed to the external scene.

The euphoria of the Cultural Revolution triggered off uncontrollable incidents involving foreign missions inside China and/or with the governments of the countries where China had a diplomatic mission. More often than not, they were relatively minor and in normal times would have been mutually nipped in the bud; but since the times were not normal in China, they were allowed to escalate, thereby increasing tensions between the governments. This was the starting point of the real build-up of Sino-West European tensions.

The second phase was the appearance of highly critical media comments about West European 'reactionary' policies. In the highly charged atmosphere of the Cultural Revolution, cool and sober analysis of Western Europe was hardly possible.

The third phase began with the intensification of the 1968 student revolts in Western Europe. They contributed to the emergence of the Chinese view that the prospects for revolutions in Western Europe were indeed real.

The example of Sino-French relations during the Cultural Revolution demonstrates all the phases described above. The whole process began with a spontaneous or well-organized demonstration by forty-nine Chinese students in Paris on

27 January 1967 to protest against 'Soviet revisionism's January 25 bloody suppression in Moscow of Chinese students'.[40] Before the demonstrators could reach their objective of arriving at the Soviet embassy, they were stopped by the police. Clashes occurred and resulted in the injury of Chinese male students, who had been 'brutally dragged by their necks or ears', and of Chinese female students, who had also been 'brutally dragged by their hair or plaits' to the police van.[41]

Nothing could be more banal than this, for in Western pluralisic societies such incidents often happen and are equally rapidly forgotten. But the Chinese response was immoderate. In fact, it was magnified into a major incident. Yi Su-chih, the first secretary at the Chinese embassy, lodged a protest with the French Foreign Ministry on the same day. Chen Yi, the Chinese foreign minister, personally became involved. He sent a message (31 January) to the Chinese students 'to express his support and sympathy for them'.[42] The All-China Student Federation went even further: it raised the 'strongest protest' against the French 'fascist attack' on Chinese students.[43] On the same day a massive demonstration was held in front of the French embassy to protest against the French government and to give vent to its anger 'against the criminal police action of tearing up Chairman Mao's portrait and trampling on Quotations'.[44] And, finally, to cap it all, Robert Richard, the French commercial counsellor 'recklessly, driving a car through the crowd and injuring several demonstrators', was hauled up and forced to stand in the cold for seven hours along with his wife.[45]

The press articles on France lost their earlier friendliness. Though in 1967 they still had not become sulphurous, they were none the less indicative of the direction towards which they were heading. If an editorial in the People's Daily was in June 1967 reproaching 'French imperialism' for 'standing on the side of US–Israeli aggressors' in the Middle East,[46] only a few weeks earlier the 'Commentator' of the same newspaper was still highlighting French resistance to British entry to the Common Market and was still supporting the French 'struggle' against the United States regarding its control and domination of Western Europe.[47]

Chinese attacks against Britain was even more ferocious, following more or less the same pattern. By far the most serious attack concerned Hong Kong. A relatively small labour–management industrial dispute in factories producing artificial flowers in the Kowloon area in May 1967 was escalated into a major crisis. Action by the Hong Kong police to quell the disturbances outside the two factories was used as a pretext to spread disturbances to other parts of the colony. Chinese reaction was certainly disproportionate to the events. It began with critical articles in the press, developed into a massive demonstration of more than 100,000 people at the British Embassy in Beijing, escalated into sharp diplomatic exchanges and finally climaxed into a very tense situation with the arrest of Reuters correspondent Anthony Grey and the burning of the British Embassy. The situation had gone totally out of hand. The Chinese leadership was no longer in a position to halt demonstrations against the British in Beijing and were not able to exercise authority in the outlying cities, including Shanghai and Guang-Zhou, where attacks against British interests had got totally out of hand.[48]

Similarly escalated reaction also occurred in Macao. Tensions against Portugal were built up in the wake of a small incident regarding the establishment of a 'patriotic school' in Taipa, a small island off Macao. The authorities tried to stop the Chinese residents from establishing such a school.[49] The residents 'armed with the thoughts of Mao Zedong' carried out a very broad mass action of sanctions against the Portuguese authorities beginning on 25 January 1967.[50] Protests were made and sanctions were taken that finally compelled the Portuguese authorities 'to fully admit their crimes of massacring and persecuting Chinese nationals'.[51]

The Cultural Revolution did not spare other West European countries either, not even those who did not have any conflict with China. The Danes were lambasted because the Danish Social Democratic Party paper had carried (9 August) a cartoon of Mao being swallowed by a dragon. The Italians were attacked because the captain of a Chinese freighter was forced by authorities in Genoa to choose between taking down propaganda posters or leaving the port.[52] The Swedish cultural attaché Jan Sigurdson and a Swedish journalist were accused and detained by Chinese authorities for having engaged in 'illegal activities'. And the Swiss were severely criticized for admitting Tibetan refugees to Switzerland.

On the bilateral diplomatic front, China was isolated. Whatever advances she had made in this sector in the past were seriously jeopardized by the excesses of the Cultural Revolution. In fact, in some ways, China was back to square one — a situation comparable to the period that followed immediately after the 1949 revolution when China was cut off from Europe. What made things worse than that phase was the Chinese decision to formulate a two-pronged revolutionary policy that was even unacceptable to the radical fringes of West European politics. So the isolation became not only *vis-à-vis* the established West European governments, but also *vis-à-vis* political forces that had previously been well-disposed towards China — a situation far more uncomfortable and far more difficult.

Western Europe: the two-pronged revolutionary strategy

Splinter Communist groups

The first part of the revolutionary strategy was directed at establishing secessionist parties or party-like organizations to range behind Beijing. Though a warning hint about the promotion of this type of factionalism had been given in 1963 in a letter addressed to the CPSU,[53] the process was greatly accelerated as China moved in the direction of the Cultural Revolution. Dissident parties or associations were then openly encouraged in the whole of Western Europe (see Table 6.1).

Most of these splinter groups presented great diversity in their origins. While some used legalistic processes to justify their split, others simply broke with the established party in the name of Marxism–Leninism and announced the

Table 6.1 Pro-Beijing parties or groups in Western Europe

Country	Party	Year established
Austria	Marxist-Leninist Party	1967
Belgium	Communist Party	1963
Denmark	Communist Study Circle	unknown
Finland	Helsinki Marxist-Leninist Group	1969
France	Marxist-Leninist Communist Party	1967
Great Britain	Communist Party (Marxist-Leninist)	1967
Greece	Communist Party (Marxist-Leninist)	1966
Italy	Communist Party (Marxist-Leninist)	1966
Luxemburg	Luxemburg-China Society	unknown
Norway	Young Socialist League (Marxist-Leninist)	unknown
Netherlands	Marxist-Leninist League	1966
Portugal	Communist Party of Spain	1964
Sweden	Marxist-Leninist League of Communists	1967
Switzerland	Swiss Communist Party (Lenin Centre); Organization of Communists (Marxist-Leninist)	1963
West Germany	German Marxist-Leninist Party	1965

formation of a rival body. Some of them were founded through local initiatives, while others received the necessary impetus from outside.

China took an active interest in these parties. In fact, their existence was often proclaimed in the Chinese press, where propaganda coverage regarding their activities and their clout was out of proportion to their actual strength. 'The Marxist-Leninist Parties and organizations of European countries', wrote an 'observer' in the *People's Daily* 'are growing in strength. We are convinced that these parties and organizations, under the guidance of Marxism–Leninism, Mao Zedong's thought, and by rallying and leading the working class and other labouring people of Europe will surely be able to overthrow the reactionary rule of imperialism, capitalism and revisionism and achieve their own complete emancipation'.[54]

It is important to note that many of these splinter groups were further split into different contending groups that mirrored the confusion and disagreement of the Chinese party, were heavily dependent on Beijing for financial support and could hardly survive the withdrawal of such support. Consider for example the pro-Maoist Belgian Communist Party, the most important of them all.[55] Founded in 1963, it went through as many as five splits in two years, the most important of which was of its party secretary, Jacques Grippa who fell out with the CCP over his support for the disgraced Liu Shaoqi.[56]

When financial support was withdrawn from Grippa's group, his weekly organ which had had as many as twenty pages in the beginning of 1968 was reduced to four pages and was finally suspended in December of that year. Grippa also ceased receiving further telex transmissions from the New China News Agency making it very difficult for him to continue to function.

New left

The second Chinese revolutionary strategy was directed towards the new left student movement of 1968. At first when this movement began to spread in Western Europe, the Chinese paid no attention to it. This was partly because of their heavy involvement with their own turmoils, but also because it 'seemed to concern only a movement of students'.[57] When the new left movement finally exploded in May 1968 as a spontaneous rebellion on the Left Bank in Paris, Beijing became interested and they came out in favour of what was happening in Western Europe.

Chinese interest went through three stages. The first was the organization of massive demonstrations in support of the 'progressive student movement in Europe and North America'.[58] On 21 May, according to the Chinese statements, more than half a million Chinese demonstrated in Beijing.[59] The following day 'more than 700,000 revolutionary people' held a great demonstration in the great square before the Gate of Heavenly Peace. Vowing their support for the French uprising, they carried banners and sang revolutionary songs, including the one based on Mao's exhortation that 'to rebel is right'. Similar demonstrations took place in other cities — in Shanghai, in Tianjin, in Wuhan and in Nanjing. During the few days of these demonstrations between 21–6 May, twenty million people were reported to have displayed their own support for the French students.[60]

The second stage was coverage, analysis and comments in the Chinese press of what was happening in Western Europe. For fourteen consecutive weeks the Chinese press, particularly *Peking Review*, carried articles on the subject. Some analysis was made of the new left, but what was particularly interesting was the avoidance of any major criticism of de Gaulle, with the attacks focused on 'US-led imperialism', and the 'Soviet revisionist renegade clique'[61]. The 'French revisionist clique' (the French Communist Party) was not spared; it was particularly berated for not having done anything to transform the revolt into a full-fledged revolution. It is also interesting to note that while the Chinese press laid particular stress on the participation of workers in the student unrest, it did accept the fact that the 'students stood at the forefront of this revolutionary struggle'.[62]

Chinese interest in student upheavals in Western Europe was essentially due to the mounting instability these movements generated in West European politics. In a country like France, where discontent was widespread, the established system of authority did become wobbly during the student-initiated revolt of 1968, leading many to think that revolutions in affluent societies were not that remote after all. It would seem that extremist groups who had the upper hand in China were more interested in the process of European destabilization as such rather than the ideals for which the European students had created a tumultuous situation; for the new left student movement, the real source of all the troubles, represented ideas and a system of values that were antagonistic to Chinese thinking. They were inspired by leaders (for example, Che Guevara) whose ideological beliefs and political behaviour had been challenged by the CCP. Furthermore the philosophy the new left represented in Western Europe was fairly close to that of the ultra-leftist group, *Sheng-wu-lien* (Hunan Provincial

Proletarian Revolutionary Great Alliance Committee), founded in the autumn of 1967 and which the Chinese authorities was seriously trying to suppress.[63]

The third stage in this interest in the student movement was to highlight Mao Zedong's role in all this. On 27 May, the *People's Daily* carried an editorial claiming that Mao was the source of inspiration for the new developments in France and elsewhere. It declared:

> The extensive dissemination of Mao Zedong's thoughts throughout the world has spurred the development in depth of the contemporary world revolution. The tremendous victory of China's great proletarian cultural revolution has inspired the people of all countries.[64]

European intellectuals were certainly taken by the dimension and the ideas of the Cultural Revolution. Although a fascination had also existed during the earlier stages of the post-1949 revolution, it resumed at the time of the Cultural Revolution. One author confirmed it in the following terms:

> Not unlike the Soviet Union in the 1930s, China had something for everybody: for the puritan, a hard-working, simple, efficiently modernizing country; for the cultural connoisseur, thousands of years of Chinese culture; for the frustrated leftist, a Marxist-Leninist regime restoring the good name of Marxism; above all, and for most visitors, there was a land of mystery, beauty, purpose, and order, a former victim acquiring power and dignity, a nation seemingly possessing all the virtues Americans sorely missed in their own society during and after the war in Vietnam.[65]

According to another author, this fascination with China was particularly relevant among the French intellectuals. She wrote:

> More than the messages, China was emitting ultrasonic sounds and simple stereotyped formulas: 'the east wind prevails over the west wind' was then something that seemed to overthrow classical political coordinates. The one who thought about China first was Althusser with the cover of a flame on his *cahiers marxistes-leninistes*. One who had studied in depth was Lecan who began to once again involve himself in Chinese, a language he knew since the last war . . . China became a new theoretical dawn, a sort of reference for new knowledge. One was supposing that China would have a role in the West that was comparable to that of Greece for our neo-renaissance. The intellectual idols, the pop-stars saw a utopia where the revolution of language, of psychoanalysis, of justice, of science would go hand in hand with the revolution of action. This idea came from the surrealists of the twentieth century, and it is perhaps for this reason that the nervous and the most sensitive centre of the Chinese Cultural Revolution is Paris.[66]

But all these revolutionary poles of attraction came to nothing. The pro-Marxist parties were too marginal, the new left movement was too brief and the pro-Peking intellectuals really too ineffective to have any impact on Western Europe. It was a short episode whose impact was much less than was suggested in China.

Eastern Europe

In Eastern Europe, China was even more isolated. 'Revolutionary' activity was hardly possible. In fact, it was almost non-existent. First of all, once again this may be attributed to the simple fact that the Chinese leadership was totally embroiled in keeping control over its domestic situation. Despite all the anti-East European polemical rhetoric that made the Chinese headlines, the hard-pressed Chinese leaders had neither the time nor the inclination to be active in areas where they were isolated.

Second, 'revolutionary' activity was simply not possible. Unlike those in the West, the East European authoritarian political systems did not lend themselves to any political dissonance, least of all of the Chinese brand. The only examples of such an attempt that were cited in the Chinese press were those of the Provisional Communist Party of Poland established in 1965 by Kazimierz Mijal, a former member of the Central Committee of the Polish Communist Party and the so-called Duro Djakovic group of Yugoslav Marxist–Leninists. But this could hardly be compared to events in Western Europe, since the Polish group was established in Albania and no information was given on the Yugoslav group. Besides, from what one knows of the party, it was even more marginal than any of the pro-Maoist groupings in Western Europe.

Third, the Stalinist groups on whom China could have relied to establish pro-Beijing groups had been discredited and suppressed even before the Cultural Revolution. There was not much left in the way of political forces with whom China could forge ties. The students and the intellectuals were even less disposed towards Beijing. For one thing, large numbers of them were operating within the framework of the communist parties and were obviously in total disagreement with the Cultural Revolution. And those who were in the opposition were searching for more liberal solutions to socialist problems.

Even in Albania and Romania, the scope for pro-Beijing revolutionary activities was limited—in fact, even more so than other socialist countries. Albania was in total agreement with the CCP and had placed Mao on the same pedestal as Marx, Engels, Lenin and Stalin; and Romania was neutral in the Sino-Soviet dispute, a situation that the Chinese leaders hardly wished to rock at a time when their isolation from the rest of East Europe was so widespread. Besides, any forceful attempts would have only caused the Romanian leaders to distance themselves from Beijing.

Conclusion

It would obviously be an exaggeration to conclude from the catalogue of events listed in this brief chapter that Europe was important in Chinese diplomacy during the Cultural Revolution. It was not. In fact, no other countries were really important to China during this tumultuous period, least of all Europe, for the Cultural Revolution was essentially an internal phenomenon. Foreign Affairs—with the sole exception of the Soviet Union—was not a priority for the Chinese leadership.

Locked in a severe intra-party battle for power within the country, none of the leaders was really very much concerned with what was happening outside, or with what was or what should be China's foreign policy. If the Chinese foreign minister, Chen Yi, was completely engaged in the politics of survival, and if the Chinese prime minister, 'in addition to his full time job of running the State Council . . . was frequently called to meetings to deal with pressing problems thrown up by the factional fighting between Red Guard groups',[67] can one really talk about foreign policy—particularly if one considers that foreign ministry personnel too were paralysed into inaction by the Cultural Revolution?

Besides, can one really talk about foreign policy during the Cultural Revolution? Was it really possible, during the tumultuous phase, even to imagine that a coherent and a well-concerted policy was conceivable? Where was the time to do all this? Would it not be more correct and more appropriate to suggest that what China was indulging in was an aggravated and highly disproportionate response to her external environment? Even China's anti-Sovietism, around which much of her foreign policy was constructed during the Cultural Revolution, had already been conceived and operationalized in the early sixties and was continued during the Cultural Revolution—only more dramatically and more venomously. Seeking out the Third World was another major external objective that was pursued during the Cultural Revolution. It too had its origins in the sixties and was continued—also more dramatically and more vehemently.

Europe was even less important during the Cultural Revolution. Having failed to create a dent on that continent during the early sixties, the whole relationship with Europe, during the Cultural Revolution, was reduced to a confrontational policy towards the established states of Europe and to establishing or developing relations with pro-Maoist groups, both of which never got off the ground.

Chapter 7
Inauguration of a new policy

The euphoria of the Cultural Revolution did not last long. It was a brief interlude whose militant phase was finally halted in 1969 following a decision by those who had originally unleashed it in 1966. A number of factors contributed to this decision—a decision that must have been taken at the highest level.

Reasons for change

First, a 'near state of anarchy' had set in throughout the whole country.[1] The radicals and the moderates—who seemed to be equally divided—were continuously fighting one another all over China 'with batons, old bits of furniture, not to mention rifles and machine guns'.[2] Stories of disruption of the economy, of the breakdown of public order, of suspension of all education above the primary level and of rampant fears of mass actions even led Mao Zedong to characterize it as a civil war. Many of his successors—long after the events—considered these events as 'domestic turmoil' and admitted that they 'brought catastrophe to the party, the state and the whole populace'.[3]

Second, by the summer of 1968, the Cultural Revolution had served its purpose. If one accepts the hypothesis advanced by many in the Western World—that the whole objective of these tumultuous events was to isolate and then exclude Mao's adversaries in the party, then there was really no point in continuing the Cultural Revolution, since Liu Shaoqi and the others had disappeared from the political scene. At a special meeting of the Central Committee from 13 to 31 October, a resolution was passed unanimously purging Liu. He was dismissed from party and state posts and was described in a joint editorial of *People's Daily*, *Red Flag* and *Liberation Daily* as 'the most insidious and vicious counter-revolutionary chieftain'.[4]

He was incarcerated in Beijing for two years, and was then bundled away to Kaifeng (Henan Province) where he died in prison. His 'counter-revolutionary accomplice', Deng Xiaoping, also characterized as 'number two capitalist roader' was disgraced at the same time and was sent to an agricultural commune where for a time he served meals to peasants and worked in the fields.

Third, if the Cultural Revolution had served its purpose of isolating those who were on Mao's right, it had, on the other hand, consolidated the power of Lin Biao and other military leaders on his left, and who, it is now known, were out to remove him.[5] The continuation of the Cultural Revolution in its original militant form could only prove counterproductive and dangerous. The sooner it was reined in, the better it was for those who wanted to block its further radicalization.

Fourth, foreign relations had come to a complete standstill. What was even worse was that the aggressive attitude of Chinese diplomats abroad, and the concern for the safety of their foreign missions in China had prompted a number of governments to reconsider their relations with Beijing. Some had even initiated withdrawals of their personnel. Paradoxically the first to do this was Sihanouk, who was known for his friendly disposition towards the Chinese. On 13 September 1967, he announced that the Cambodian Government was withdrawing all but one of its diplomatic staff from Beijing. The Chinese, he declared, 'are off their heads' and 'have lost their self-possession'.[6] Two days later, the Indonesian government announced that it was withdrawing its entire mission. And a spokesman of Denmark went on record—also in September—to declare that his government was contemplating considerably reducing the size of its mission in Beijing.[7] What probably triggered a new process of high-level stocktaking was the burning of the British embassy on 22 August 1967 by the Red Guards. According to some reports, Zhou Enlai tried, between that date and 30 August, to persuade Mao Zedong to take steps, and stake his prestige, power and influence to put an end to the state of anarchy, at least in foreign affairs.[8]

Fifth, the rapidly changing international situation also caused the leaders to scrutinize the Cultural Revolution more closely. By September 1968, the Chinese perceived a real threat from the north and began to consider the Soviet Union 'as our principal and most dangerous enemy'.[9] And between September 1968 and April 1969, the Chinese press was awash with articles, commentaries and declarations that did not leave any doubt regarding this threat from the north.[10] During this period the number of anti-Soviet comments in the Chiness press far exceeded the anti-American attacks.[11] Thenceforth, the dispute was no longer viewed as a simple matter of polemical exchanges, but something more real which could seriously undermine China's security.

The new perception regarding the Soviet Union was influenced by a series of factors. There was, first of all, the Soviet armed intervention in Czechoslovakia in August 1968. This was a clear warning to the socialist countries of the risks they were likely to run in the event of any major transgression of the political guidelines and the broad foreign policy framework established by the Soviet Union. Then there was the proclamation of the so-called 'Brezhnev doctrine'—also in 1968—under which the Soviet Union arrogated to herself the right to intervene in socialist countries 'when internal and external forces hostile to socialism, seek to reverse the development of any socialist country whatsoever in the direction of the restoration of the capitalist order'.[12] There was also the important reinforcement of Soviet military presence along the Sino-Soviet border in 1969, the outbreak of actual border clashes on Chenpao Island on the Ussuri River in March of the same year,[13] and the widespread circulation of Soviet-inspired rumours of a possible Soviet pre-emptive attack on China's nuclear installations.[14] There was also the Brezhnev proposal, made at the international conference of Communist and worker's parties in June 1969, for the establishment of a 'system of collective security in Asia',[15] which, in Chinese eyes, was 'another unbridled step taken by Soviet revisionism in its collusion with US imperialism in recent years to rig up an anti-China ring of encirclement and to make war clamours and threats of aggression against China'.[16]

The situation thus had changed. For the first time, since the Korean War, the Chinese felt seriously threatened—and by a major land power with a large frontier with China. If one were to add to this the growth of Soviet influence in Afghanistan, India and Vietnam, security must have become a major element of concern for the Chinese leadership despite its heavy involvement in the Cultural Revolution.

The combination of all these factors must have contributed to the Chinese decision to put an end to the militant phase of the Cultural Revolution, the Chinese leaders were shaken out of their excessive involvement in domestic affairs. The perception of a security threat from the north was perhaps the most important factor that catalysed the Chinese leaders to break out of their external isolation and to do something to neutralize the threat.

It was of course much easier to implement a decision involving foreign policy as opposed to domestic affairs. For one thing, the different radical groups were less interested in foreign affairs than in what was happening in China. For the Chinese leaders, therefore, local resistance to any new diplomatic posture would be much less. For another, the main Chinese leadership was not seriously divided on international issues, and it was thus much easier to reach a broad consensus on the new guidelines for foreign policy.

Repeated proclamations of China's adherence to revolutionary goals were no longer considered adequate, though they were not completely jettisoned. Revolutionary friends, isolated and scattered all over the world, were no longer viewed as viable contenders against the established pro-Soviet Communist parties, although they were not completely disowned. Something more palpable, more pragmatic and more national was needed to meet the rapidly changing situation.

Signs of change

The first major sign of change was the Chinese decision to return ambassadors to the missions abroad from which they had been re-called to undergo a programme of 're-education' during the Cultural Revolution. As many as thirteen new ambassadors were sent out in May and June 1969. All of them were experienced diplomats, and two of them were former deputy foreign ministers (Keng Piao in Tirana and Huang Chen in Paris).

The second major indicator of change was the re-opening of boundary talks with the Soviet Union on 20 October 1969, and the re-commencement of Sino-American ambassadorial talks in Warsaw on 11 December. The first began after an interval of five years, while the second followed a break of nearly two years.

The third sign was a flurry of diplomatic activity in Beijing. The number of foreign delegations coming to the Chinese capital had grown. But the most important landmark was the well-publicized meetings that Mao Zedong, Lin Biao and Zhou Enlai had jointly with the ambassadors of Albania, Pakistan, Zambia, Sweden, Kampuchea, Congo, Tanzania and New Guinea. All of them were received on the Tiananmen rostrum on 1 May, and photographs were taken with each of them.[17] This was perhaps the most important and obvious signal of the revival of Chinese interest in foreign affairs.

What were the broad orientations of this new opening up? Was a clear direction discernible? And what was the real pivot of this new diplomatic strategy?

China's foreign policy was centered around anti-Sovietism and all thoughts of the outside world were underpinned by this phenomenon. The post-Cultural Revolution perception was heavily coloured by an increasing conviction that the Soviet Union was no longer socialist, and, within the international system the tilt towards the Soviets had made the Soviet Union the principal threat not only to China but also to the world. The geopolitical reality that the Soviet Union is China's principal northern neighbour, with thousand of miles of contested frontier, had contributed heavily to building up this image. If the Soviet Union was the main determinant that launched a new diplomacy, it was also China's main target.

The new strategy

The Chinese response was multifarious in character. An external strategy was designed, with four broad objectives. The first was rhetorical in character and directed principally against the two superpowers. The Chinese leadership and the press harped on the existence of revolutionary movements that would 'determine the destiny of the world'[18] and urged that 'all countries and people subjected to aggression, control, intervention or bullying by US imperialism and Soviet revisionism unite and form the broadest possible united front and overthrow our common enemies.'[19] This was the standard refrain of most Chinese declarations, press comments, editorials and authoritative articles. Whether the Chinese leaders really believed in such rhetoric—inaugurated with Lin Biao's report and continued right up to 1973—it is of course impossible to say with any certitude. But in the wake of the Cultural Revolution, it certainly served the purpose of convincing the active proponents of the Cultural Revolution of the Chinese leadership's revolutionary credentials.

The second component of this strategy was to accept a *rapprochement* with the United States. Begun very discreetly and confidentially—while the Cultural Revolution was still on—it gathered speed and momentum reaching a climax with Nixon's visit to China in February 1972. The obvious and most evident reason for this turnabout was to counterbalance the growing Soviet power.

Formally, all sorts of reasons had been invoked for what was the most significant change in Chinese foreign policy—a change, furthermore, that had been introduced in record time. It has been suggested that Chinese overtures in the direction of Washington were very much in line with Mao's tactics of 'exploiting contradictions, winning over the majority, opposing the minority and destroying them one by one'.[20] Also, it was argued that *entente* with the United States was politically acceptable because the latter was 'going downhill more and more'.[21] Such reasoning was based on domestic conflicts such as black power and anti-war resistance, 'insoluble economic crisis',[22] rivalries resulting from the resurgence of the European and Japanese economies and the dangerous growth of Soviet influence.

Much of the formal argumentation advanced is very long-winded—its main purpose was to influence the party militants. Although the real factors that resulted in the change were more pragmatic, down-to-earth factors did not go down so well, and a whole spectrum of argumentation, theories, analysis and rationale had to be invented to give some degree of legitimacy to their action.

In any event, the Chinese leaders had convinced themselves of the need for some normalization of relations with the United States. There were, none the less, limits beyond which China could not possibly go in this process of normalization—limits imposed by years of uninterrupted rhetoric stating that the United States was an imperialist nation with whom China would have nothing to do. Besides, what would the Third World—itself usually anti-American—think of a Sino–American understanding? Would this act not tarnish China's image among those very nations towards whom bridges were being built, and who had been finally successful in getting China into the United Nations despite ferocious American opposition? Furthermore, how could China become friendly with the United States, the principal obstacle to the integration of Taiwan to the mainland—an issue perceived as highly important at the time? All these considerations militated against too close a relationship with Washington.

So China's goal was a limited and prudent *entente* with the United States—an *entente* sufficiently developed to push Washington to consider that China's independence was now within the framework of its security interests, but, at the same time, an *entente* ambiguous and distant enough to permit China publicly to criticize Washington—in sum a delicate balance between friendliness and unfriendliness and between some *entente* and some political distance was established. In this China was successful. In fact, even before the inauguration of the process of Sino–American normalization, the United States 'could not accept a Soviet military assault on China'.[23] After the formal commencement of that process this view became even more pronounced.[24]

The third component of China's new foreign policy strategy involved relations with the Third World. Relations with a vast group of new actors was viewed as vital in this phase of opening up to the world. On many occasions, the Third World had served China well, and its members could perhaps in the future use their moral force to deter any forceful Soviet initiative against China. Besides, in the game of numbers in the United Nations, close cooperation with Third World countries is most useful to counter Soviet and American attempts to dominate international organizations.

But relations with the Third World also had limits. These were fine when China hardly had any relations with any one else. But now that China was moving into international politics with a heavy involvement in triangular diplomacy (the United States, the Soviet Union and China), and once again increasingly concerned with national security problems, the Third World had lost some of its glitter. China certainly could not ignore the Third World, but at the same time could hardly afford to rely principally on the Third World as in the past. Thus the two urgent goals of security and modernization had returned and were pushing China more into the central balance of international politics and away from the Third World.

The importance of Europe

In China's new foreign policy strategy, the European continent was once again, as in the early sixties, beginning to occupy a central position—more central than the United States because there were no inhibitions in turning towards that area and more important than the Third World because it had much more to offer.

Varyingly characterized as the 'second intermediary zone',[25] or 'the second world'[26], or as one of the five major centres of the international system,[27], Europe thus became one of the centre pieces of Chinese diplomacy.

First of all, China no longer really had any conflict of interest with Europe. There were no major issues that remained outstanding and no major controversies that needed to be resolved. In the wake of African and Asian decolonization, the ex-colonial European powers had no imperial interests to defend, no discernible ambition to dominate the Third World economically and no apparent capacity or inclination to assert themselves in the international system. In fact, Europe was viewed as having become a victim of superpower contention, and as such a potential partner offering considerable scope for dialogue, understanding and even some joint action. 'These countries too', wrote a Chinese observer, 'were subjected to other control, intervention and bullying of the two overlords to varying degrees, and the contradictions between these countries and the two superpowers are daily developing'.[28]

Often much has been made of the conflictual interests between China and British and Portuguese residual interests in Hong Kong and Macao. But since China extracted more economic benefit from the European presence than would have occurred otherwise, were they really conflictual? Besides, Beijing was well aware that it could take over the two colonial outposts without any resistance from the two countries. Yet it had not done so—not even during the height of the Cultural Revolution. In fact, what was even more indicative of the absence of any perception of conflict was the Chinese behaviour at the United Nation: the Chinese delegation refused to accept the inclusion of Hong Kong and Macao in any multilateral discussions on decolonization on the grounds that the matter had to be dealt with bilaterally by Great Britain and Portugal.

With East European countries too, China had no real conflict. For none of them—not even historically—had any interests on China's periphery. In fact, many of them had long considered the emergence of China as a boon, since it gave them greater leverage in their relations with Moscow. The only conflictual element was the Sino-Soviet dispute in regard to which most of the countries had to follow Moscow, and in which China, with its very rigid attitude, had left them no choice but to continue to follow Moscow. After the Cultural Revolution, however, the overall situation changed for the better. China adopted a more flexible position, and the possibilities of making a dent improved distinctly.

Second, Europe had indeed evolved since the days of the cold war. Many of the nations, which had hitherto constituted integral but subservient parts of the two blocs, had begun to assert themselves. In the economic and political domains they were no longer prepared to go along completely with the views and objectives of the superpowers; and some of them were no longer willing to subscribe to the foreign policy frameworks designed by their senior partner. Admittedly, there were a number of political, military and economic factors—more in Eastern than in Western Europe—that constrained them from cutting themselves off from Moscow or Washington, but the fact remains that the alliances had changed.

The Chinese leaders, concerned as they were with the dangerous escalation of the Sino–Soviet dispute, viewed this as an important development in Europe. In most of the post-Cultural Revolution Chinese writings and declarations that contained a general evaluation of the constellation of forces in international politics, Europe as an independent phenomenon was given the pride of place. *Beijing Review* in the early seventies, to take just one example, continuously highlighted and welcomed the strengthening of the Common Market with the entry of Great Britain, Denmark and Ireland,[29] the establishment of the free trade area involving ten West European countries, the increasing trade problems between the United States and Western Europe,[30] and the 'drifting away' of Great Britain from the United States.[31]

For the Chinese, the importance of these developments could be gauged from the fact that both superpowers were against the establishment of Western Europe as an independent force within the international system. 'The United States and the Soviet Union', wrote *Beijing Review*, 'were extremely dissatisfied over the prospect of a West European Free Trade Area. As early as November 1971, the United States lodged a protest with the Common Market and the European Free Trade Association saying that the projected establishment of a free trade area constituted a "discrimination" against Washington. The Soviet newspaper, *Pravda*, had also "warned" and attacked some West European countries which would join the free trade group'.[32]

At the same time, the Chinese also underlined the surge of contradictions within the Soviet bloc. Moscow, in their view, was 'sitting on the volcano of resistance of the people of the East European countries'.[33] 'Uneasiness', in their view, 'was growing among the East European people and the struggle to defend their independence, security and equal rights is gaining momentum.'[34]

Third—another source of Chinese interest in Europe—was the traditional European fear of Soviet expansionism. Most of the European nations have always viewed Russian policies, behaviour and intentions with considerable alarm. In the nineteenth century, Russian objectives had haunted a number of European countries. After the Bolshevik revolution, the level of mistrust in Soviet intentions rose; and with the Soviet acquisition of superpower status, in the aftermath of World War II, European apprehensions regarding Soviet intentions reached new heights which even the recent atmosphere of *détente* had not been able to obliterate completely.

For China, this was another major source of attraction, particularly when one takes into account the new Chinese perception of a growing American–Soviet collusion on a wide spectrum of issues. With the escalation of the Sino-Soviet dispute, some similarity had thus emerged in Chinese and European perceptions in so far as the former had ceased to make any distinction between the old Tsars and the 'new Tsars in the Kremlin'.[35] A Chinese commentator wrote:

> Two dynasties, the Romanov dynasty and the Khrushchev–Brezhnev dynasty, are linked by a black line, that is the aggressive and expansionist nature of great Russian chauvinism and imperialism. The only difference is that the latter dons a cloak of 'socialism and is 'social-imperialism' in the true sense of the word.[36]

Fourth, Europe was important because of the implications that East–West *détente* of the sixties and early seventies could have on Soviet policy towards Europe. The Chinese attitude was contradictory and confusing, to say the least. On the one hand, they feared the acceleration of Soviet pressures on China as soon as *détente*—already operational—had set in; on the other hand they advanced the curious argument that 'strategically the key point of superpower contention was Europe',[37] and that the Soviets 'were making a feint to the East, while attacking the West'.[38] However, this contradictory argumentation notwithstanding, Europe had suddenly acquired an unusual importance in China's foreign-policy calculations.

Fifth, for a nation like China, which was in the throes of economic development, Europe was also perceived as an important economic partner. With the abandonment of the autarkical policy of the 1960s, and the launching of an ambitious developmental programme in late 1972 involving the importtion of complete factories and power plants, Europe, with its remarkably developed base in aerospace, communications, transportation, shipping etc., was viewed as an area from which China could obtain important economic benefits. In fact, Europe appeared to offer the only sensible and viable option. Curiously enough, the Japanese were regarded in some sectors as technologically inferior to the Europeans, and the United States viewed as politically unattractive as a supplier of capital goods.[39] Already in 1974, next to Japan, Europe had become China's biggest trading partner,[40] and according to information that had appeared in the European press, trade prospects had become even greater with the emergence of new Chinese wealth in oil and natural gas.[41] Besides—this was important after the Soviet experience—China could easily avoid becoming dependent on one nation by spreading her purchases around to a number of European countries.

Finally in the military field, Europe could replace the obsolescent elements of China's armed forces. Dwindling air power through obsolescence was China's most critical military problem. China's 3,000 Soviet-built MIG-17s, MIG-19s and 200 MIG-21s could not match Soviet aircraft. Despite relative success in building missiles, and nuclear warheads,[42] the Chinese had been unable to develop on their own the difficult metal technology and high-altitude test chambers to make high-performance jet engines,[43] But obsolescence was not only limited to airpower. China's ground forces and naval equipment were also based on the technology of the 1950s. Only seven of the 156 Chinese divisions were armoured, and their equipment was much inferior to modern Soviet designs. China's navy, though the world's third largest, was about twenty years out of date in anti-submarine warfare and other underwater sensing devices.

Europe clearly was the only developed area that could meet China's needs. There was no one else. The United States—at least in the seventies—was politically unacceptable, and Japan was militarily unable.

What about Europe? Were the European nations also interested in developing relations with China? Did they consider that Beijing could be helpful in advancing European objectives and interests? Evidently not all European nations considered that development of relations with China was vital. There were differences in perspectives and goals. There were, for instance, a number of East European nations who were either unable or unwilling to go beyond a simple normalization of relations. Either the Soviet constraints were too stupendous or ideological differences were too basic. But the majority of them—principally in Western Europe though some in Eastern Europe too—seemed to have realized the vital importance of Beijing for the advancement of their interests in economic as well as political sectors.

There were none the less areas of disagreement too between the Europeans and the Chinese. With the sole exception of Albania, none of the European nations seeking some understanding with China were willing to accept the rather extremist and highly belligerent position that China was taking regarding the Soviet Union. Since 1970 China had consistently attacked the whole gamut of international negotiations and agreements in which the Soviet Union had been directly involved and which had resulted in the improvement of the international political atmosphere.

For the Chinese, this was a smoke screen for ultimate Soviet domination; whether it was disarmament negotiations, or SALT or MBFR or the European Security Conference, they spared no effort and no media to attack scathingly Soviet motivations and European naïvity. To cite just a few examples, the Soviet-West German Treaty of 1970 was characterized as a 'betrayal of interests of the German people, of the Soviet people, and of all the peoples of Europe';[44] and the European Security Conference was viewed as a Soviet attempt 'to consolidate its hegemony in Eastern Europe, extend its sphere of influence to Western Europe and to squeeze out United States influence there'.[45]

Almost all the European leaders who streamed through Beijing were informed with disconcerting repetition that Europe was the focus of superpower contention, that it was 'still in a state of aggravating armed confrontation', and that the objectives of Soviet diplomacy were nothing more than a concerted attempt to dominate the entire world. To encourage the Europeans to adopt an anti-Soviet stance, the Chinese even abandoned their own repeatedly proclaimed view that their country was Moscow's principal target,[46] and replaced it with a new line which stressed that the 'Soviet Union's strategic offensive' was 'spearheaded in the first place against the West'.[47] Two-thirds of the Soviet armed forces, the Europeans were warned, were concentrated along the Soviet western frontiers and were all set to establish 'a military hegemony on the continent'.[48].

All Europeans (with the exception of Albania) disagreed with the Chinese, not so much with the Chinese evaluation of Soviet motives but regarding the strategy they should follow to meet the Soviet threat. Their reaction to the 'era of negotiations' was as follows: we grant, they argued, that the Soviet Union should be regarded with some mistrust, and we admit that there often does exist a wide gap between Soviet declarations and real Soviet intentions. We are therefore on our guard and are trying, as recommended by the Harmel report and approved by the NATO ministerial meeting of 14 December 1967, to preserve our security by all means including military force. But, in our view, as highlighted by this report 'military security and a policy of *détente* are not contradictory but complementary'.[49]

The Chinese Cassandra-like cries did not go down well with the Europeans. They were at variance with mainstream European thinking and aspirations; for practically all the political forces on the continent favoured the idea of pushing even further the new 'era of negotiations'.

However, notwithstanding all these pressures and warnings,[50] the Chinese were sufficiently realistic and flexible not to permit these differences to interfere with their policy of seeking a *rapprochement* with Europe—for within the framework of the existing international situation and the changing constellation of international forces, an understanding with Europe had become a vital necessity for China's national and security interests.

Therefore, with a thoroughness that was impressive and a perception that was remarkably free from rigid ideological preconceptions, a new framework of foreign policy was designed in the post-Cultural Revolution period for Eastern as well as Western Europe.

New operational diplomacy in Eastern Europe

The first signs of change in the Chinese attitude towards Eastern Europe became visible after Soviet intervention in Czechoslovakia. Most of the region, hitherto considered hopelessly tied to the Soviet orbit, was perceived, rapidly after 1968, to be showing varying signs of autonomous behaviour on an impressive array of issues: East European disenchantment with the Soviet Union had further increased, and disappointment with Western Europe's abstentious attitude during the Czech crisis had become widespread. Besides, the Chinese were also noticing an emergence of envious fascination by East Europeans with the successful Chinese defiance of the Soviet Union.[51]

Even more significant, in the Chinese view, was that the continuously expanding Soviet 'colonialist economic control' over Eastern Europe[52] had increased the level of discontent and had given a new impetus to the 'separatist tendency among the exploited nations'.[53] In the new line of Chinese thinking, the most important sign of this new trend was the increasing determination of CMEA nations to tap their own energies and to develop their economic relations with Western Europe as well as with the Third World.[54]

It was perhaps this new evaluation, compounded with the perception of the Soviet threat to their own security, that served as a major catalyst to the Chinese activation of their hitherto dormant policy towards the area as a whole. This does not of course mean that the Chinese suddenly began to have visions of possessing any great capacity of rocking the Soviet boat in Eastern Europe, or of having developed a military capability strong enough to come promptly to the assistance of small nations who were threatened by their powerful neighbour. Far from it. They were only too conscious of their limitations.[55] But the new situation in Eastern Europe was perceived by the Chinese leadership to merit a new response—even if this could not be effectively backed by a credible military policy in the area.

The first visible sign of this change was the Chinese extension of radio transmissions (previously limited to Russian and Serbo-Croat) to include the Czech, Slovak, Polish and Romanian languages. To emphasize the importance Beijing attached to these broadcasts, they were relayed by Albanian radio transmitters during the peak hours of the evening to provide a clearer reception in the target areas and to reach a wide number of listerners.[56] The contents of the broadcasts were carefully selected to respond to the mood of the area. Having realized the ineffectiveness of ideologically orientated transmissions, the main Chinese propaganda thrust was on denouncing Moscow, on comparing the Soviet invasion of Czechoslovakia with American actions in Vietnam and on underlining the details of Soviet 'colonialist' plunder of the region.[57]

Though it would be difficult to evaluate the effectiveness of such transmissions on East European listeners, the pattern of such broadcasts and the importance accorded to it by the Chinese is a significant indicator of the new and the rapidly growing Chinese interest in Eastern Europe.

A campaign was also initiatied to normalize inter-state relations. First of all, ambassadors were once again despatched to Eastern Europe. The first to receive a Chinese ambassador was Albania in May 1969, while the last was Czechoslovakia in June 1971 (see Table 7.1).

Table 7.1 Chinese ambassadors to Eastern Europe

Name of ambassador	Country	Departure from Beijing
Geng Biao	Albania	15 May 1969
Zhang Haifeng	Romania	17 June 1969
Zheng Dai	Yugoslavia	15 August 1970
Lu Jixien	Hungary	15 August 1970
Yao Guang	Poland	23 August 1970
Sung Jiguang	East Germany	20 September 1970
Zhao Jin	Bulgaria	25 March 1970
Song Kewen*	Czechoslovakia	June 1971

* Already in Czechoslovakia as chargé d'affaires.

In the economic sector too there was some progress. The conclusion of trade agreements was by no means a sign of this progress—since annual trade agreements were also concluded during the height of the Cultural Revolution—some economic interaction, however, did pick up after 1969 and then continued to increase uninterruptedly (see Table 7.2).

The third striking change was regarding attacks directed against Eastern Europe. They were slowly abandoned, with the main thrust now directed at Soviet 'colonial rule' in Eastern Europe.[58]

Table 7.2 Trade between China and Eastern Europe (US$ million)

	1972	1973	1974	1975	1976
Eastern Europe*	495	605	765	985	1075

* Excluding Yugoslavia and Albania.

The evolution of the Chinese attitude towards events in 1968 in Czechoslovakia exemplifies this change very well. On the first anniversary, two articles appeared in the *Peking Review*, denouncing the Russians as well as the 'Czechoslovak revisionist ruling clique'[59] — a line that was identical to the one taken in 1968. For the second anniversary, the *Peking Review* did not publish any Chinese article, but reproduced excerpts from an article that had appeared in the Albanian paper, *Zeri i Popullit*, in which Moscow was attacked, but, in which, at the same time, such expressions as 'Czechoslovak stooges', and 'quisling Husak' were also included. On the third anniversary, *Peking Review* ignored the event completely. On the fourth and fifth anniversaries only the Soviets were denounced; nothing was said about the Czechoslovak leaders.[60]

A similar behaviour pattern was also visible during the December 1970 Polish crisis when massive demonstrations in the Baltic ports finally resulted in the downfall of Gomulka. The Chinese welcomed the change. Though the Russians were not spared, the main denunciation was directed against the 'Polish revisionist ruling clique', with the *People's Daily* commentator,[61] expressing the hope that 'the working class and broad masses of the people in Poland will certainly win great victories'.[62]

The focal point of Chinese attacks in the beginning was essentially the Polish leadership.[63] The most dramatic of these was the publication of a letter from a dissident Polish Communist who was described as the 'general secretary of the Central Committee of the Polish Worker's Party', in which he had underlined the necessity for the Polish party to model 'itself on the revolutionary mettle of the heroic Chinese working class and its party'.[64]

Bellicose attacks on the Polish leaders, in the middle of the crisis, were unavoidable. China really had no choice but to take a position. With the Cultural Revolution domestically still in operation, the CCP could not ignore what was happening in Poland. But as time passed, the Chinese position became more and more low-keyed with inter-state relations holding sway over inter-party relations.

It is interesting to note that in the very year China was denouncing the Polish leaders, Sino-Polish trade relations were expanding rapidly. In fact, in 1971, Poland emerged as China's leading partner in Eastern Europe with trade reaching $58 million, a 16 per cent increase over 1970.[65]

What is perhaps even more significant is that within the broad framework of change towards the whole area, the Chinese government attempted to design a new two-pronged diplomatic strategy; one narrowly focused on the three Communist dissident states of the area and the other broad enough to encompass even the non-Communist countries of the Balkan peninsula.

The three dissident Communist states

The main thrust of China's foreign policy was directed towards Albania, Romania and Yugoslavia. The policy pattern towards the three historically different Balkan nations mirrored the sophistication that had now emerged in Chinese diplomatic initiatives so soon after the militant phase of the Cultural Revolution.

Policies towards Albania and Romania of course were not new. They were a continuation of a very warm relationship that already existed during the turmoil; what was really innovative was the rapid incorporation of Yugoslavia in this new and very systematic Chinese venture of countering the Soviet Union in the very heart of its empire.

The new policy was facilitated by a number of considerations that China had not taken into account earlier owing to her deep ideological immersion during the militant phase of the Cultural Revolution. Such traditional and down-to-earth factors as balance of power, or the large leeway these countries had developed in foreign policy, became more important and more relevant.

The three nations had acquired varying degrees of independence from the Soviet Union. The Albanians had successfully defied Moscow and were carrying out an intense polemical campaign against the Soviet 'revisionists'. The Yugo-slavs—more 'revisionist' than the Soviets—had successfully resisted all Soviet attempts to make them toe the line. Besides, Yugoslavia had become a leading member of the non-aligned nations, while, at the same time, continuously interacting with the Western world. The Romanians—without cutting themselves off from Moscow—had successfully assumed an independent posture on a wide array of international issues, including the Sino–Soviet dispute. All these independent or autonomous voices had contributed to the erosion of Soviet influence in the area—an area in which Moscow had hitherto exercised considerable authority.

The successful projection of a nationalist image by the three defiant Communist states had given them a level of legitimacy and popularity which was—relatively speaking—far more deep-rooted and far more widespread than the other Communist states of the region who were known to be generally under Soviet control. Since 1969 the three countries had increasingly turned to each other, thus creating a new autonomous web of interactions distinct from other socialist countries. This process had begun with the forging of ties between Romania and Yugoslavia, including regular consultations at the highest levels and joint economic and military collaboration on a few projects.[66] Each country, furthermore, tended to view threats to the other as threats to their own security, a situation that was clearly exemplified by the sharp Yugoslav reaction to the Soviet campaign against Romania after Ceauşescu's return from Beijing in the summer of 1971 (see Table 7.3).

In addition to this growing bond, caused by the fear of the Soviet Union, this 'deepest and most fertile collaboration',[67] was made possible because the two countries had a history of unclouded friendship, and by the geopolitical fact that while Romania separates Yugoslavia from the Soviet Union, Yugoslavia is for Romania the only neighbouring country which is not a member of the Warsaw Pact and thereby forms a bridge with the Mediterranean and the West.

Table 7.3 Mutual high-level visits between Romania and Yugoslavia, 1970–1

January 1970	Romanian Premier Maurer visits Belgrade
May 1970	Yugoslav foreign minister visits Belgrade
July 1970	Standing Presidium-member Bodnaras visits Yugoslavia
July 1970	Premier Ribicic visits Bucharest
November 1970	Ceauşescu visits Yugoslavia
December 1970	Yugoslav Defence Minister Ljubicic visits Bucharest
June 1971	Romanian Defence Minister Ionita visits Belgrade
November 1971	Tito meets Ceauşescu in Romania

Source: Radio Free Europe Research, East Europe, Bulgaria, 1971

The process of normalization also included Albania. Since the 1968 invasion of Czechoslovakia this inward-looking and isolated country had been forced to widen its contacts with the outside world.[68] Relations with Romania had steadily improved, particularly in the economic field. Ties with Yugoslavia were also forged. The gradual improvement of relations began with the formal establishment of diplomatic relations between the two countries, and with the conclusion of a five-year trade agreement in 1971. This was an important milestone in so far as the two countries had been in a continuous conflictual state for a number of years over the problem of the large Albanian minority in the autonomous Yugoslav province of Kosovo; and that they still regarded each other with considerable misgivings and distrust.[69]

One of the first manifestations of Chinese interest was that the three countries were the first in the area to whom Chinese ambassadors were despatched—in May 1969 to Tirana, in June to Bucharest and in August 1970 to Belgrade. The three countries also had the important distinction of being accredited with ranking diplomats or important political personalities who probably had an easy and direct access to decision makers in Beijing. Keng Biao—sent to Tirana—already had a long experience as a diplomat, since he had been ambassador to Sweden (as well as Minister to Denmark and Finland) between 1950–5, to Pakistan between 1956–9 and to Burma in 1963. Additionally, he was vice-minister for foreign affairs between 1960–3 and was—even more important—a member of the ninth Central Committee of the CCP when he was sent to Tirana. The Chinese ambassador to Romania, Zhang Haifeng, had been ambassador to East Germany for three years (1964–7) and had been for four years (1959–63) secretary of the Kweichow Provincial Party Committee. Zheng Dai—ambassador to Yugoslavia—was the first Chinese ambassador to Belgrade since 1958. Though he was not a senior party man, he had held a number of powerful positions before—ambassador to Algeria (1962–7), adviser to the Chinese delegation (led by the Chinese foreign minister, Chen Yi) to the Geneva Conference on Laos (1961) and director of the New China News Agency bureau in Havana in 1960.

The ambassadorial appointments to the three states were significant from another angle. While treating the three states on an equal basis diplomatically, they were treated differently from the perspective of inter-party relations. Since Beijing, at the time, scrupulously wanted to avoid any inter-party relations with 'revisionist' Yugoslavia, of the three ambassadors only the one to Yugoslavia did not appear to have any strict and formal party connections. This distinction can be attributed principally to the basic guidelines that China had established regarding relations with the outside world. Whereas a remarkable flexibility in openly developing inter-state relations with all states had been practised, irrespective of their socio-economic structures, China showed an equally remarkable degree of consistent flexibility in abstaining from establishing inter-party relations with 'revisionist' parties even if they had defied Moscow.

There were other imparities in Chinese attitudes and behaviour. Interestingly enough the country with whom China was the closest (Albania) during the Cultural Revolution was the one with whom relations were distinctly on the downgrade. Since the Albanian leaders had expressed their alarm over the new Chinese policy of meeting the Russians, of talking to the Americans, of opening up to Eastern and Western Europe, the Chinese were discreetly distancing themselves from Tirana. In the midst of all the ostentatious display of mutual friendliness,[70] they were drifting apart. Already towards the end of 1969, Enver Hoxa was manifesting—though not publicly—his irritation at the Chinese for ignoring Albania, for hobnobbing with the Yugoslavs, for being too friendly with the Romanians and for urging him to seek an alliance with Belgrade and Bucharest. Commenting on Li Xiannian's visit to Albania in December 1969, he had this to say: 'This Chinese delegation has been the most negative, the worst, with evil and provocative aims. But we did not lose our aplomb.'[71] And yet, despite these undercurrents of tension, China continued to give economic aid and to develop all forms of cooperation.

China was still interested in maintaining ties, but was rapidly abstaining from attributing to Tirana the status of a special friend. Romania and Yugoslavia were becoming more important. Relations, which were already close, took a very friendly turn. It seemed as if the Chinese leaders had decided to give them far greater importance than previously. The vice president of Romania, Emile Bodnaras, was given an exceptionally warm welcome, but the real peak was reached with Nicolae Ceauşescu's visit in 1971.[72]

It was perhaps with Yugoslavia that China's relations took the most dramatic turn. From almost no relations they leaped forward to something close to an *entente*.[73] The first major contact was established as early as February–March 1969, when Yugoslavia's assistant federal secretary for foreign trade, Atanas Ikonomovski, arrived in Beijing to conclude a new Sino–Yugoslav trade and payments agreement that provided, for the first time, for exchange payment in pounds sterling or any other convertible currency, undoubtedly a major change in the Chinese mode of trade.[74] There had been no ministerial contact between the two countries since 1958, and the agreements up to then were annual protocols laying down commodity lists (without fixing the value and clearing quotas) based on payments through a clearing account, signed every year between the embassies and competent Ministries.

After the trade agreement and the appointment of ambassadors, there were concerted attempts to increase economic and political interaction through regular exchange of high-powered delegations, through mutual participation in their trade fairs, through an agreement on scientific and cultural cooperation

(12 November, 1975), it was the exchange of journalists, cultural delegations etc.,[75] that was perhaps the real inauguration of a new phase in Sino-Yugoslav diplomatic relations.

The first major interaction was the visit of Yugoslav Secretary of State for Foreign Affairs Mirko Tepovac to China in June 1971 who was accorded honours 'fully in keeping with his status as foreign minister',[76] and whose visit was 'more significant' than that of Ceaușescu, during the same month, in so far as it was 'a sign of changed Chinese attitudes.[77] In one of his public speeches—probably the most important in China—he revealed that the main purpose of his visit was to discuss with the Chinese leaders 'the further development of our political, economic, cultural and other forms of cooperation'.[78] Li Xiannian, China's vice-minister, reciprocated by assuring the Yugoslav delegation that it 'can expect firm support from the Chinese people' in the event of any foreign aggression towards Yugoslavia.[79] The joint communiqué, published at the end of his visit, underlined 'with satisfaction that recent years have witnessed a smooth development in relations between China and Yugoslavia on the basis of the five principles of co-existence'.[80] This was the starting point of the establishment of Sino-Yugoslav relations which then continued to develop on an even keel.

In addition to working towards the establishment of close bilateral relations with the three Communist States, China strove to encourage them to interact with each other and to establish their relations on a firmer footing. Mindful of their own incapacity to assist them militarily, the Chinese particularly tried to push them to seek some mutual *entente* in the military sector; in the Chinese view, this was the only viable way of meeting their mutual concern. Therefore, when the Albanians sought increased security support from China, Zhou Enlai was reported to have pressed the Albanian prime minister to enter into a military alliance with Yugoslavia and Romania.[81] Similar advice presumably was given to Romania and Yugoslavia.

Broad Balkan cooperation

The second major manifestation of Chinese interest was to work towards the establishment of a broader grouping that would encompass even some of the non-communist countries of the Balkan peninsula. The advantages of such a broad cooperative effort were obviously greater than the clustering together of the three dissident Communist states—though the latter process was by no means discouraged. Since the number of countries involved in such an enterprise would be bigger, their capacity to resist the Soviet Union would be correspondingly greater, and such a grouping would tend to lessen the doubts of those dissident Communist states reluctant to join each other. Albanian hesitations would logically have been removed in a larger grouping. Yugoslavia might feel that such an enterprise would be more in accord with a non-aligned status than an alliance with the Communist states only. And Romania—reluctant to defy the Russians— might consider a larger union less provocative than one limited solely to some Communist states.

The most weighty consideration for Balkan cooperation, in Chinese calculations was the presumed greater security protection it would give to all the counries of the region. The United States had already become fairly active in the region as exemplified by Nixon's visits to Romania in August 1969 and to Yugoslavia in October 1970. With Turkish and Greek participation in such an alliance American interest would naturally increase, thus giving even greater protection to the area.

The idea of a broad-based Balkan grouping, it should be noted, was not a Chinese invention. It was already being bandied around by the states of the region. The perception of a growing Soviet threat probably acted as a catalyst for the emergence of an autonomous geopolitical approach by the Balkan nations.

Despite the numerous issues that divided them, a two-phase process of drawing together was inaugurated.[82] The first phase was characterized by greater bilateral interaction. Beginning around 1970 this had finally resulted in the re-establishment of diplomatic relations among the Balkan nations, in the development of economic ties and in the exchange of high-level political visits, often culminating in joint declarations upholding the familiar principles of respect of sovereignty, territorial integrity and non-interference in each other's affairs.[83]

Even Albania—the most reluctant and isolated of them all—joined this bilateral process. After a hiatus of almost thirty years, diplomatic relations were resumed with erstwhile adversaries, Greece and Yugoslavia. Even with Bulgaria—a Soviet client state—relations were normalized, though at the chargé d'affaires' level.

The second phase, which began in 1975, was characterized by multilateral consultations that led to a conference in January 1976. It was attended by Bulgaria, Greece, Romania, Turkey and Yugoslavia and non-political issues were discussed.[84] Albania did not join the second phase principally because of an internal power struggle between Enver Hoxa and his defence minister, Bulluku, who had different views regarding the structure of the armed forces, and the type of foreign policy Albania should follow in the light of the rapidly changing situation in Europe. Since Enver Hoxa, the proponent of the hard orthodox line of party hegemony and of self-reliance, had emerged as the winner, it was hardly possible for Albania to be present at the conference. Though present, Bulgaria was not very cooperative, pro-Sovietism inspiring the creation of procedural difficulties at all attempts to give a more concrete or institutionalized form to Balkan multilateral cooperation.[85]

The fact that such a conference was held was of greater significance than the fact that it was not very successful: it ended without even taking a decision regarding another meeting. In China, the conference did not go unnoticed. In a constant search for counterweights against an expanding Soviet influence, the Balkan get-together was probably perceived as another important edifice for the advancement of such an objective. It is an interesting coincidence that an important statement on Balkan multilateral consultations was made by Ceauşescu soon after his return from a triumphant tour of China. 'Romania', he declared, 'is situated in the Balkans, and is therefore devoted to an understanding and cooperation in the area'. As a 'splitting policy', pursued by 'imperialist powers' has often, he continued, harmed Romania, it was important for 'the people of the Balkan countries to seek ways of cooperation and unity'.[86] On the following day,

Scinteia, the Romanian journal went further by suggesting 'that time has come to go over from the phase of agreement in principle to that of practical and concrete enactment'. The journal then invited Yugoslavia, Bulgaria, Albania, Greece and Turkey 'to join together' for 'Balkan cooperation'.[87]

China's relations with all these countries also picked up during this period— including the establishment of diplomatic relations with Greece and Turkey.[88] At the same time, China actively came out in favour of Balkan cooperation and presumably took some initiatives in this direction. An article in a Chinese newspaper stated:

> The Balkan peninsula belongs to the Balkan people, and the Balkan problem should be solved by the Balkan countries themselves. No outside force whatsoever has the right to interfere in Balkan affairs or encroach upon the Balkan countries' sovereignty and independence. The Balkan countries are daily strengthening their relations and are taking effective measures to safeguard their national independence.[89]

China, however, did not succeed in persuading the dissident Communist states or the Balkan countries to institutionalize their multilateral consultations. The repeatedly announced goal of establishing viable counterweights in the region failed because the strategy conceived to achieve this objective was flawed.

Most of the countries—at least the ones on which China was focusing her attention—probably shared the same objective, but differed with China about the manner of achieving it. Whereas, China was openly pushing them, the geopolitical constraints were indeed too great to permit any one of them to adopt policies that would be perceived by Moscow as inimical to its interest. Establishment of normal and even friendly bilateral relations between these countries and China was something to which Moscow could hardly object, but getting too close to Beijing would have been viewed as an inadmissible provocation. Indeed that actually happened in the case of Romania. Following Ceauşescu's visit to China in the summer of 1971, a well-concerted *Nervenkrieg* (war of nerves) was launched against China for interfering in Balkan affairs and against Romania for cooperating with China in this endeavour. The pro-Soviet East European press was awash with such articles. The Hungarian newspaper *Magyar Hirlap* condemned what in its view was becoming a 'Peking–Belgrade–Bucharest–Tirana' axis. The East German *Berliner Zeitung* berated Beijing for striving 'to drive a wedge against socialist states'. The Slovak Daily *Smena* was even more direct. It wrote: 'A shift on the part of the Romanian leadership to the Chinese platform . . . as can be judged from the communiqué issued at the end of the visit of the Romanian Socialist Republic's delegation to Peking and from the course of the visit itself—would mean a deviation from the principle of proletarian internationalism'.[90] None of these countries therefore really wanted to 'cross the Rubicon' as this might have proved dangerous to their own national interests. Greece and Turkey were too tied to the Western world, and were, at the same time, too eager to establish friendly relations with Moscow, to have indulged in a dangerous policy of getting close to anti-Soviet and faraway China; and non-aligned Yugoslavia and autonomous Romania in the face of such an offensive did not wish to go any further than they had already gone. Even Albania—the most anti-Soviet and most pro-Chinese of them all—was well aware of the dangers of such a policy.

The reluctance of the East European and Balkan countries to establish anti-Soviet counterbalances is certainly attributable to the geopolitical reality, but their reluctance to get too close to China was also because Chinese diplomacy was too stridently anti-Soviet. The risks of Soviet displeasure were too great, and any gains from an *entente* with China were too marginal. Besides, Chinese ability to come to their assistance was severely limited; for after all was it not Zhou Enlai himself who had declared to a Yugoslav journalist in August 1971 that China was 'far away from Europe . . .' and 'distant water cannot quench fire'—clear message to the states in the region that they could not expect any serious military aid from China in the event of Soviet aggression.[91]

New operational diplomacy in Western Europe

Change towards Western Europe was also significant—in fact, even more so, since the area was outside the Soviet sphere of influence, and since it was less inhibited and less constrained than Eastern Europe in voicing anti-Soviet views. Besides, Western Europe had a far greater military clout, undoubtedly a weighty consideration in Chinese diplomatic calculations.

Patterned more or less after the framework established for socialist countries of Eastern Europe, China sought to focus attention on another—hopefully more viable—counterweight to expanding Soviet influence.

China's interest was very different from what it had been in the sixties. Whereas a decade earlier the ideological component heavily coloured China's perception of the outside world, it was minimal in the seventies, and had been replaced by pragmatic considerations of national security and modernization. The significance of this major transformation does not reside so much in the upgrading of national interest—for this had occurred before—as in the fact that so soon after the termination of the Cultural Revolution, ideological consider-ations had been jettisoned in the foreign-policy sector.

Formally, of course, nothing had been abandoned, and nothing had been changed. The rhetoric continued unabated. Zhou Enlai, in his report to the tenth congress of the CCP (August 1973), spoke about the 'great disorder on earth',[92] and called upon 'all genuine Marxist-Leninist parties and organizations the world over' to 'carry the struggle against modern revisionism through to the end'.[93] The real change was elsewhere—in the situational analysis and the discrete formula-tion of actual foreign policy.

From the multitude of media comments, official declarations, private con-versations of Chinese leaders with their West European counterparts one can trace three broad and successive phases in the development of China's policy towards Western Europe in the seventies. The first was a situational analysis of Western Europe, followed by the formulation of a broad foreign policy strategy, and then finally its implementation.

Situational analysis

Western Europe, in the new Chinese thinking of the seventies, had become more important than ever before since World War II. This was not only because it had gained considerable economic clout, but also because the Chinese were convinced that the basic superpower conflict was going to be played out in that part of the world, for it was there that the United States and the Soviet Union were often competing with each other and sometimes colluding with each other. The possibilities of a conflict breaking out in the area were, therefore, far greater than elsewhere. Zhou had underlined this particular point at the tenth party congress through his statement that 'strategically the key point of their contention is Europe'.[94]

In this Soviet–American contention, the balance, in the Chinese analysis, had heavily tilted in favour of Moscow, and the danger of the Soviet Union finally coming out as the winner was real, if the Western world was not vigilant.

Of course, Europe in general and Western Europe in particular—ran the Chinese argument—was in the process of acquiring its own personality. There were, in fact, visible signs of it wanting to play an autonomous role within the international system. The Gaullist policy of national independence, culminating in the French withdrawal from NATO and the building up of the *force de frappe tous azimuts* (multi-directional nuclear strategy) was fairly advanced. The problem of Britain's oscillation between the Commonwealth, the United States and Europe was finally resolved in favour of her European partners with entry into the Common Market in January 1973. For the Federal Republic of Germany, a choice between a Bonn–Washington axis and its European partners had become even more problematic. Increasing signs were indeed building up of a consensus among the West Germans that their fate was linked with their West European partners. Italy, drawn more deeply into the domestic whirlpool of instability and rising communism, was no longer able to voice openly and clearly transatlantic loyalties. Besides, the Italian government had already taken the decision (January 1969) to recognize the PRC. And the process of democratization, in full swing in Portugal and Spain, had brought to the fore political forces which appeared to be more interested in seeking close ties with Western Europe than with the United States.[95]

For the Chinese, by far the most significant development in the early seventies was the intense West European activity to strengthen the European Economic Community as a distinct unit. The series of measures that were agreed upon at the Hague summit meeting in December 1969 to intensify political cooperation, to take appropriate steps for the eventual establishment of a European economic and monetary union, to initiate the process of enlarging the Community and to extend the budgetary powers of the European Parliament were viewed as landmark decisions in the ongoing process of West European unification.

Though all these developments were welcomed, Western Europe, in the new Chinese perception, was still not sufficiently strong to face the Soviet Union independently. The presence of the United States in Europe was, therefore, the only effective way of withstanding Soviet expansionism. The major conclusion drawn from this assessment was that should Moscow succeed in achieving its 'expansionist' aims in Europe, it would finally constitute a major security concern for China. For Moscow then would be able to focus its attention on China, 'an attractive piece of meat coveted by all'.[96]

China's interest in Western Europe was thus heavily influenced by a quest for security. A successful Soviet expansion into Western Europe, the Chinese were apparently convinced, would only clear the road for Soviet expansion in the east. Though security concerns clearly dominated Chinese thinking, economic recovery was also viewed as significant. The 'acute deterioration' of the national economy during the Cultural Revolution finally pushed the Chinese leadership to develop a new plan for the national economy (1970) and to expand China's 'economic and technical interflow with other countries'[97] in order to place China on the path of what Zhou Enlai later declared as the 'four modernizations' to be achieved before the end of the century.[98] Clearly at the time, Western Europe was viewed as the most politically acceptable economic partner.

Foreign-policy strategy

China's foreign-policy strategy towards Western Europe was clearly influenced by the Chinese situational analysis of the region. To risk a generalization, it could be argued that in the seventies there were three specific strategies in the security sector so far as Western Europe was concerned: (a) to support the ongoing process of West European integration in all sectors; (b) to persuade the West Europeans — pending the achievement of integration — to continue with American protection; and (c) to block the acceleration of East-West *détente* in Europe. In sum the whole Chinese strategy was to get closer to Western Europe, and, at the same time, to ensure that the Soviet Union remained preoccupied with Europe.

Preliminary steps

To implement China's foreign policy strategy effectively it was obviously important to normalize relations with Western Europe. The first major initiative was the establishment of diplomatic relations with all the countries of the region irrespective of their socio-economic systems, and irrespective of their political orientations. This was clearly perceived to be crucial, for no viable and institutionalized relations were really possible without a physical diplomatic presence. The process was inaugurated with the full establishment of diplomatic relations with Italy in November 1970 and was completed with the forging of similar ties with Portugal in February 1979. (see Table 7.4)

The only point on which China insisted in negotiations for recognition was the unconditional acceptance that Taiwan was an integral part of the mainland. Though different formulas were used to announce the establishment of relations, the basic objective clearly was the same. Those countries which had no ties with Taiwan were required to issue statements containing a bland announcement on the establishment of relations (West Germany) or containing a brief statement to the effect that the government in Beijing was 'the sole legal government of China' (Austria, Turkey and Luxemborg).[99] For those countries which had diplomatic relations with Taiwan or which had indicated in the past their preference for a 'two-Chinas' formula, the Chinese insisted on the inclusion of a clear paragraph which not only reaffirmed Beijing's declared policy that Taiwan was 'an inalienable part of the People's Republic of China' but also contained a sentence that the West European government concerned took 'note of the statement of the Chinese government'.[100]

By far the most difficult negotiations on the subject were with Britain; and the final formula agreed upon was slightly different from the ones agreed with others. It was more elaborate. After 'acknowledging the position of the Chinese government that Taiwan was a province of the People's Republic of China', Britain decided to withdraw her official representative from Taiwan.[101]

Accepting the Chinese formula on Taiwan was not much of a problem for most of the West European countries, since very few of them maintained any ties with Taiwan from which they could not extricate themselves (Table 7.4).

Table 7.4 West European countries establishing diplomatic relations with the People's Republic of China (from 1970)

Italy	November 1970	Greece	June 1972
Austria	May 1971	West Germany	October 1972
Turkey	August 1971	Luxemburg	November 1972
Belgium	October 1971	Spain	March 1973
Iceland	December 1971	Portugal	February 1979

The establishment of diplomatic relations was only a first step, for soon after in 1972 China began a systematic campaign of establishing meaningful contact by receiving a host of West European public figures: Beijing received Maurice Schuman, Walter Scheel and, Sir Alec Douglas-Home in 1972. In 1973, George Pompidou was given the red carpet treatment. In 1974, Edward Heath arrived in Beijing. In 1975, it was the turn of Chancellor Helmut Schmidt, Dom Mintoff, Franz Josef Strauss, Max van der Stoel, Sauvargnes and Leo Tindemans. In 1976, Anthony Crosland and Margaret Thatcher arrived in Beijing.

Nowhere else in the world were they given such a warm and enthusiastic reception as in China. And nowhere else in the world did they hear such profuse language underlining the past sufferings of the European people, the present importance of the continent and the future role it could play.

Though all of them were well received, the French delegations were given exceptional treatment. This was perhaps natural, given that the Chinese were very supportive of France's foreign policy after de Gaulle returned to power in 1958. For example, while personally receiving the French foreign minister, Maurice Schuman, in July 1972, Mao Zedong paid an unprecedented homage to France. He said, 'I cannot receive foreign ministers who visit China, only heads of state. But you, Mr Schuman, are not the same thing. You are not any foreign minister. You are a minister of France.'[102]

Table 7.5 Visits of West European foreign ministers to China, 1972–5

Maurice Schuman	France	July 1972
Walter Scheel	West Germany	October 1972
Alec Douglas-Home	Great Britain	October – November 1972
Giuseppe Medici	Italy	January 1973
K.B. Anderson	Denmark	May 1973
Gaston Thorn	Luxemburg	May 1973
Dagfinn Vaarvik	Norway	May 1973
Krister Wickman	Sweden	May – June 1973
Max van der Stoel	Netherlands	January 1975

Table 7.6 Visits of West European heads of state or government to China, 1973–5

Georges Pompidou	France	September 1973
Helmut Schmidt	Germany	October 1975
Leo Tindemans	Belgium	April 1975

Table 7.7 Visits of Chinese leaders to Western Europe, 1972–5

Bai Xiangguo	foreign trade minister	January 1973
Ji Pengfei	foreign minister	June 1973
Deng Xiaoping	deputy prime minister	May 1975

Return visits were also made by Chinese dignitaries. These were systematic and well organized and as enthusiastic as the ones made by the Europeans to China. Some of the European countries received Qiao Guanhua (deputy foreign minister) in 1972, Ji Pengfi (foreign minister) and Bai Xiangguo (minister of trade) in 1973, and Deng Xiaoping (deputy prime minister) in 1975 (see Tables 7.5, 7.6 and 7.7)

Most of the meetings in China, concluded with an audience with the top Chinese leaders, who displayed a singular tendency for indulging in long monologues, the centrepiece of which invariably was their deep concern regarding Soviet intentions.[103] One wonders whether this pattern of Chinese behaviour might not be attributable to a tendency towards decreeing even the details of what the leaders were going to communicate to their interlocuters', to some insecurity regarding their knowledge of international affairs', and to the general Chinese predilection for asserting as opposed to discussing their views about international affairs.

None the less, it is undeniable that these visits did serve a useful purpose, for they gave the Chinese and their European counterparts, the opportunity not only to evaluate each other in person (undoubtedly a vital element in the game of diplomacy), but also made it possible—Chinese monologue notwithstanding—for them clearly to define the limits beyond which they were not prepared to take any political and military risks. Although it could be argued that visits did not have to be made to comprehend the clear reluctance of the Europeans to rock the boat of *détente*, the occasions of these talks permitted the Chinese leaders to grasp the degree of this reluctance, and to understand the West European political atmosphere, which did not lend itself to any confrontation with the Russians. Besides, these visits must have also given the Chinese an idea of American–West European relations which they had been trying to congeal into a set pattern in their ideologically based writings for so many years.

Foreign policy goals

West European integration

Within the broad framework of China's security concern, West European integration was viewed as of prime importance. Perceived as the most efficacious way of containing Soviet expansionism, it became the focal point of Chinese diplomacy. Chinese interest in the European Economic Community[104]—the most important example of such integration—first became discernible in the summer of 1971 with the publication of a series of rather objective news items regarding its development.[105] On the occasion of the Pompidou–Heath talks in May 1971, a Chinese weekly declared that the 'trend of these countries getting united to challenge contention by US imperialism is developing further'.[106] During Ceaușescu's visit to Beijing in June 1971, Zhou Enlai, while welcoming the trend towards greater autonomy for medium-sized and small countries, stated that 'a new development has also taken place in the multifarious struggle of many European countries which are uniting to resist the aggression, control and interference of big powers'.[107] And on the successful conclusion of United Kingdom–Common Market negotiations in June 1971, the Chinese press became even more categorical. It declared:

> With the relative strengthening of the Common Market and the weakening of US imperialism, the trend has become increasingly evident in which these countries strengthen their union politically so as to oppose jointly the power politics of US imperialism and domination and control of Europe by two overlords—the United States and the Soviet Union.[108]

It is significant that in all these initial declarations, the Chinese highlighted what they considered to be the anti-American aspects of West European integration. Reviewing the Pompidou–Heath conversations, *Beijing Review* expressed the view that Britain's participation in the Common Market 'will cause further disintegration of the imperialist camp and will put US imperialism in a more isolated and difficult position'.[109] For the Chinese—at least until 1973—the development of the Common Market was more a setback to American imperialism than an effective countervailing power against the 'social imperialists'.[110]

Thereafter, the stress was shifted; China decided to focus more on the importance of the community to contain 'Soviet hegemonism, rather than US imperialism', to which only a ritual reference was made.

In line with promoting the strength of the European Community, the Chinese, it should be noted, perceived of a closer collaboration between the 'Second' and the 'Third' Worlds, both of which, in their view, had the common goal of disengaging themselves from the control or the influence of the 'First' World. In numerous declarations on this point, the Chinese, therefore, welcomed the Euro-Arab dialogue in the summer of 1974,[111] affixed their stamp of approval to the Lomé convention[112], approved the negotiations between the EEC and the five-nation Central American Common Market, and congratulated West European countries for having reached some preliminary agreement in October 1975 at the North–South meeting in Paris.[113]

Chinese activities were, however, not limited to rhetorical declarations; they were also operational. Discreet contacts were established with the EEC at different levels. In London contacts were established with the representative of the Community.[114] In 1973 the Chinese took three initiatives in Brussels, all of which were directed at the Community. The first was in the form of visits to the Commission's press bureau in January 1973 to obtain documentation on the Community;[115]. the second in October 1973 was directed at the Commission itself;[116] and the third, also in October, was by the Chinese correspondents who were assigned to the EEC and who established an office in the Belgian capital.[117]

By far the most significant initiative, however, was an unofficial invitation to Christopher Soames, the Commission's vice-president, in charge of foreign affairs, to visit China in 1973. The trip finally took place in May 1975 and resulted in an agreement for the establishment of official relations between China and the European Community.[118] China's reasons for seeking out the European Community were 'more political than economic.'[119] It was perceived 'as a first step towards an independent Europe'[120] with a political identity and a defence clout of its own,[121] and with the possibility of being able 'to play a positive role in international affairs'.[122]

Every step that pushed Western Europe towards integration was welcomed, and everything that surfaced in the Chinese press on the region conjured up visions of a politically united Europe as distinct from the two superpowers. The British entry into the Community was viewed exclusively in terms of the enhanced strength that it would give to Western Europe against the Soviet Union. And the establishment of a 'European nuclear force based on existing atomic weapons of Britain and France' was welcomed as a very favourable development.[123]

So the main thrust of Chinese diplomacy was to push the West Europeans in every way it could to extend the process of economic integration in to political and military domains. All the Chinese declarations and informal conversations with West European leaders was principally geared to this objective. This had, in fact, become a normative goal of Chinese foreign policy.

The American presence in Europe

If the Chinese favoured West European integration, it did not take them long to realize that it was not possible. It was not in the cards for the moment. For the West Europeans were simply not ready to accelerate the pace of unification. There were indeed too many obstacles for this goal to be realized, at least in the foreseeable future.

Therefore, while continuing to proclaim the importance of integration, China moved on to the next best option, the option of the continuation of an American military presence in the area. Since the Soviet Union was perceived as the most dangerous and expansionist adversary, it was better for the West Europeans as well as the Chinese to encourage the maintenance of an American presence in Europe.

Thus, instead of continuing to proclaim the crucial necessity of autonomous integration, China began to support the maintenance of a powerful NATO; instead of demanding the departure of American troops, she now came out in favour of their continued presence; and instead of considering the whole NATO military might as a threat to world peace, she now advanced the argument that it met the interests of many countries.[124]

The process of change first became visible during the second half of 1972, particularly on the occasion of West German Foreign Minister Walter Scheel's visit to China in the autumn of that year.[125] Thereafter, on a number of different occasions they gave their approval to the American military presence in Western Europe.[126]

It was on the occasion of Tindeman's visit to Beijing in 1975 that the Chinese attitude became more than apparent on the question. Since the West Europeans, they argued, were unable to unite 'it was better for them to continue their support to NATO in the face of Soviet political and military pressures.'[127] During German Chancellor Helmut Schmidt's visit in October–November 1975, they made it clear that they were satisfied with the close defence collaboration between the United States and Europe. In fact, Schmidt stated in a press conference that he had 'not heard one negative remark about the United States'.[128]

How could the Chinese leaders explain this volte-face to the country, and particularly to the militants of the party, who for years had been fed with the argument that the United States was the principal enemy; and then with the thesis that both the superpowers were out to dominate the world, and finally with the new theory that the Soviet Union was the principal threat and the principal adversary? Furthermore, how could the party leadership square such a position with its Marxist framework, in which the United States together with the Soviet Union were dubbed as the two expansionist superpowers in almost all of Chinese declarations—even when the Chinese in fact were becoming more and more anti-Soviet?

It would seem that the Chinese leadership did not do much explaining during the period in question. Most of the remarks favouring an American presence, it should be noted, were made privately to West European leaders. If the Chinese position finally filtered into the press, this happened in the non-mainland press, probably revealed by the West European leaders themselves.

Whatever appeared in the Chinese press on the subject was of a very general nature in which the Chinese leadership continued to be critical of both super-powers.

Much has been made of the so-called 'Kunming Documents' in which the military leaders in the Kunming military region tried frankly to explain the reasons behind the Chinese decision to inaugurate a bilateral process of normal-ization with the United States.[129] Nowhere in this document does the military leadership accept that the United States is China's ally; a detailed explanation is given only as to why the Chinese leaders deemed it necessary to accept American overtures. Besides, it should be noted that the document was confidential, and was designed for restricted distribution. Much has also been made of Zhou Enlai's report to the tenth CCP Congress in which he talks about the 'necessary compromises' that 'revolutionary countries' had sometimes to make with 'imperialist' powers.[130] But, here, as well, the statement is very general. Besides, the 'Hegemonism' of both the powers was severely criticized. In sum, China's foreign policy objective of encouraging the maintenance of American troops in Western Europe was handled very discreetly, far away from the limelight of the media.

Blocking East–West *détente*

The early seventies witnessed a remarkable growth in East–West interaction, and East-West *détente*. Though such a process was already inaugurated by de Gaulle in the mid-sixties, it gathered momentum when other West European nations followed suit—with West Germany designing her own *Ostpolitik*,[131] and with even traditionally anti-Soviet Great Britain moving in the same direction, the most dramatic manifestation of which was Prime Minister Harold Wilson's visit to Moscow in February 1975.[132]

To cap it all of course was the important Helsinki conference in July 1973 that was attended by all the European countries, with the exception of Albania. This important conference had moved the whole process of European *détente* from the bilateral plane to the multilateral one—undoubtedly a major Soviet achievement, since Moscow had been working for it for many years.

The Chinese were alarmed by this process. Its repercussions for the Sino-Soviet border could only be horrendous. For *détente* in Europe would give Moscow additional leverage to manipulate the already tense situation on the Sino–Soviet border. Conscious as China was of the asymmetry that existed between the Soviet and Chinese military power, the new situation served to enhance China's security concerns.

To face this new threat, the Chinese leadership came up with a curious assessment of the overall situation—an assessment that finally resulted in the formulation of another component of China's foreign policy towards Western Europe. Instead of publicly expressing their security concerns, the Chinese argued that the real Soviet threat was not to China, but to Europe, since the latter is 'strategically the key point of superpower contention'[133]; the Soviets were 'making a feint to the east', but were really preparing themselves to 'step up their contention in Europe'.[134]

Once this conclusion had been reached, and repeatedly reiterated—almost in the same language—persuading Western Europe to discontinue with process of *détente* became the third goal of Chinese foreign policy. The Chinese diplomatic machinery was then put in full gear to 'impress' upon the Europeans 'the dangers of Soviet threat to Western Europe'.[135]

In sum, what the Chinese were saying was that the focal point of the 'Soviet Union's strategic offensive' was directed at the West,[136] where, through a well-organized carrot-and-stick policy, the aim was to drive a wedge between the West Europeans and Americans in order 'to disintegrate Western Europe and dominate the whole of Europe'.[137]

Economic modernization

The forging of economic ties with Western Europe was China's fourth foreign policy goal. Years of isolation after the Sino–Soviet rupture and during the Cultural Revolution had left the country very much behind in the economic sector. Technologically, China had not made much progress, and in many sectors was simply unable to provide even basic technical know-how. Some relationship with the outside world was viewed as vital even for minimal economic growth.

Economic ties with Western Europe were obviously viewed as important, since it was politically more acceptable than the United States and, since in certain economic sectors that China needed to replenish, it was more advanced than Japan. For the aerospace and communication technology that the Chinese regarded as essential—not only to build a modern defence capability but also to spread the fruits of economic development to the whole of China—Western Europe in the early seventies offered China the only sensible option.

But expansion in the economic sector was not easy. The opposition of the radicals to any economic interaction with the outside world, compounded with the fact that the ideal of self-reliance was still very much a part of basic Chinese thinking, made it very difficult for the pragmatists to take another course. In fact, it was more difficult than the political opening up, since self-reliance was a fundamental principle whose abandonment could hardly be explained in tactical terms as was done with the political aspects of Chinese foreign policy.

So Zhou Enlai, who took charge of 'the day-to-day work of the central authorities' after Lin Biao's death in September 1971, had cautiously to wade his way through on the delicate question—in fact more cautiously than with political issues.[138] It was only in 1972 that more outward looking orientations were slowly implemented, and it was only from 1973 that these gathered steam. It was in that year that China imported machinery and complete sets of advanced equipment, including thirteen giant chemical fertilizer plants, four giant chemical fibre mills, three petroleum chemical industrial works, forty-three sets of coal combines, three giant power stations and a 1.7-metre rolling machine for Wuhan steel.[139]

China was able to implement this policy of importing machinery and of signing joint venture agreements only by accepting the principle of 'deferred payments, for it was clearly not possible for the Chinese to develop a policy of economic interaction with Western Europe in view of its lack of convertible currency. Since

Table 7.8 Industrial projects concluded with principal West European firms (in excess of US$50 million)

Year	Company (by country)	Product	Cost
	West Germany		
1972	Demag AG	Ball-bearing factory	$80 mln
1974	Demag AG	Steel complex	$198 mln
1974	Demag AG	Moulded cast steel	$58 mln
	Italy		
1973	Gruppo-Electro Mechnichi per Impianti al Estero	Electric power plant	$86.2 mln
	France		
1972	Technipand Speichim	Petro-chemical complex	$1,200 mln
1974	Heutrey	Fertilizers	$106 mln
	Great Britain		
1973	Hawker-Siddeley Aviation	Fifteen aeroplanes	$80 mln
1975	Rolls Royce	Spey engines	$120 mln

Table 7.9 Trade between EEC and China (in million ECUs)*

Year	1969	1970	1971	1972	1973	1974	1975
Imports	370	348	362	418	544	722	667
Exports	432	461	397	369	607	807	1,153
Balance	+ 62	+ 113	+ 5	− 49	+ 63	+ 85	+ 486

Sources: SOEC *Special Issue* 1958–1976; SOEC *Monthly Bulletin*

* One ECU = approximately US$1.40.

the whole controversy regarding self-reliance was raging between the radicals and the pragmatists, this was done rather discreetly in the beginning of 1973 when Bai Xianguo, China's minister of foreign trade, surprised his British hosts by informing them that Beijing would make 'deferred payments' for heavy equipment instead of conducting virtually all her trade in cash. The foreign trade minister asked British officials to price the cost of industrial plants on the assumption that payments would be made in instalments. In order to maintain discretion on this controversial issue on which serious disagreements had emerged between the pragmatists and radicals, an agreement was reached that the interest charges would not be listed separately but would figure in the proposed yearly payments.[140]

Western Europe thus was very much in the picture. Although Japan had the geographical and competitive edge, it was not far behind. In any event, it was

Table 7.10 Trade with principal West European countries (US$'000)

Year	Italy	Great Britain	France	West Germany
1969	10,995	40,347	12,906	24,645
1970	10,183	48,951	17,283	27,502
1971	10,553	28,975	17,736	23,082
1972	16,266	31,988	21,796	27,391
1973	19,318	63,216	64,841	51,934
1974	20,492	72,587	91,448	61,915
1975	24,959	48,576	50,391	81,554

Source: Barbara Krug, 'The PRC's Foreign Trade' in Yu-ming Shaw (ed.), *China and Europe in the Twentieth century*, Taipei, Institute of International Relations, 1986

ahead of the United States. A number of economic agreements were concluded with West European firms (see Table 7.8), overall trade too was boosted (see Table 7.9) particularly with the four major countries of Western Europe (see Table 7.10).

Focal point: Great Britain

Though China showed interest in all West European countries, Britain was given special attention. In fact, she had become a focal point of Chinese diplomacy during the period in question.[141] There were possibly three reasons for this. The first was the general reserve that the conservative government had towards the Soviet Union. Though this was generally the case, it was perhaps more pronounced in Britain than in other West European countries. The Chinese press had noted this state of affairs. It had, in fact, given prominence to the 1973–4 British defence budget, which was £523 million higher than 1972–3. At the same time, it had underlined those features of the British White Paper that were critical of the increasing Soviet military presence in Europe.[142]

The Chinese interest in Britain really began with the establishment of full diplomatic relations in March 1972, and with the final acceptance by London of the Chinese position on Taiwan—a position, interestingly enough, that a number of other West European countries had declined to accept. Whereas most West European governments had only 'noted' the Chinese claim to Taiwan, Britain had gone much further in 'acknowledging the position of the Chinese Government that Taiwan is a province of the People's Republic of China'.[143] This was undoubtedly a major concession, which was much appreciated by the Chinese government.[144]

The first major sign of Chinese interest in Britain was the strong support extended to the British demand for admission to the EEC. This was clearly in sharp contrast to the position taken in the sixties when Beijing approved de Gaulle's blockage of British admission to the Community. The negotiations of the seventies were largely commented upon,[145] and their successful conclusion was viewed as an important step to 'the further development of the economic and the defence and "the diplomatic" union of West European countries'.[146]

The Western press generally accepted the thesis that the genesis of the special Chinese interest in Britain could be traced to the establishment of full diplomatic relations between the two countries, and, more particularly, to the British admission to the European Community. One sharp observer, for example, expressed the view that 'Peking has a hope that Britain will soon play a major role in the Common Market, which it has just joined . . . because China appears to doubt the vigour of Bonn or Paris towards Moscow. London has been on rather bad terms with the USSR during the past few years'.'[147] Another journal went even further and devoted an editorial to this development. It wrote :

> China thus appears to have made a more optimistic assessment of Britain's role within Europe than those who believe that Britain's economic ills are endemic. China's estimates of the status which London will command within the Common Market and of the influence it will enjoy at the expense of its former rival has encouraged Peking to establish a special relationship with London in the hope that China's interest will not be forgotten in Europe.[148]

The second reason for this 'special' interest, paradoxically, was the very one that hitherto pushed China to distance itself from Britain, and which had hitherto supported the French determination to keep Britain out of the Common Market, i.e. Britain's close relationship with the United States. Now that China had veered around to the idea that an American military presence was necessary to contain Soviet 'expansionism' in the area, it was thought that Britain's entry into the Common Market would make the United States more vigilant, providing an additional reason to be concerned about West European security. Besides, ran the Chinese argument, it might even deter the Soviet Union from taking any military initiative.

The third consideration was economic. Britain appeared to be the right partner, at least during the first half of the seventies, because it, alone among the West European states, possessed the aerospace technology China badly needed to expand her backward internal air services, and to build up a much needed international service. This, at the time, was considered as a top priority since China was opening up to the European countries, with whom a number of direct air link agreements had already been concluded.[149]

The 'real breakthrough' in Sino-British relations, however, came in June 1972 with Anthony Royle's (British parliamentary under-secretary for foreign and Commonwealth affairs) visit.[150] The 'breakthrough' was attributed to the fact that, in this first important Sino-British meeting, the two parties—though disagreeing on Vietnam—found a convergence of view on the Soviet military presence in the east as well as in Europe and on the importance of building up a real confederation of European states as a 'welcome balance to the economic, military and political pressures exercised by Washington'.[151] For the Chinese, this was indeed very important, since the other powers (France and West Germany) were more eager to seek an understanding with the Soviet Union.

In addition to the general exchange, the talks centred on two main topics. One pertained to specific ideas on cultural exchanges, and the second concerned the purchase of British civil aircraft. Thereafter the bilateral relations continued to improve rapidly with visits by British Foreign Secretary Douglas-Home in October 1972 and the return visit of his counterpart, Ji Pengfei in June 1973.[152]

The highlight of these bilateral relations was the British Industrial Technology Exhibition, held in Beijing, in March–April 1973. With 900 businessmen representing 346 companies and with more than 1,475 tons of highly sophisticated equipment, spread out over 15,000 square metres, it was the 'largest technical show ever put on in China by a Western country'.[153] 'The Chinese', noted a correspondent, 'had never seen anything like it.'[154] An interesting innovation introduced at the exhibition was a series of 227 lectures organized by British companies. Given by qualified British technicians, they invariably developed into round-table question and answer sessions.[155]

The Labour victory in the February 1974 elections, however, slowed down the process of Sino-British interaction. Though by no means against such a process, the Labour government had other international perspectives and other international priorities. For one thing, it wished to move away from the maintenance of a firm anti-Soviet posture. The pressure groups within the party, favouring a better understanding with Moscow, were fairly strong. Those supporting the idea of accelerating the process of *détente*, had considerable influence on the leadership. Besides, the government itself was eager to spruce up its international image by taking some foreign policy initiatives that were different from the preceding Conservative government.

The official visit of Prime Minister, Harold Wilson and Foreign Secretary James Callaghan to Moscow in February 1975 testified to this new thinking. A number of agreements were concluded on this occasion.[156] What was, perhaps, most significant was the emergence of a broad identity of view on a wide spectrum of international issues. On *détente*, the Labour government struck a note that was different from the Conservatives. The joint Anglo-Soviet statement brought this out clearly :

> The Soviet Union and the United Kingdom took note of the important and positive changes in Europe and in international relations as a whole in recent years. They agreed that these developments had significantly improved the prospects for deepening *détente* in Europe. In these circumstances they resolved upon the systematic expansion of relations between the Soviet Union and the United Kingdom in all fields.[157]

The Soviet press seized this opportunity to compare the relative stagnation in Anglo-Soviet relations under the conservatives, and the new momentum that had been given by the labour government. 'Cooperation between the two countries', editorialized the *New Times*, 'which lost momentum in recent years is being given new impetus, provided with a solid foundation and ensured good prospects. After a seven-year interval the Soviet–British dialogue at the top level has been resumed.'[158]

If the Labour party favoured *détente*, it was less enthusiastic about West European integration. For many trade unions, it was an anathema. And since they constituted the backbone of the Labour party, they successfully pushed the government to demand re-negotiation of the conditions for British entry into the Common Market. Even after the success of the national referendum in June 1976, favouring the maintenance of British membership to the EEC, Labour indifference to West European integration, none the less continued.

The new British policy thus ran counter to the Chinese objectives of slowing down East–West *détente* and of accelerating West European integration, inevitably generating considerable disappointment inside China. The high hopes they had had in Britain were being dashed to the ground. The vision that the Chinese leadership had conjured up of a new counterweight to the Soviet Union under British leadership was disappearing. The press became less enthusiastic and more critical, albeit indirectly. One of the interesting manifestations of this Chinese disappointment with British policies was the extraordinarily warm reception given in Beijing to Edward Heath in May 1974. He had been prime minister when the Chinese invitation was extended to him, but he arrived in May 1974 as the Conservative leader of the opposition. The only observable difference between his visit and that of a head of state was the absence of the Beijing diplomatic corps at the welcoming ceremony. The visit included a meeting with Mao Zedong. At a welcome banquet on 25 May 1974, Deng Xiaoping noted that Heath 'consistently stood for the unity of the West European countries, and for the strengthening of their independence and sovereignty'. By bringing Britain into Europe, Deng continued, Heath had contributed to the people's struggle against 'hegemonism'.[159]

Clearly Heath was regarded more favourably in Beijing than Harold Wilson. Without commenting on the latter's visit to Moscow in February 1975, Chinese sources subsequently tried to put it in a bad light. An NCNA commentary from London on 21 April 1975, for example, warned that Britain was an 'important target of Soviet espionage'.[160]

Thus towards the end of Mao Zedong's rein, China began to lose interest in Great Britain under the Labour party. Even the arrival of James Callaghan as Wilson's successor did not change the Chinese perception. If anything, their opinion was that as long as the Labour party was in power, Chinese and British goals in Europe would not be analogous.

Conclusions

The first half of the seventies witnessed an activation of foreign relations. They were brought forward from the backburner where they had rested during the militant phase of the Cultural Revolution. The determining factor that catalysed the leadership was the growing Chinese fear that the Soviet Union was becoming dangerously powerful and aggressive, thereby increasing Chinese security concerns. Undoubtedly, this was the single most important factor that revived Chinese interest in foreign affairs, and caused them to seek friends abroad in order to countervail Soviet power.

Although a number of diverse steps were taken, including some opening up to the United States, the centrepiece of Chinese diplomacy undoubtedly was Europe because Europe was politically the most acceptable among the developed countries or areas; and it fitted very well into the broad ideological framework that China had designed—a framework of three worlds in which Europe had been assigned an acceptable and respectable role.

Economic considerations had also begun to weigh in the Chinese decisional process. A number of agreements, joint ventures, trade accords etc., were concluded with the European countries, but, in the China of the first half of the seventies, they were not assigned a crucial position in China's foreign relations. The Chinese leadership was apparently inhibited in taking bold decisions in this sector, principally because of the emergence of opposition from the radicals to any major open-door economic policy. Since the radicals had made it a major issue, the Chinese leadership, while continuing discreetly to open up, decided to play it down as long as the conflict was not settled one way or the other.

Chapter 8
The transitional years

The general confusion that marked the internal political scene after the death of Mao Zedong in September 1976 did not materially affect the foreign policy options adopted during his rein. Though the form and pattern of Chinese diplomacy had become more outgoing and more benign than before, its substantive framework was continued with the Soviet Union still the main ideological target and still the main security concern.

The only difference was the magnitude of the Chinese inquietude. It had increased and was clearly evident from the flow of anti-Soviet articles, comments and declarations in the Chinese press; after Mao's death it was the Soviet Union that formally became the prime target. The argumentation invoked in support of what clearly was a far more belligerent stance than previously was that the power balance had tilted even more in Soviet favour, thus making Moscow the more dangerous and more expansionist of the two superpowers.

The main thrust of post-Maoist diplomacy thus was directed at the objective of forging a united front with all nations to contain, as the deputy chairman of China, Li Xiannian, put it, the 'threat' of 'Soviet imperialism'.[1] The editorial department of the *People's Daily* in an important article on the Third World characterized the Soviet Union—of the two superpowers—as 'the more ferocious, the more reckless, the more treacherous and the most dangerous source of world war'.[2] The Chinese foreign minister, Huang Hua, was even more categorical—and in the presence of a high American official. At a reception organized in Beijing for the national security adviser, Zbigniew Brzezinski, he declared:

> The world is full of contradictions and the international situation is undergoing swift convulsions and changes. The struggle for hegemony is the principal source of anxiety in the world. The shadow of social imperialism is to be seen in all the changes and unrest taking place in different parts of our planet. Under the guise of '*détente*' 'cooperation' and 'disarmament', it is preparing for war everywhere, and it is everywhere engaged in expansion and aggression to establish its supremacy in the world. In the face of this reality all nations should unite, be prepared for sudden developments and not let themselves be deceived by illusions of peace. They should act against the policy of appeasement and pursue 'spear against spear' policy to wreck the strategic plan of the hegemonists.[3]

If Huang Hua is categorical, Deng Xiaoping was precise, and this too, significantly enough, during his 1979 visit to Washington. Both on the eve of his visit and during his visit he openly called on the United States, Europe and Japan to forge an anti-Soviet alliance with China.[4] The clarion call was audible, and the adversary, even though not named was identifiable. In sum, the Chinese were proclaiming that 'imperialism of the old type' was being replaced by 'Soviet social imperialism . . . that sprang up in the latter half of the 1960s.'[5]

Clearly, Chinese leaders were concerned. They were particularly fearful of a repetition of a Munich-like scenario of the thirties in which they might eventually become Moscow's target.[6] Though they repeatedly warned the Western world that the real Soviet threat and interests were in Europe, they could hardly exclude the prospect that they too could become victims of the Soviet Union. The proclamation of the Brezhnev doctrine, and the mounting rumours of Soviet temptation to strike at China's nuclear installations gave some credibility to Chinese fears.

What did China do to confront what it regarded as a new and dangerous situation? How was this translated in terms of a concrete foreign policy? And where did Europe stand in Chinese diplomatic calculations? China operated at two levels: the rhetorical and the operational. At the rhetorical level, the particular importance of the Third World in containing the Soviet Union was ceaselessly harped upon as well as the vital necessity of forging 'the broadest international front.'[7] This had become so much a standard refrain of Chinese rhetoric that the Chinese media, official declarations, reports, comments, etc. were awash with such themes.[8]

But those who were in charge in post-Maoist China were realistic enough to realize that their normative goal of forging the 'broadest international united front'—however desirable—was hardly feasible. The Third World had neither the clout nor the inclination to stand up to the Soviet Union. Besides, most of these countries were on friendly terms with Moscow and really did not see any point in standing by China in a dispute that did not concern them directly. It is hardly possible that this view went unnoticed by the Chinese leadership who were usually realistic in assessing international situations and particularly percipient of the power element.

Unity with the Western world was even less possible either at governmental or at grassroots' level. Besides, the Western world was too divided, and its perception of the Soviet threat too diverse to permit any unity. Furthermore, why should the Western world—hitherto castigated—forge ties with a weak and insecure China? What would they get in return? For many, it would have been a gratuitous and provocative act which—if operationalized—would have rendered their task of handling the Soviet Union even more difficult.

The only possible explanation for this pattern of behaviour at the declaratory level was that the Chinese leaders had become prisoners of their own rhetoric from which any extrication was indeed difficult, particularly during the transitional years when the power struggle within the Chinese leadership was being played out. For so long had the Chinese people been exposed to a radicalized picture of the world, and for so long had the Chinese leaders carefully cultivated their own revolutionary image, that any other form of behaviour, soon after Mao's death, would have been ruinous. In fact, one wonders if some degree of legitimacy for those who were attempting to preside over the destiny of China was not dependent on such a behaviour.

At the nuts-and-bolts level, however, Chinese diplomacy was very different. It had to take into account a wide series of already existing situations, coolly assess the real configuration of international forces and realistically define its own foreign-policy goals within this broad framework. This is what the Chinese leaders apparently did at the operational level. Despite a raging struggle for power even after the swift dethronement of the 'Gang of Four', a broad agreement was reached to continue the basic pattern of foreign policy that had been decided upon when Mao was still alive. The only difference perhaps was that this basic pattern was operationalized with greater applicability and with greater audaciousness than before—at least so far as the anti-Soviet component was concerned. This was indeed paradoxical, for the uncertain and rather volatile domestic situation would normally have constrained the Chinese leaders to be more prudent *vis-à-vis* their northern and more powerful neighbour.

Two different and even contradictory hypotheses can be advanced for this unusual Chinese behaviour. The first explanation could be that the siege mentality, from which the Chinese leaders were known to be suffering, catalysed them to take bold steps to neutralize any Soviet pressure. They were convinced that Moscow had for years systematically followed a policy of encircling China by an important presence in Afghanistan (and finally its occupation) in the west, India in the south and Vietnam in the south-east, not to speak of the massive Soviet military presence in the north. If one were to add the active Soviet attempts to stabilize her Western flank, then the Chinese geopolitical concern to do something on the diplomatic front to break out of the encirclement made sense.

Retrospectively, another argument could be advanced to explain the activation of Chinese policy to contain the Soviet Union. It is now known that Leonid Brezhnev, after his reportedly near death in 1976, had become so irredeemably weak and so physically feeble that there was no coherent leadership to effica-ciously run the important affairs of state. The power struggle was on for his succession, and policy was increasingly delegated to an ever-growing bureaucracy which apparently was in no position to give decisive leadership against China.[9] Could it be that the Chinese knew this and estimated that they had a freer hand to take initiatives in Europe? Whatever may have been the real explanation—on which opinions may differ—the indubitable fact is that Europe did not go unnoticed during the transitional period.

Eastern Europe

Eastern Europe particularly the Balkans, was the area towards which China began to show a special interest. The policy of surrounding the Soviet Union with a hostile or a neutral zone in the Balkans was, in Chinese thinking, one efficacious way of countering the increasing Soviet encirclement of China. Already during the Maoist period, the Chinese leadership was conscious of the strategic importance of the region; after Mao, it became even more so. Romania and Yugoslavia were in fact made the focal points of China's diplomatic strategy in the Balkans.

Table 8.1 Sino-Romanian trade
relations (in US$ mln)

1975	435.49
1976	450.78
1977	512.35
1978	787.15
1979	1056.13
1980	1126.02

Source: Economic Commission for Europe

Romania

For Romania this was nothing new. It was a continuation of the already existing smooth bilateral relationship that Romania's successful defiance of the Soviet Union had made her the envy of other East European countries which were overly tied up with Moscow. On the other hand, the geopolitical reality had made the Romanian leaders fully aware of how far they could go. They could not, for example, ally themselves with China against Moscow; and they could not take a pro-Beijing position in the Sino–Soviet dispute. But such a state of affairs perfectly suited Romania; for it provided maximum leverage — in any event much more than it would have been possible to obtain otherwise. Much of the Romanian diplomatic effort naturally was devoted to the delicate task of resisting Soviet pressures. This was by no means very easy given Romania's proximity to Moscow. None the less, they did succeed in doing so.

With the Chinese it was more problematic, since they had the tendency to make strong anti-Soviet statements while visiting foreign countries, the Romanians had to be very much on their guard and often had to dissociate themselves from what the Chinese had said about the Russians. Therefore, whenever any Chinese leaders while visiting Romania went too far in their assailment of the Soviet Union, the Romanian leaders took a very firm stance. This was done when Zhou Enlai came to Bucharest in June 1966 and was repeated during Hua Guofeng's visit in September 1978. After Hua fired his opening salvo on the very first evening in Bucharest by declaring that 'imperialism and hegemonism are spreading out their hands to undermine and commit aggression and expansion',[10] the Romanian government wound up the official talks forty-eight hours after his arrival, though he stayed on three more days.[11] At the same time, the Romanian press considerably toned down its coverage of the visit.

In effect, Romanian diplomacy was quite successful; for it did allow tensions to be built up with Moscow by their independent stance on many issues, but always succeeded in preventing the situation from getting completely out of hand. If the Romanians practised some degree of restrain in their political relations, they were much more outgoing in their economic relations with China. In fact trade shot up from US$ 435.49 million in 1975 to US$ 1,126.02 million in 1980 (see Table 8.1), making Romania China's biggest trading partner in Eastern Europe. The importance attached to expansion of this sector by the two countries can be gauged from the fact that as many as ten agreements were concluded between them to boost trade and economic cooperation during Hua Guofeng's visit to Romania in 1978.

Yugoslavia

Sino-Yugoslav state relations rapidly picked up, too. They were, in fact, more crucial than relations with Romania. For one thing, the relations had been at a low ebb for so long that any improvement would be beneficial to the anti-Soviet component of Chinese diplomacy in the Balkans; for another, Yugoslavia was really independent of the Soviet Union, and did not, therefore, have to show the same level of caution as Romania did in formulating foreign policy.

Relations with Yugoslavia had begun to improve in the early seventies, and there had been a stream of exchange visits between the two countries. Already in 1973, Mao Zedong had confidentially declared to a small circle of Chinese leaders that Tito had been right in 1948 and that he should be invited to China. In 1975, he went even further and actually informed the Yugoslav prime minister, Bejedic, during his visit to Beijing in October 1975 of his wish to meet Tito.[12]

The most spectacular event of course was Tito's visit to China in August 1977. To say that he was well received would be an understatement, for he was given unprecedented red-carpet treatment that was incomparable to the visit of any other head of the state. 'Filled with profound friendship for the Yugoslav people', declared Xin Lua, 'one hundred thousand people in the Chinese capital today performed songs and dances to give a warm ceremonious welcome to President Josep Broz Tito of the Socialist Federal Republic of Yugoslavia'.[13]

This really was the galvanizing factor for setting off a process of exchange visits of ministers, trade-union leaders, war veterans, scientists, cultural leaders, etc. In fact, from that point on nothing interfered with 'the development of mutual relations in all domains'.[14] The field was wide open; and the Chinese—having made this their main objective in the Balkans—systematically tried to open all avenues for an all-directional improvement. The most important of these visits was that of Hua Guofeng in August 1978. In many ways, this was even more important than Tito's visit to China. For Hua Guofeng, as the head both of the party as well as the government, was visiting an area that the Soviet Union had jealously guarded as its sphere of influence. In many ways it was like touching the tail of the Soviet tiger.

In any event, this is how the Soviets took it—as a provocative act. The Soviet news agency, Tass, bluntly announced that the term 'hegemonism'—repeatedly used by Hua—was in fact a code word for 'anti-Soviet' slanders.[15] *Pravda* accused Hua of using every opportunity during his visit to the Balkans to make crude attacks on the Soviet Union. The Western press reports appeared to confirm that this visit had 'alarmed' and 'thrown' the Soviet Union 'off-balance'.[16]

However, not withstanding that Moscow had 'worked itself up to such a fury',[17] there was little likelihood of a real Soviet initiative to destabilize these two countries. The constraints were too great. For one thing both countries would have resisted any punitive Soviet action. By adopting autonomous policies on a wide spectrum of issues, they had been able to gain the support of their population, at least so far as the Soviet Union was concerned. A repeat performance, similar to the ones taken in Hungary in 1956 and in Czechoslovakia in 1968, was, therefore, not possible. Second, Soviet interventions had taken place when the targeted countries were in a state of crisis either internally or externally. This was hardly the case in Yugoslavia and Romania. Both countries were pursuing the same foreign policies that they had followed for many years. Besides, Tito had no intention of allying himself with China, for he had made clear to the Chinese, during his China visit, that non-alignment constituted the 'lasting Yugoslav option, which is deeply rooted in the core of our revolution'.[18] Third, international reaction would also have been vigorous in the event of any Soviet intervention. Even if one were to exclude the possibility of military action by Beijing in the event of Soviet attack or a Soviet attempt to destabilize Yugoslavia, some Chinese initiative to counter Soviet action could hardly be excluded. Their non-intervention in 1956 and 1968 (Hungary and Czecho-slovakia) was primarily due to the fact that the two countries before the crisis were allied to Moscow whereas Yugoslavia and Romania during the period in question had a record of pursuing autonomous or independent foreign policies. Besides, practically all the members of the Atlantic community had close ties with both.

All these factors must have restrained the Soviet Union from any temptation to take any punitive action. China, therefore, continued to remain active in the Balkans. While relations with Romania continued to advance on an even keel, as they had in the past, interaction with Yugoslavia was accelerated. In fact, in many ways Yugoslavia's role was more crucial in influencing Chinese perspectives in international affairs, now that the Beijing government had decided to open up to the outside world. Broadly it involved three sectors: ideology, domestic options and the commercial sector.

The first and perhaps the most important development was in the ideological sector. Although, during Tito's August 1977 Beijing visit, the CCP had accepted in principle 'gradually to embark upon the resumption of relations between the CCP and the Yugoslav League of Communists',[19] there was none the less some reluctance within the CCP actually to do so. Forging interstate ties was one thing, but developing party relations with the most 'revisionist' of them all was another matter, especially at a time when the CCP was still harping on adhering 'to proletarian internationalism' and the need to 'strengthen our unity with the international proletariat . . .'[20] In this connection it is important to mention the Chinese foreign minister's secret speech of 30 July 1977 in Beijing a month before Tito's visit in which he had highlighted the CCP's dilemma. Though he had clearly stated that Yugoslavia 'was of course revisionist then and it still is now', it was very important for China to have close relations with that country because of its anti-Soviet credentials.[21]

The real decision to develop inter-party relations came in June 1978 when the CCP finally accepted the Yugoslav League as a Communist party.[22] And by the time Hua Guofeng came to Belgrade in August 1978, the balance had clearly tilted in favour of the proponents of inter-party relations, for in his very first public statement, he showered praise on Yugoslavia as 'a heroic country' where 'the League of Communist, on the basis of Marxist scientific theory . . . has built up a system of social management'.[23] At the same time, in his conversations with Yugoslav party leaders he 'stressed in particular the need to develop party relations'.[24]

The forging of inter-party ties opened for the Yugoslav leaders the prospects of discussing with the Chinese leaders the West European Communist parties, of informing them of the new roads they had embarked upon, and of impressing upon them the dimensional steps they had taken to become more independent of Moscow. The many hours of 'informal and intimate' talks that Tito and Hua had, reportedly contributed 'to a kind of "bridge building" between some Euro-communists and the Chinese leadership'.[25] The Yugoslav influence in the demotion of the ideological factor in Chinese diplomatic behaviour and in the Chinese opening up to Eurocommunism was probably crucial. Signs of some change became visible during Tito's China visit in August 1977 and became clearly evident during Hua's visit to Belgrade a year later.

The second dimension in Soviet-Yugoslav relations was the burgeoning Chinese interest in the Yugoslav economic model of organization and development. Having increasingly come to the conclusion that the 'advanced foreign experience' needed to be learnt and used for reinvigorating the battered Chinese economy,[26] the most logical step obviously was to examine closely other socialist systems. Though some interest was shown in how the Hungarians and Romanians were restructuring their economies, the principal focus clearly was on the Yugoslav model — a model that had incorporated new concepts and generated new thinking.[27]

It is important to note that only after China had taken the decision to open up politically to Yugoslavia and, after the Yugoslav system had been pronounced as socialistic in a conference convened in May 1978 to examine the Yugoslav economy,[28] did the party and the press began to show interest in the Yugoslav system of self-management; it was then identified as one of the key factors that had contributed to economic success. Many of the Chinese comments considered them as democratic innovations that enhanced the power of the workers in economic decision-making.

Even more attractive for China was Yugoslavia's growing involvement in foreign economic relations. Apparently the Chinese learnt in this sector more from Yugoslavia and other East European countries than in the area of industrial management. The Yugoslav influence can be discerned from the fact that the 1978 party documents plainly stated that there was much to be learnt from Yugoslavia about foreign affairs; and when the Chinese joint-venture laws were passed by the People's Congress, the Chinese commentators made it a point to quote the Yugoslav experience in support of the measure[29]

The third dimension was commercial. Years of political freeze had stagnated relations in this sector. The conclusion of the March 1969 trade agreement was not much of a booster, since economic exchanges remained on the low side, oscillating between a few million dollars to about 30 million in 1975 and 1976, the sole exception being 1974 when trade exchanges shot up to 140 million.[30] The trend, however, moved upward in 1977, when commercial figures shot up to 90 million dollars, and thereafter maintained that trend.

Tensions with Albania

The Chinese abandonment of a radical ideological posture and the burgeoning Chinese interest in Romania and Yugoslavia frayed Sino–Albanian relations and finally resulted in a rupture in the summer of 1978.

Already, during the post-Mao struggle, the Albanians were unhappy with the rapid removal of the so-called 'Gang of Four'. For them this was a bad omen, since they had been on the same ideological wavelength. The new benign foreign policy towards the United States and the established 'bourgeois' Third World governments aggravated their fears about the direction China was taking. But what really galvanized them to break with China was the new friendly attitude towards Yugoslavia—their worst adversary. It was this that tilted the balance.[31]

On 7 July 1977, the Albanian party decided to bring its differences out in the open because, in the words of Enver Hoxa, 'the Chinese revisionists were doing increasing harm, stepping up the struggle against Marxism–Leninism and especially against the Albanian party of labour'.[32] The party organ, *Zeri-i-popullit*, splashed out with an editorial entitled 'the theory and practice of revolution' through which they signalled an open ideological break. In a very clear and sharp tone it rejected Beijing's 'theory of three worlds'—a theory that underpinned China's foreign policy. Characterizing it as 'anti-revolutionary' and 'a flagrant departure from the teachings of Marxism–Leninism', it argued that

> it leads to the weakening of the dictatorship of the proletariat in the countries where socialism is being built, while calling on the world proletariat not to fight, not to rise in socialist revolution, and this is not to be wondered at: departure from the proletarian class criteria in assessing the situation can lead only to conclusions in opposition to the interests of the revolution and to the proletariat.[33]

Though the Chinese were surprised at the virulence of the attack, they gave vent to their irritation only privately;[34] in public they played it down and denied that they were 'estranged' or that there were 'basic divergences' between them.[35] However, when Albanian assaults became more and more persistent, and particularly when unqualified support was extended to Vietnam in its conflict with China[36]—an unpardonable act from the Chinese viewpoint—the Chinese government retaliated by terminating all economic and military aid and by recalling all Chinese specialists working in Albania. In an official note, the Chinese Ministry of Foreign Affairs declared:

> All the facts show that the Albanian leadership has decided to pursue the anti-China course, deliberately abandoned the agreements signed by the two sides providing Chinese aid to Albania, slandered and tried to fabricate charges against Chinese experts, and sabotaged the economic and military cooperation between China and Albania in a planned and systematic way, making it impossible for our aid work to go on while you blocked the way to a solution of the problems through consultations . . . The disruption of the economic and military cooperation between China and Albania is wholly the making of the Albanian side, which must bear the full responsibility.[37]

The timing of the China initiative was significant (7 July 1978). It took place more than a month before Hua Guofeng's visit to Romania and Yugoslavia. Presumably, Beijing did not wish to convey the impression of ambivalence on Albania. The stakes were indeed too high and the visit indeed too important for Chinese interests to allow the situation to perpetuate itself. The decision to focus on Romania and Yugoslavia had been taken, and the Chinese leaders did not, therefore, wish to allow the Albanian discontent to get in the way, least of all now that the divergences had intentionally been brought out in the open by Albania.

The CMEA countries

What about the other East European countries, the ones which were pro-Soviet (Bulgaria, Czechoslovakia, East Germany, Hungary and Poland)? Can one also discern any change towards them? Did China make any special effort to cultivate them?

At the broad diplomatic level there was not much of a change. No attempts were really made to warm to them. And no initiatives were taken to wean them away from the Soviet fold. The post-Maoist leadership had apparently become realistic enough to realize the futility of such an attempt towards Soviet client states, particularly those which were geopolitically vulnerable to the Soviet Union. Besides, even if China wanted to this was not possible, since most of Soviet client states in 'Eastern Europe had once again . . . launched in a rather animated way their attacks against the Maoists without Mao'.[38] Jivkov of Bulgaria had, for example, on 14 September 1977 compared the Chinese leaders to the 'worst reactionaries and fascists'.[39] Kadar of Hungary and Husak of Czechoslovakia in a joint statement of 16 September of the same year had strongly attacked China for having come to the rescue of 'extreme imperialist forces'[40] while *Neues Deutschland*, an organ of the East German party, had on 20 September noted that 'unfortunately no change has taken place in the fundamental orientations of the Chinese leadership'.[41]

None the less, there were three changes—albeit timid and subtle—that slowly did emerge in Chinese behaviour towards the five CMEA countries. The first pertained to a change in the pattern, scale and direction of Chinese attacks. They became more selective. Whereas before China invariably made across-the-board polemical assaults on all of them, the main thrust of Chinese criticism was now no longer directed at them, but at the Soviet Union's role in their affairs: how the Soviets were exploiting the CMEA countries; how East European economies were tied to the Soviet Union; and how little leverage they had in designing their own internal and external policies.[42]

If the virulence of Chinese attacks on Moscow had become more trenchant, they had correspondingly become more benign towards the established governments of Eastern Europe. There were of course brief periods of irritations and attacks on some of them—particularly Bulgaria—specially known to be pro-Soviet, but on the whole the main target of Chinese polemical assaults was the Soviet Union itself.

Table 8.2 Trade with CMEA countries (US$ mln)

Country	1976	1977	1978	1979	1980
Bulgaria	35.92	51.62	91.37	77.34	67.57
Czechoslovakia	125.89	161.70	263.71	283.43	201.27
German Democratic Republic	182.18	225.14	271.12	242.04	263.61
Hungary	70.29	72.65	130.33	129.15	114.52
Poland	102.66	114.97	188.50	245.17	242.11

Source: Economic Commission for Europe

Second, to improve the performance of their economy, the Chinese showed a particular interest in the innovations that had been introduced in Eastern Europe. Yugoslavia and Romania, as noticed above, were at the top of the Chinese interest list for obvious political reasons, but the others were not completely ignored. Of particular interest were the Hungarian reforms, which were apparently more advanced than in other countries. The articles in the Chinese press showed an interest in the Hungarian attempts to replace budget appropriations for investments by bank credits, to allow enterprises to invest freely, and to develop foreign economic relations. Especially interesting was the new Hungarian price system which took market forces into account. An article in June 1979, for example, focused on the three-tier price system that divided prices into fixed, fluctuating within limits and those freely set and which gave the proportions for each. Another article (November 1979) dealt with the criteria for setting fixed prices and stressed that decentralization of price setting authority was a key component of the reform,[43] while a third a month later underlined the Hungarian price reforms and the expansion of the powers of the enterprises as the two most important Hungarian innovations in the economic sector.[44]

The third change was in the domain of commercial relations with the five CMEA countries. With China's new determination to develop economic relations with the outside world, Eastern Europe was not ignored. In fact, China hardly could do that, given that most of the technology had come from the socialist countries, including Eastern Europe, and it would have been cheaper to replace it with the same—but more updated—version, at least so far as existing industries were concerned. Trade relations, therefore, increased with each of the CMEA countries during this brief period (see table 8.2).

The contours of what subsequently became China's policy towards Eastern Europe in the eighties were thus already visible during the transitional period. The basic foundations were laid then. What is perhaps more important and more striking is that—the power struggle not withstanding—a wide consensus was established on foreign policy. And this was evident regarding Eastern Europe.

Western Europe

In Western Europe, the broad foreign policy framework, established in the early seventies, was continued during the transitional period. The situational analysis was the same as before, with Western Europe as the centre of superpower contention, and with the Soviet Union perceived as the main threat to all nations, including the United States.

The prescription for the strategy proposed was identical to the preceding period: forging an international front to contain Soviet expansionism. And the four foreign-policy goals were identical (European integration, maintenance of an American presence in Europe, blocking East–West *détente* and seeking European assistance to modernize), and were perceived to be still valid.

The number of declarations made and the interviews given underlining these goals were indeed considerable. They were no longer as discreet and subtle as they had been during the time of Mao and Zhou; for the latter—even when seeking out Western Europe to countervail the Soviet Union—carefully avoided mentioning it in so many words, and never openly suggested that China was prepared to openly join hands with Western Europe or the United States. After 1976—at least during the transitional period—they were more outspoken, more direct and more urgent. In the very first foreign policy statement made on behalf of the post-Maoist leadership, Li Xiannian declared 'we want Europe to be powerful, and would like to see it bolster its defences against the Soviet Union'.[45] Hua Guofeng told British Air Vice Marshall Neil Cameron that 'We hope that Western Europe will unite'. And Deng Xiaoping, speaking to a group of visiting UPI correspondents, declared on 19 May 1978 that he was basically in agreement with US Ambassador to Japan Mike Mansfield's remarks that China's the 'eastern Nato'.[46]

Hao Deqing, chairman of the PRC National Society for the Study of International Relations at the German Foreign Policy Society in Bonn, on September 1978 depicted most aptly this new and more direct attitude of the post-Maoist leadership. He said:

China has opened its doors to the West as the leadership has come to the conclusion that only close cooperation with the West will enable it to reach its national goals. This intention applies not only to the economy, but also to foreign policy and security, about which Peking official have stubbornly kept silent until now.[47]

The actual policy was a continuation on the political front. Now that bilateral diplomatic relations had been forged with most West European countries, an intensive campaign was launched to encourage Western Europe to integrate, to discreetly push them to maintain the American presence and to warn them openly of the Soviet threat. All this—as before—was rhetorical diplomacy. China did not have any real means to achieve these goals. But in the sector of real policy, there were two major initiatives taken in the late seventies. The first was a growing interest in buying arms from the West, while the second pertained to a concerted attempt to build up relations with the European Economic Community.

West European arms

China became interested in buying military hardware from Western Europe—
certainly a change from the Maoist period when such a policy was not followed,
despite an obvious and urgent need for such sophisticated weaponry. After the
political elimination of the so-called 'Gang of Four' who favoured 'a revolutionary
army with politics in command', a consensus emerged that modernization of the
armed forces was indeed necessary.[48] There was apparently no disagreement on
this point. The military leaders did not have any difficulty in persuading the
party leaders about the principle of giving a more sophisticated and more
efficacious military clout to the Chinese armed forces. There was apparently
a consensus among the Chinese leaders. The problem arose regarding the
allocation of financial resources for the achievement of this goal. While the army
leaders obviously wanted more money and larger resources, the civilian leaders
were of the opinion that modernization of the armed forces would take time, and
could best be attained 'with the faster growth of economic construction',[49] for
only when this goal had been reached would it be possible to allocate the
resources to modernize the armed forces technically.

Although it was finally agreed that China's defence modernization would take
years owing to the country's fragile technological and managerial infrastructure,[50] it was none the less decided at a series of four important military
conferences, held in February 1977, that some purchases should be made rapidly
for use in defensive land warfare against an enemy having air and armoured
superiority.[51]

Clearly this was a compromise. Give and take was unavoidable during the brief
uncertain period when the power struggle was in full swing. Hua Guofeng
probably calculated that some concession to the armed forces would strengthen
his position *vis-à-vis* his political adversaries. China thus decided to turn to
Western Europe to explore different ways and means of obtaining some of the
sophisticated material that was urgently required. As has often been the case with
the Chinese pattern of diplomatic behaviour, once an internal decision is taken, a
concerted campaign is then launched to communicate this decision through a
series of inspired leakages, through interviews given or declarations made by
Chinese leaders.

This is what was done.[52] The Western press was awash with this news,
including some indications regarding the type of arms in which China was
interested.[53] Since the United States at the time was unwilling—and Japan
unable—to provide arms, the only option left was to turn to Western Europe—an
option that was extensively aired in the Chinese press towards the end of 1977.[54]

A number of factors favoured such a choice. The Chinese themselves were
optimistic that agreements to this effect might be possible with some West
European countries. First of all, the circumstances had changed: the United
States had withdrawn objections to arms' transfer. Though the United States
itself had ruled out any 'thought of any military aid' to China for the time being,[55]
the green light had apparently been given to its West European allies to go ahead
with the sale of weapons, as long as they were defensive in nature. Undoubtedly,
this was a major development, since this in effect meant that COCOM would no

longer create obstacles to the export of arms. In fact, to some extent the United States had set the precedent with the sale of two computers (Cyber 172) to China a week after the removal of the 'Gang of Four' in 1976.[56] Also, at about the same time, the Department of Commerce's export control regulations and the Department of State's 'munition control list' were modified so that China was assigned a new 'P' classification for arms transfer rather than the previous Warsaw Pact 'Y' classification. The 'P' designation meant that export applications by American firms for technology transfer to China would no longer be refused because the end use could be military.[57]

The second major development was the emergence of proponents for the greater Sino-West European military cooperation in Europe itself. Apart from leading conservative political figures (Franz Josef Strauss, Alfred Dregger,) or leading military leaders (Neil Cameron, British Air Vice Marshall), who realized the strategic importance of Sino-West European *entente*, there were powerful and organized military or political institutions who favoured either an explicit or implicit understanding with China in the military sector.

Though NATO could not make a formal declaration to this effect, it could hardly be against any such cooperation. How could it be, considering that a significant Chinese military presence along the Sino-Soviet border would have probably resulted in the diminution of Soviet military pressure on its weak and highly exposed Western flank?

In any event, views to this effect were openly expressed by Alexander Haig, the former Commander-in-Chief of NATO in Europe. In his view, the Sino-Soviet border tensions constituted 'a clear benefit to us in military terms'.[58] Later he characterized the PRC as the 'sixteenth member' of the North Atlantic bloc.[59]

The West European Union, however, was more explicit on the question of Sino-European military *entente*—at least some of its important members. The General Affairs Commission of the Union, in fact, submitted a report on 'China and European Security' in May 1978 to the 24th session of the Western European Union underlining the importance of the Sino-Soviet dispute to the West. The original draft of the recommendation was much stronger, for Sir Frederic Bennet—the rapporteur of the General Affairs Commission—had specifically recommended the sale of arms to China. Though it was finally deleted at the request of other members of the Commission[60] all this had generated a great deal of controversy within the press and in the national parliaments of various members of the W.E.U.[61] The Commission also tabled a 'draft resolution' at the 24th plenary session recommending that it 'examine carefully the role China can play regarding European security' and 'favourably consider the rising Chinese demands for industrial technology'.[62]

The third factor was the interest of the West European countries themselves in selling military hardware. Economic benefits were considerable, especially when one takes into account the widespread rumours that were circulating regarding all that China wished to buy. In fact, there were already some signs of fear among the main arms producing countries of being left out of the game—not so much because they were producing the same items,but because they were sure that the limited Chinese financial resources would force them to slow down their plans of going on a buying spree. Though the report and the recommendations of the

Commission were vetoed by a majority of thirty-four to twenty-one, it is important to note the seventeen-member Commission had adopted the recommendations and the report by a majority of fourteen with no one against and with three abstentions.

The pressure groups in Western Europe favouring an understanding with China were therefore not that insignificant. They generated a great deal of discussion on China among the countries concerned. They succeeded in publicizing the whole issue of NATO-PRC relations in the West European press. What is more, they encouraged the West European Union a few years later (1983) to publish a more elaborate report.[63] Though it was by no means pro-Chinese, it did none the less recommend the Council to 'start regular consultations with the Government of the People's Republic of China in the most appropriate framework on matters relating to the maintenance of peace in the world',[64] and to see to it that 'any negotiations on intermediate-range nuclear weapons do not allow the Soviet Union to deploy in Asia weapons withdrawn from Eastern Europe'.[65]

Whether the pressure groups played a decisive role may be a debatable question; what is not debatable was the sharp Soviet reaction to the activities of the pressure groups. Moscow intervened in three West European capitals (Bonn, London and Rome) to demand that the forthcoming debate on military relations between China and Western Europe be withdrawn from the agenda of the WEU Assembly.[66] The Soviet chargé d'affaires in London in fact warned the Foreign Office that any recommendation by the Assembly on the lines recommended by the General Affairs Commission would be considered 'a collective hostile declaration which would considerably undermine international security'.[67] Later two Soviet specialists on military affairs wrote a book on China charging that 'Today the Peking leaders and NATO top brass are drawing closer together on the common ground of hostility to *détente* and international cooperation. They are hoping to form an alliance in which China is assigned the unseemly role of NATO's military outpost in the Far East' . . .[68]

From the different military missions sent to the region, particularly in the summer of 1978, it would seem that Beijing had made up an impressive shopping list of highly sophisticated items. From the British, they were interested in buying Harrier jump jets and Chieftain tanks. From the French, they wanted to buy anti-tank and anti-aircraft missiles and the Mirage fighters 2000. From the West Germans they wanted to acquire equipment like inertial guidance platforms and range finders, the highly effective Leopard tank and some anti-tank mobile artillery.

When the dimensions of the Chinese list became known, the West Europeans, however, began to show some signs of hesitation. Their enthusiasm for selling military hardware began to flag. Consider, for example, the Sino-British negotiations on the question. The Labour government, under James Callaghan, became increasingly reluctant to proceed with the arms sale. It was showing 'all the uneasiness of a clergyman hesitating outside a massage parlour'. [69] It did everything to avoid any parliamentary debate on the question, and gave evasive answers whenever the question was forced on the government. Finally, it hid behind the argument that the Chinese had not made a formal request, knowing full well that the Chinese negotiatory style invariably made them reluctant to make formal requests as long as they were not sure that the opposite party would agree. Finally, when negotiations reached a critical stage in early 1969, the Callaghan government stipulated that five conditions would have to be met before an agreement could be sealed.

1. The Coordinating Committee for Export of Strategic Materials (COCOM) would have to give its approval to each British arms transaction;
2. Only those weapons systems that were defined as 'defensive' in nature would be sold to China;
3. The supply of British arms would have to be a part of a general Sino-British trade agreement;
4. China would have to make a payment as work on the system progressed;
5. The Chinese must submit a formal written proposal to the British government specifically outlining their weapon requirements.[70]

By the spring of 1979, China satisfied the first three requirements to the satisfaction of the Labour government. On the other hand, it would seem the Chinese were hesitant regarding the financial stipulation, and were frankly reluctant to send the formal written proposal.

A number of reasons could be advanced for such hesitations. First, domestic financial stringencies were making it difficult for the Chinese to make the type of advance payment that the British government was insisting upon. And second, the Chinese were reluctant to place their weapon requirements on a piece of paper. This was not their style of operating or of carrying out negotiations. Besides, one cannot exclude the possibility that this reluctance might in part be attributable to some uncertainty or even disagreement regarding their weapons requirements.

The French were also hesitating. While, on the one hand, the minister of state in the French Foreign Ministry (Olivier Stirn) was declaring that France envisaged cooperation with the Chinese 'in all domains', the foreign minister (Louis de Guiring) declared that France was willing to 'sell certain defence' items but not offensive weapons 'such as airplanes'.[71] At a press conference in Paris in October 1978, he declined to elaborate on the question.[72]

West Germany was of course the most reluctant of them all to sell weapons directly to China. Her method of operating on such a sensitive issue was to finance or to contribute components to a weapons system manufactured by multinationals headquartered in other West European countries.

These general signs of West European vacillation can be, first of all, attributed to intense Soviet pressures against the conclusion of such agreements with China. Brezhnev threatened James Callaghan with serious consequences for Anglo-Soviet relations if Britain went ahead with the Harrier sales.[73] Gromyko reportedly pressured the French to sell only defensive weapons.[74] West Germany did not really need any great pressure, for it was quite clear that it could hardly afford to annoy the Soviet Union, given that developing relations with Moscow was one of the major West German priorities.

While the West European governments formally resisted all external pressures, and invoked their sovereign right to take any decisions that accorded with their national interests, pressures from Moscow did have some effect in dissuading them—at least in the seventies—from concluding any major arms deal with China.[75]

The United States, too, played some role. Though generally no longer opposed to the sale of arms by the West European governments, there was, according to some reports, a sudden change of attitude while the Sino-British negotiations were under way. The American State Department—known for its opposition to all such deals, in contrast to the White House—suddenly came up with the argument that the SALT talks with Moscow were at such a delicate stage that nothing must be done to endanger them. Selling arms to China, it feared might do just that.[76]

Though it is difficult to assert that this new and sudden American objection did play a role, this argument cannot be excluded, at least so far as the British government, which was already hesitating, was concerned.

The domestic dimensions were not insignificant—though their impact varied from country to country, these were very much there. Apart from the British bureaucracy that was worried about selling the production process to the Chinese, for fear that they might make their own planes and compete with Britain, or was concerned with the technical perspective of British airmen having to train Chinese pilots, who might one day fly against the Soviet airforce,[77] James Callaghan had to reckon with powerful pressures from the pro-Soviet lobby within the Labour party restraining him from taking any action to which Moscow might strongly object.

The domestic dimension was perhaps less important in the case of France. With the exception of the French Communist party, there was no other political force that really opposed any Sino-French military accord, though all of them realized that France could not completely ignore Soviet objections. The domestic French doubts stemmed essentially from the French uncertainty regarding China's capacity to pay, and from the French fear that the Chinese might use advanced French technology to produce the military items themselves and eventually compete in the Third World.[78]

In West Germany domestic constraints were strongest. For one thing, Moscow was generally viewed by German economic groups as potentially a major economic partner that hardly any country was prepared to forsake for a few military contracts with China. Besides, there was no certainty that these would come their way, since the major Chinese priority was in the aviation sector, in which the Federal Republic was unable to compete with France or Great Britain. Politically, too, there was apparently a consensus regarding the folly of seeking out China in the military sector, as it might upset her *Ostpolitik*, the linchpin of its foreign policy. Very few agreements thus were concluded during the transitional period (see Table 8:3), for in addition to West European hesitation, the Chinese began to lose interest in buying arms-related technology.

The last reason was economic. At the April 1979 working conference, convened by the CCP, the focus was shifted to economic matters, particularly to the goal of 'readjusting, restructuring, consolidating and improving', the national economy. The defence budget for 1980, for example, was trimmed. The Chinese then began to show 'remarkable sales resistance' to concluding any major

Table 8.3 Agreements for the sale of arms and military-related technology, 1977–80

Items	Year	Seller	Value (US$ mln)
Alouette and Super Frelon helicopters (approx. 30)	1977	France	*
Anti-tank missiles (600)	1978	West Germany	*
Bo-105 helicopters	1978	West Germany	*
Marconi Space and Defence System, field artillery control equipment sets (5)	1979	United Kingdom	2.2
Co-production deal for model 212 helicopter	1980	France	
Marconi Avionics—modernization of communications, gear and fire control on Chinese jets	1980	United Kingdom	92
Société Nationale Industrielle Aérospatiale et Société Turmomeca, Dauphin II helicopters under licence (50)	1980	France	98.4

* Price unavailable

arms deal, 'because the price was too high'.[79] This became particularly apparent after the British conservatives returned to power in May 1979 and the new British government had indicated that no onerous strings were attached to the sale of British military equipment.

Institutionalization of relations with the EEC

The second major foreign policy development was the rapid expansion of relations with the European Economic Community. Both political as well as economic considerations galvanized China to forge ties with the Community.[80]

Politically,the regional organization was perceived as an important step in the eventual integration of Western Europe and as an eventual counterweight to the Soviet Union. According to one observer,the Chinese interest in seeking out the Community was 'primarily political'.[81]

But the economic component was no less important. Within the new Chinese framework of economically opening up to the outside world, the Chinese concluded bilateral economic cooperation agreements with the Community members in the late seventies (except for Ireland and Greece) (see Table 8.4).

What was really significant was the institutionalization of relations between China and the Community with the establishment of three accords or pieces of legislation. The trade agreement, concluded on 3 April 1978, was clearly the most important accord. For it was this agreement that opened the prospects of an upswing in trade relations, making the Community China's second biggest economic partner after Japan.

Table 8.4 Economic cooperation agreements between China and EEC members

Belgium–Luxemburg Economic Union	27 June 1979
Denmark	14 September 1979
France	4 December 1978
Great Britain	March 1979
Ireland	–
Italy	23 April 1979
Netherlands	30 October 1980
West Germany	24 October 1979

Source: Hunggah Chiu, *Agreements of the People's Republic of China: A Calendar of Events 1960–1980.*

Table 8.5 The development of China–EEC trade relations (in million ECUs)

	1978	1979	1980
Total volume	2,426	3,425	3,613
Imports	937	1,324	1,888
Exports	1,489	2,101	1,725
Balance	+ 552	+ 777	– 163

Source: Monthly Statistical Bulletin of the European Communities

Immediately, trade between the two parties increased significantly, even during the first three years after the treaty was signed. China's exports doubled from ECU937 million in 1978 to ECU1,888 million in 1980. Imports from the Community rose rather slowly from ECU1,489 million to ECU1,725 million during the same period (see Table 8.5). The agreement also made it possible under article 4.2 for the EEC to extend the list of items that could be imported from China. For example, on the recommendation of the Commission, the Council introduced new regulations to permit China to export to the Community, with effect from 1 January 1979 more than twenty additional products which had hitherto been governed by restrictive regulations applicable to all state trading countries.[82] The European Parliament attempted to go even further in facilitating the expansion of trade. In a report on the trade agreement, its External Economic Relations Committee expressed the hope that the Commission would give preferential agreement to Chinese imports over imports from countries which had not recognized the Community.[83]

The textile agreement was the second agreement, concluded for two years between the two parties.[84] It was initiated on 18 July 1979 and fully implemented with effect from 1 January 1980. Though China did not achieve what it wanted to achieve, it none the less doubled textile exports from 21,000 tons to 41,000 tons.

The third major development was the Community's decision to include China in a preferential agreement with effect from 1 January 1980. Accorded unilaterally, it involved full exemption from customs duty for all industrial goods and for

Table 8.6 Medium- and long-term loans from EEC countries, 1977–80

Country providing official credit	Amount/terms of interest	Date
Belgium	$13 million	November 1979
Great Britain	$1,200 million (7.50% interest)	December 1978
France	$7,000 million (loans 7.25%; for less than seven years at 7.5%; for between seven and ten years at 7.75%)	May 1979
Italy	$1,000 million (7.5% interest over five years)	May 1979
Belgium	$170 million (7.75% interest)	October 1979
West Germany	$235 million	November 1980

Source: World Bank Report, 1 June 1981

partial exemption for certain processed agricultural products exported to developed countries.[85]

The cumulative effect of these bilateral arrangements or unilateral EEC decisions was impressive. The trade between the two parties increased considerably between 1975 and 1980. It doubled, reaching the figure of ECU4,378 million, an increase of more than 41 per cent in 1980 alone.

The opening up of China also resulted in the conclusion of a wide range of whole-plant imports and licensing and co-production agreements. Contracts for the import of machines and equipment worth $2,500 million, for example, were signed in 1978 and 1979. Since China was unable to meet the capital outlay from domestic funds needed for all these projects, important credits were sought from the Community members. The principal source was the banks. A number of credit agreements to the tune of $30,000 million were concluded with the Community. State guaranteed and tied-up exports accounted for two-thirds of the overall amount. The rest were either untied, marked or easy-term loans. The principal creditor was West Germany, followed by France and Great Britain. (see Table 8.6).

Conclusion

During the transitional period, Chinese foreign policy was very politically oriented. Heavily influenced by Chinese determination to forge an international united front against the Soviet Union, the main thrust of its activity in Europe was principally geared to the task of countering Soviet actions. In practical terms, this meant that Chinese policy in Eastern Europe was essentially to reinforce further relations with Romania and to seek out Yugoslavia more and more. The importance that China attributed to building up this relationship with the two dissidents can be determined from the way Albania, an ideological ally and friend of many years was abandoned when it became increasingly evident that Albania opposed such opening up towards Yugoslavia.

In Western Europe, Chinese policy translated itself into two objectives: (a) to seek military hardware from Western Europe; and (b) to support the integration of Western Europe.

Chapter 9
New directions in foreign policy

The eighties witnessed a major transformation in Chinese perceptions of the international system. This was not so much because the international configuration of forces had radically evolved since the seventies or that the foreign-policy behaviour of European governments had materially changed and to which China had felt the need to respond differently. The change was essentially Chinese: for one thing, the transitional period, with its intense power struggle and its political uncertainties, had come to an end thereby allowing the introduction of necessary revisions. For another, a new breed of political leaders, with Deng Xiaoping in command, had come to power. These leaders considered China's existing foreign policy as being far too restrictive, far too ideologically oriented and far too categorical.

Change

The basic and the most important change was regarding the Soviet Union. The politics of anti-Sovietism, inaugurated in the sixties and built up into a prime strategy during the transitional years, was slowly abandoned.

This was not simply another of those policy changes comparable to the numerous fluctuations that China had gone through in the past. It was much more than that—a sort of landmark, a precursor to the new thought process. The whole pattern of the Maoist way of thinking and of looking at the world, of simplifying international politics in terms of friends and foes, of distinguishing between minor and major contradictions, of designing foreign policies against real or imaginary adversaries was slowly abandoned.

The process of change began slowly in mid-1981 with the publication of articles and the voicing of declarations that no longer solely assailed the Soviet Union, but once again included attacks on her in general broadsides against the two superpowers. And in the fullness of time even this was abandoned and was slowly replaced by mild criticism or by a new approach of even extending support to one power or the other on some specific issue.

Although the debate, to some extent, still continues in China on 'whether the *perestroika* of Soviet foreign policy is strategic or tactical', whether the warmer atmosphere in international relations can be attributed to the weakening of the superpowers or the strengthening of the 'forces of peace', the press comments on the whole are increasingly becoming indulgent to Soviet diplomatic activities—in any event more than towards the United States.

After the mid-eighties even this balancing act was to some extent abandoned by the appearance of statements in the Chinese press to the effect that the CPSU 'has fairly and realistically analysed the international situation' and that the Soviet leadership 'has markedly advanced in the all-round correction of foreign policy'. Well-known diplomats, Gong Dabei, and Huan Xiang even went to the extent of stating that Moscow's initiatives and the Chinese response to these are qualitatively different from what they had been a few years earlier. Foreign and domestic policies, in their view, were going through 'a sort of new revolution whose global significance should not be underestimated', and that the Soviet leadership's current course 'is an important new factor affecting China's foreign policy'.[1]

The whole process of analysis and looking at international developments consequently became more benign than previously. The new catchword in the Chinese lexicon was 'independence'. The official stamp of approval of what had slowly and clearly become the new line was given at the twelfth party congress in September 1982, where Hu Yaobang, the party general secretary, declared that China intended to follow an independent foreign policy,[2] and where Deng Xiaoping made it clear that 'no foreign country can expect China to be its vassal or expect it to swallow any bitter fruit detrimental to its interests'.[3] This was confirmed by foreign minister Huang Hua from the podium of the United Nations General Assembly (4 October 1982) when he declared that 'we adhere to an independent foreign policy'.[4] The implication of all these writings and official declarations was obvious: a united anti-Soviet front at the international level was no longer China's official policy.

Determinants of change

It is of course impossibl to unravel the mysteries of the Chinese process that resulted in the decision to slow down, and to finally end the continuous assailment of the Soviet Union. Mao's disappearance in 1976 and Hua Guofeng's removal in 1979 opened a new perspective for pragmatically evaluating the wisdom of continuing an anti-Soviet stance with the same acerbity as before.

A number of factors had contributed to its abandonment: first, and perhaps the most obvious was that this policy had failed. In fact, it had never got off the ground. None of the three major world powers were prepared to forge ties with China against the Soviet Union. The developed nations did not see any point in doing so, for China really had nothing to offer in return, not even a viable defence system on the border with the Soviet Union. In fact, China's anti-Soviet stance was so unbridled and so vociferous that many of the European nations considered an open alliance with China as counterproductive to their own national interests. Besides, thought many of them, with China's heavy record of see-saw diplomacy since 1949, there were no guarantees that there would not be another change in attitude in due course. The West European reluctance to sell arms to China during the post-Maoist transitional period was perhaps the most striking indicator of the limits beyond which they were not prepared to go along with China and against the Soviet Union.

Furthermore, linking up with China would have amounted to a renunciation of the flexible NATO strategy of seeking relaxation of tensions while continuing to strengthen Atlantic defences—a strategy that was clearly embodied in the Harmel report of December 1967 and that was formally approved by the NATO ministerial meeting of 14 December of the same year.[5] The report had clearly recommended that *détente* with the Soviet Union must be an important part of NATO strategy, and that it 'must end the unnatural barriers between Eastern and Western Europe which was clearly and most cruelly manifested in the division of Germany'.[6] The West Europeans had, in fact, gone much further than the United States by suggesting that since the nature of the Soviet threat had changed, a permanent relaxation of intra-European tensions was imperative.

Second, China's defence system was not adequate to meet any security threats from the north. The numerous discussions that took place within the Chinese leadership in the relatively more free atmosphere of the post-Maoist period had frankly brought out most of the weaknesses of the Chinese armed forces: they had, for example, come too much under 'the pernicious influence of the ultra-leftists during the Cultural Revolution'.[7] They were at least two decades behind the developed countries in technological and military infrastructure which they were unable to neutralize owing to the lack of any cooperation from the developed world. Besides, the army had become too politicized as a result of which its capacity to defend itself or to carry out efficacious military campaigns beyond China's borders had been severely jeopardized. In effect, the Chinese armed forces were not in a position to measure up to the Soviet forces of which as many as forty-seven divisions were deployed on the Sino-Soviet border. The Sino-Vietnamese conflict of February 1979, in this connection, was very instructive, for it revealed China's incapacity to fight a sophisticated war. Neither the Chinese equipment nor combat performances had improved materially since the 1950 Korean War.

So the only rational strategy that China could envisage, under the existing circumstances, was to avoid a military confrontation by politically seeking out the Soviet Union; in sum, launching a process of normalizing relations with Moscow that would diminish—if not remove—the military danger from the north.

But this new policy of seeking out her northern neighbour cannot be explained purely in security terms or in terms of the failure of the previous policy. The post-Maoist 1980 leadership had also come to the conclusion that China had indeed gone too far in her assailment of Moscow, and in her characterization of the whole Soviet system as 'fascist', 'expansionist' and 'anti-socialist', etc.[8]

The first major initiative that was taken was to admit China's errors, for only by doing so publicly would the Chinese leaders be able to signal their willingness to open up, albeit slowly, to Moscow. Through an editorial of 2 April 1980, published in the *People's Daily*, it was therefore declared that the nine articles published in 1964, which contained all these epithets and had highlighted the expansionist character of the Soviet system, were incorrect.[9] 'The origin and characteristic of revisionism', admitted the editorial, 'were presented in an erroneous manner'.[10] Undoubtedly the publication of this editorial was a landmark decision, for it set off a slow process of leading China away from the confrontational path.

Having taken such a decision—undoubtedly a concerted move—it was hardly possible to continue to proclaim that the Soviet Union was the main enemy and the main threat to China and the rest of the world.

Third, the abandonment of the 'united front' line can also be attributed to the new Chinese reading of the international situation, according to which the balance of power had shifted. The United States had apparently recovered her economic and military clout after the advent of Ronald Reagan, while Soviet growth during 1981–5 had decreased to its lowest point since the 1960s.[11]

Fourth, China realized the futility of the continuous assault on the Soviet Union. For the embarkation on such an anti-Soviet strategy had led the Chinese leadership to peculiar and apparently uncomfortable situations of supporting or normalizing relations with Pinochet in Chile, Marcos in the Philippines, the Shah in Iran, Mobutu in Zaïre and Franco in Spain. It had led them to regard with approval an American military or political presence in the Third World, particularly in Asia and Africa. Rather than oppose the United States as they had in the past, the Chinese considered the American presence as a necessary evil to be tolerated for the time being as a countervailing force against the Soviet Union. In fact, they had often found themselves in the uncomfortable position of criticizing Washington for not being vigorous enough in its policy towards the Third World.

Such a stark anti-Soviet policy, the Chinese leadership realized, could not be continued any longer if China wished to accelerate the momentum of the 'great leap outwards', particularly when it was mending fences and building bridges with the established governments of the Third World countries.

A new foreign policy

The abandonment of the 'united front' policy had a major impact on basic external strategy. This was inevitable for once the focal point is abandoned around which a whole policy had been constructed no nation can logically continue with the same policy. The whole edifice has to be restructured. Practically all the components were therefore modified, and even radically changed. Whether it was at the behaviourial, decisional, analytical or the normative level, everything altered, so much so that a break with the Maoist period was indeed visible by the mid-eighties.

Behaviour level

At the behavioural level the most conspicuous transformation was in the very style of Chinese diplomacy. The revolutionary and the acerbic tone that hitherto had been an integral part of Chinese press comments, analytical articles and declarations on foreign affairs was slowly replaced by moderate, pragmatic and even neutral language. The whole emphasis shifted from what China was against to what she was for. Even an impressionistic analysis of the Chinese press revealed the dimension of change. The harsh rhetoric had gone, and the focus was more on describing and analysing international issues rather than simply expressing views.

The nature of China's diplomatic behaviour also qualitatively changed. Having become one of the principal actors in the mainstream of international politics, China's pattern of diplomatic behaviour was not materially different from other main actors. On numerous issues, China talked and listened, and more often than not sought a consensus or a common ground on a wide spectrum of international issues. In sum, Chinese diplomacy had become much more interactive with national and international units and much more responsive to international opinion than ever before.

The level of presentation of Chinese views on international issues became more sophisticated. The daily press became more analytical and the academic journals more sedate. It is important to note that the very first group that benefited from this process of change was the academic world, and that it was deliberately encouraged by the Chinese authorities. This can principally be attributed to the increasing and untrammelled involvement of the academic world in internal foreign-policy debates on the grounds that the outcome of all this opening up would be beneficial to the formulation of consensus politics; and also on the grounds that an encouragement to think and to deliberate openly if left solely to a small group would be tantamount to drawing a line between acceptable free discussion and unacceptable political agitation.

The style of diplomacy and the form in which a nation presents its viewpoint or interacts with other nations can have a strong impact. It can bring it into the mainstream of international politics. It can arouse confidence. Others listen much more eagerly and the position that a nation has taken on any contentious issue may get across more efficaciously.

The decisional level

The second broad change was in the decision-making process. New elements were involved, and greater interaction was discernible than before. To risk a generalization, it could be argued that the change was discernible in three aspects: the input of other international actors or institutions on Chinese decisions; the institutionalization of foreign policy decisions; and the quantum increase in those actually involved in the process.

The Chinese decision-making process became more interactive with other international actors. Since the early eighties, China's foreign policy behaviour has become not only more reactive to external variables, but apparently when designing foreign policy has taken into account the feedback it has received. This is particularly true in the economic sector.

Years of virtual isolation from international economic interactions, compounded with ideological orthodoxy, had made China a virtual prisoner of its own rhetoric. The Chinese leadership was either indifferent, or contemptuous or even unaware of the functioning of the international economic system.

With the shifts from a command method of running the economy to the economic method of running it in the early eighties, it stands to reason that the Chinese leadership began to take a greater interest in the international economic system, and was no longer indifferent to absorbing or seeking advice on a wide spectrum of international issues.

Simply taking administrative decisions or just announcing that foreign capital or foreign technology would be welcome and foreign trade would be expanded was obviously not enough to inspire confidence among foreign economic interests. Concrete economic measures were required to overhaul the Chinese economy, and some interaction or feedback with international institutions, foreign experts, recognized academic institutions, etc. was deemed necessary before deciding on issues of foreign economic policy. In sum, a whole new learning process had to be set in motion for a nation which had lost the habit of such behaviour since the 1949 revolution. Consider the continuous international expertise that China has sought on a wide spectrum of technical issues to ameliorate the functioning of her economy.[12]

The second major innovation was institutional. Within the Chinese political system a wide network of institutions and a highly structured decision-making process were established that dealt with foreign policy in a regular and coordinated manner. Consider, for example, the establishment of a 'foreign affairs small group' within the CCP in which 'all organizations concerned with foreign affairs' participated. Though this body did not take any decisions,it is more than likely that any conclusions drawn in the meetings of this group carry a great deal of weight with the decision-makers.[13]

The Centre of International Studies, established directly under the authority of the State Council, also plays a crucial role. Involved in writing papers on different aspects of international affairs, it is probably in a position to swing the Chinese decisions in one direction or the other. In many ways, its role is comparable to the policy planning units within the foreign ministries of other countries; and its real importance can be gauged by the fact that it was headed by Huan Xiang, a well-known personality with a long diplomatic experience.[14]

The Institute of International Studies, a research arm of the Foreign Ministry, should also be mentioned in this connection. Established in the 1950s and reactivated after the Cultural Revolution, it is perhaps the most influential organization in the Chinese decisional process. With a staff of about one hundred, it carries out research on different aspects of international affairs, which is ultimately used as background information by the ministry when taking decisions on foreign affairs. It is headed by a Wang Xhu, a veteran diplomat who played a crucial role in the development of Sino-German relations, and who, in fact, was instrumental in making the Chinese leadership accept the view that Europe was the centre of superpower conflict, a view which became the foundation-stone of China's foreign policy in the seventies.[15]

The China Contemporary Institute of International Relations in Beijing is another important institution that contributes to the input that goes into the decisional process. Activated in 1980, it works directly under the State Council. This organization with 300 staff is, according to one source, 'China's principal foreign intelligence analysis agency and the analyses generated by it are used to brief the senior elite'.[16] The Director of the Institute is Liu Seqing.

There are numerous other institutions involved in China's decisional process. There is the foreign-affairs coordination unit of the State Council that is presided over by Ji Pengfei (a former foreign minister), whose primary responsibility seems to be one of high-level coordination of policies involving the foreign ministry and the ministry of foreign economic relations and trade.[17] There is the foreign affairs standing committee of the National People's Congress, headed by Geng Biao (former defence minister) which has become increasingly active in discussing foreign affairs.[18] It has established international contacts and prepares reports for leading party and government bodies.

The third major innovation in the foreign policy decisional process in the eighties is the marked involvement of the bureaucracy and academia. During the Maoist period, all decisions, whether 'high' or 'low' were taken—or at least had to be cleared—at the highest political level. For obvious political reasons, none of the members of the bureaucracy were willing to take autonomous decisions on any foreign policy matter. The political risks were indeed so great that hardly anyone was prepared even to offer any independent expert advice to political leaders on specific issues when called in. The fear of giving an opinion that was counter to the views held by the political leaders literally paralysed the bureaucracy.

The distinction often made in the Western decisional processes between 'high' and 'low' policies was thus virtually non-existent in China since the highly rigid and highly conformist political atmosphere generated reluctance among the bureaucrats to venture out even on 'low' policies.

Since the commencement of the eighties, some significant changes are increasingly becoming visible in this aspect. The distinction between 'high' and 'low' policies has been established. The high-policy decisions are clearly taken at the apex of the political hierarchy. This is centred in the standing committee of the Politburo of the CCP. Here within the framework of this important and powerful institution most of the crucial decisions are taken collectively pertaining to China's 'independent' and 'open door' foreign policies[19] with a minimum of factionalism.[20] Though Deng Xiaoping is clearly the paramount authority in foreign policy, it is unlikely that his authority and his role are analogous to that of Mao Zedung. For one thing, his personal propensity for delegating decisional authority is far greater than that of his predecessor. For another, it is difficult to imagine that Deng could take major foreign policy decisions in the post-Maoist period, solely on his own, without involving some of his contemporaries in the process.

Another important characteristic relating to 'high' policies is the new process of interaction between the political leaders and bureaucracy. This has become more common and more important than previously. In part this may be attributed to the fact that in the relatively freer post-Maoist atmosphere, the bureaucracy can give its uninhibited expert advice without being disowned or criticized; and also owing to the fact that the political leadership felt the need of more information and more data in order to design the new 'open-door policy'— information and data that could come from the government or party bureaucracy.

Decisions on 'low' policies were taken more autonomously at the ministerial or bureaucratic levels. The 'bewildering number of national agencies, as well as provincial and local units' of the administration with their horizontal command structures, their vertical bargaining systems compounded with informal personal connections (*guanxi*) have created an enormous network where more and more low-policy decisions are taken at the administrative levels.[21] Should China continue to evolve in this direction, the level of bureaucratic influence in the decisional process is bound to increase even further in the future.

Even more remarkable is the increasing involvement of the academia in the decisional process. Academia[22] has, of course, always commented on foreign affairs. The press was always awash with its views and with its analyses. What is new is the quality and the character of its intervention. Earlier, it followed to the last detail the decisions taken by the upper echelons of the party, or gave the type of advice that the party leaders wanted to hear, but their role was marginal, and their assigned objective generally was to give intelligent justifications for decisions already taken.

All this has apparently changed. Academia's leeway has become much larger and its right to air contradictory views has been officially recognized by the Chinese authorities. Their impact on or their interaction with the decisional process is channelled in three ways: the first is their direct and uninhibited interaction with the Chinese foreign-affairs bureaucracy or even directly with the Chinese political leaders. Specialists in different sectors either participate on a permanent basis in the vast institutionalized network of coordinated bodies belonging to the party and/or government, or alternatively are called in to give advice on specific issues on a very *ad hoc* basis. The second is closed, concerted discussion among the specialists themselves who have been specially commissioned by the party or the government. For example, before the then General Secretary of the CCP Hu Yaobang's visit to Western Europe in 1982, one of the major research institutes in Beijing was commissioned by the party to get leading European specialists together to discuss and present views on Western Europe and on the broad options that China could consider regarding that part of the world.[23] Such a method is often employed by Chinese political leaders either before their departure for important foreign visits or when important international developments require China to take a position. The third innovation is the development of the phenomenon of public debate among academic specialists on 'non-sensitive' issues. Following the September 1986 decision encouraging 'free discussion of academic problems between different schools'[24] diverse views have often publicly aired regarding issues that are generally viewed as 'non-sensitive' and regarding the policies that China should adopt towards these issues.[25]

Analytical level

The third major foreign policy innovation was at the analytical level. From the wide array of declarations made, interviews given, and views expressed in bilateral conversations by Chinese political leaders, four broad perceptions emerge regarding the international system.

First, the multipolar trend, already visible in the seventies, became, in the Chinese view, well established in the eighties. Relatively autonomous political forces had begun to assert themselves. Although the two superpowers were still the two major components of the international system, they were finding it increasingly difficult to control completely all political situations and all political allies.

Second, the conflictual element in American-Soviet relations had, in the new Chinese perception, levelled off. A parallel process of *détente*, mutual understanding, etc. had lessened the dangers of global conflict. 'We now think', declared Deng Xiaoping to this effect in March 1985, 'that although there is still the danger of war, the forces that can deter are growing and we find them encouraging.'[26]

Third, though the dangers of global war had declined, regional conflicts had become more and more rampant. Attributed to dimensional Third World problems, all the 139 conflicts that have had an international impact between World War II and 1983 were regional in character.[27]

Fourth, China had become fully involved in the international system as a major power. The eighties, in the Chinese view, had pushed the country into the high and inner circles of the great powers, where it was constantly called upon to act with other great powers. However, if China was in such a position, its capacity for playing an efficacious role was seriously undermined by the lack of economic or political clout for playing a role commensurate with its legal position and equal to that of other major powers.

Formulating a strategy that would respond to these four aspects of situational analysis was difficult in the eighties. It was easier during the Maoist period since China always had a recognized adversary or adversaries against whom policy could be constructed. In the situational analysis of the eighties, there was neither a recognized adversary nor even a real security threat.

The whole Chinese way of thinking regarding strategic goals thus had to be shifted from the concept of rallying the country against a real or perceived adversary to a more positive objective of making China economically powerful and politically viable enough not only to achieve domestic prosperity, but also to play the more important role that corresponded to the recognized status as a major power.

Normative goals

The whole weight of Chinese diplomacy was therefore geared to seek out the outside world economically, and to deploy full diplomatic weight to establish the appropriate international environment necessary for economic development.[28] 'China', declared Deng Xiaoping, 'must concentrate on economic development if it wants to become a modern powerful socialist country. Therefore, we need a peaceful international environment and are striving to create and maintain it. Economic development is our primary objective, and everything else must be subordinated to it.'[29]

In this major normative goal of economic modernization, the outside world was crucial. 'Reviewing our history,' confirmed Deng in October 1984, 'we have concluded that one of the most important reasons for China's long years of stagnation and backwardness was its policy of closing the country to outside contact. Our experience shows that China cannot rebuild itself with its doors closed to the outside and that it cannot develop in isolation from the rest of the world.'[30]

It is important to note that the two strategic goals (modernization and a peaceful international environment) were linked. The success of one was dependent upon the other. Zhao Ziyang highlighted this point in June 1984. He declared:

Safeguarding peace and promoting economic prosperity are the two important closely related issues of universal concern to the people of the world. For all countries, a peaceful environment is an indispensable condition for their development while carrying out international economic and technical exchanges and promoting common economic prosperity can give a strong impetus to the preservation of world peace and stability and the strengthening of friendship among their people.'[31]

Conclusion

The basic framework of China's foreign policy had radically altered in the eighties. Both in form as well as in content it broke with the past—with what had been designed and followed during the entire Maoist period. The abandonment of the anti-Soviet strategy, the emergence of a more pragmatic approach, the broadening of the decisional process and the active participation in the affairs of the world had projected China on to the international stage—a China whose foreign policy behaviour was more akin and more acceptable to other established nations.

Of the three foreign policy goals (security, modernization and an 'international peaceful environment') the one that stands out as the most important was the intensification of interaction with the international economic system in order to attain China's basic goal of accelerated modernization. Security—so important during the Maoist period—had been placed on the back burner, at least for the time being.

Chapter 10

The great leap outwards

Within the broad framework of the general direction that China took in her foreign policy (analysed in the previous chapter), Europe was one of the areas that was given a special position. Under the September 1986 directive encouraging 'free discussion' among academics, it was extensively discussed, and was one of those 'non-sensitive' issues on which views were openly expressed.[1]

If one were to summarize the different debates or discussions on Europe, there appears to exist a broad consensus on three important points, and a disagreement on one basic issue.[2] The academic community generally does not appear to accept the thesis that the importance of Europe has declined in this much-discussed epoch of the Asia-Pacific region. Europe, according to this general opinion, 'is and will continue to remain one of the three major economic centres in the capitalist world', with the superpowers still perceiving 'Europe as a fulcrum of their economic and strategic interests'.[3]

Although it is generally agreed that the ongoing process of West European integration 'has come to be accepted by more and more people', its further development, in the opinion of Chinese academics, 'will be a long and slow accumulation of small steps towards the "Europe of the second generation" '.[4] West European-East European interactions in the economic and political sectors have become more and more significant. These are being increasingly encouraged by the West European states in the hope that it will 'give them more diplomatic leeway in connection with American-Soviet relations', and, at the same time, make Eastern Europe 'more independent of the Soviets'.[5]

While there is thus a broad consensus among Chinese scholars in their evaluation of Europe, there is one major disagreement regarding the state of actual relations between the Europeans and the superpowers. While some seem to consider that each of the two parts of Europe are irrevocably tied to one superpower or the other with hardly any prospects for their real disengagement,[6] the others seem to consider that Europe's political influence has extended beyond Europe itself and it can play a manifold and multiple role in major international tasks'.[7]

Given the fact that Europe is not perceived as a 'sensitive issue',[8] by the Chinese authorities, and, as such, can be discussed more frankly than other topics, the debates on Europe have become open, and have, in fact, even spilled over into the more popular press.[9]

What concrete policy has the Chinese party and the government designed towards Europe to reach their strategic goals of security, modernization and international peaceful environment? What, in the official Chinese perception, is Europe's role in all this? Can one discern the contours of a coherent policy towards that continent?

Obviously, China considers European emergence as a positive sign for the further evolution of mulipolarism. And, in this context, the Chinese political leaders agree with their academics that Europe is indeed a major centre in the international system and has not been overshadowed by the Asia–Pacific region, that the ongoing process of West European integration should be encouraged and that West European-East European cooperation in the new situation of the eighties is important.

Perhaps the most authoritative statement on Europe as a whole was made by Deng Xiaoping. Expressing his views on the subject on 12 May 1987 he considered Europe as very important in global politics, placed Eastern and Western Europe on the same footing regarding their roles in the maintenance of peace and expressed the view that both the areas were crucial for the modernization of China.

> In analysing the international situation, we pay particular attention to Europe, for Europe plays a key role in determining if there will be peace or war. For many years our relations with Eastern Europe were abnormal. Now, basing ourselves on an objective judgement, we are of the opinion that both Western and Eastern Europe are a force for maintaining peace. Both Eastern and Western Europe need to develop, and the more they develop the stronger force for peace they become.[10]

The statement is indeed a reflection of the dimension of change that has been introduced in China's foreign policy not so much regarding Western Europe—for this existed even earlier—but so far as Eastern Europe is concerned. Deng's statement is not an announcement of the change, but a confirmation of what had been slowly inaugurated in the early eighties.

Eastern Europe

China's interest in Eastern Europe thus increased considerably in the eighties. Besides the further acceleration of the already existing close ties with Romania and Yugoslavia, and the revival of relations with Albania, the real innovation was the cultivation of the five pro-Soviet CMEA countries (Bulgaria, Czechoslovakia, Hungary, Poland, East Germany). They became the focal point of Chinese interest, and this was perhaps the single most important decision that was taken so far as Eastern Europe was concerned (see Table 10.1).

As is often the case with Chinese diplomatic behaviour in such instances, all the attacks against these countries regarding their policies and their excessive links with Moscow slowly disappeared from the Chinese media. This was obviously the first step in the operationalization of a new and a more open policy towards the five countries. At the same time, the CCP began to show particular interest in what was happening to Eastern European societies. The number of favourable articles that appeared in the Chinese press on different aspects of Eastern European life increased. Of particular interest, in this connection, was the wide array of Hungarian innovations. In fact, groups of experts were sent to Hungary in 1979 and 1980 to study the mechanism of price reforms, the new

Table 10.1 Visits to China by CMEA party leaders

Wojciech Jarulzelski	Poland	September 1986
Eric Honecker	East Germany	October 1986
Janos Kadar	Hungary	October 1987
Milos Jakes	Czechoslovakia	May 1988
Todor Zhivkov	Bulgaria	May 1987

pattern of foreign economic relations and the broad reforms introduced in the agricultural sector. 'Twenty years ago', declared one article, 'Hungary launched a major economic and political reform programme that has proved to be of far-reaching significance not only to the country but to most other socialist countries as well.'[11] The number of delegates visiting Eastern Europe—also an important barometer of change—had also increased considerably, so much so that Hungarian diplomats in Beijing were declaring to foreign correspondents in 1983 that 'after not a single delegation in twenty-one years except for annual discussions of trade and technical exchanges, we suddenly had three at once'.[12]

The importance of the change can also be estimated from the modifications introduced at the ideological level. The CCP even began to gear itself up to resume party-to-party relations with the five pro-Soviet loyalists. Though it had already abandoned its hitherto hard line of 'having no truck' with the 'revisionist' parties by opening up to the Yugoslav and some West European parties by 1979, the real sign of a more generalized change was Deng Xiaoping's remarks of 31 May 1980 to 'some senior officials' of the party. On this occasion, he declared that communist parties 'should be left to find their own paths by themselves and explore ways to solve their own problems'.[13] Opening the possibility for the party to move in a more pragmatic and more tolerant direction he said: 'The correctness of the domestic principles and line of a party on a given country should be judged by that party and by the people of that country. After all, it is comrades in a particular country who know its specific conditions'.[14]

It is important to note that these remarks, made in May 1980, were published in August 1983 only after the Politbureau had apparently taken the decision in March 1983 that, with the exception of the Soviet Union, Vietnam, Kampuchea and Laos, all other countries, where the communist parties were in power, would be considered 'socialists'[15], and only after Hu Yaobang had publicly declared that the broad framework of party-to-party relations should be based on the 'principles of independence, complete equality, mutual respect and non-interference in each other's internal affairs'.[16]

So the stage was set; the high-level internal formal decision was taken to inaugurate the process cautiously, and the conditions were laid down for renewed inter-party interaction, the most important of which was that they had to be bilateral.

Much has of course been made of the inter-party interaction, and its importance in the real building up or the re-establishment of relations between the socialist countries. Some even view it a *sine qua non*, since it is expected to give a new dimension and a new qualitative character to the whole relationship.

Determinants of change

Political Factors

Why this change? What were the factors that pushed the Chinese leadership to initiate a process of seeking out the five countries that had hitherto been berated for so many years for their domestic policies and for their subservience to Moscow?

The first and most obvious reason was the failure of the old policy. The new and relatively more pragmatic leadership had realized it. To vilify the five CMEA countries for more than twenty years had really served no purpose. If anything it had proved counterproductive, since all five of them had distanced themselves even more from Beijing.

Secondly, since a process of normalization had been finally initiated with Moscow in the eighties, there was no longer any reason to maintain a critical stance *vis-à-vis* the five CMEA countries when a process of normalization had been inaugurated with the 'big brother'. In fact, one may speculate whether opening up to Moscow in the very early eighties was not partly dictated by the fact that China wished to inaugurate a new policy towards Eastern Europe; which was not possible since none of the five were prepared to risk such an interaction as long as Moscow was still rebuffed by Beijing. They had no leverage in the matter—not for such an important issue as the Sino-Soviet dispute. A veteran East European diplomat made this clear. 'All depends', he is reported to have declared to a correspondent, 'in the end on Sino-Soviet relations; we are not making peace if Moscow is still at war'.[17]

A third reason was the Polish crisis in the autumn of 1980. Perhaps this was the most ostensible and decisive reason that tilted the Chinese balance in favour of greater interaction with the established parties and governments of the five countries. Although China was initially discomfited by the explosion of the crisis,[18] the Polish leadership[19] was none the less criticized and the establishment of Solidarity was welcomed as a 'tremendous victory of the Polish people to the way to socialism'.[20] But the brunt of the Chinese attack was on Moscow. The CCP opened a concerted campaign against any Soviet armed intervention. The Chinese prime minister, Zhao Zhiyang, made it clear that the 'people of the world will not accept a repetition of Czechoslovakia', and that 'the principles of non-interference in the affairs of Poland must be observed'.[21] The *People's Daily* was even more direct:

> The people throughout the world can see that the threat to Poland comes from nowhere but the Soviet military intervention. The Kremlin's intervention in Polish internal affairs can only result in exposing further the true nature of hegemonism . . . The Chinese people support the Polish people in their just struggle to strengthen their independence and sovereignty. The Polish people cannot be bullied.[22]

But this openly critical attitude towards the Polish party and the government did not last long. As the crisis escalated, with the opposition becoming more daring in its attacks and more exigent in its demands, the Chinese party became prudent. While continuing to warn the Russians against any armed intervention, the articles and declarations favouring the opposition ceased. First, the Chinese media showed signs of caution; a little later they came out in favour of the party and the government; and finally they explicitly criticized the Polish opposition.

This more cautious attitude first became visible during the ninth extraordinary congress of the Polish United Workers' Party in July 1981, when the Chinese press began to highlight 'the democratization of social life and reform of economic structure' in Poland.[23] And when martial law was declared on 13 December of the same year, the Chinese press became even more forthcoming regarding the 'comprehensive economic reforms' carried out by the Polish government.[24] In fact, according to reports in the European media, the Chinese leaders, before the imposition of martial law, even informed the Polish Embassy that the Polish government could count on them, should it decide to take any firm action against the opposition.[25] Finally, when the martial law was lifted, the Chinese government applauded the Polish action and declared:

> After some years of unrest created by Solidarity, Poland's political and economic stability has been restored. The Polish United Workers' Party is winning back supporters and the newly organized trade union has regained more than half of Poland's work-force. Meanwhile, the influence of Solidarity is diminishing. Last year when it called for strikes and demonstrations to commemorate the fifth anniversary of the August labour uprising, it received little public response. Despite Solidarity's appeal to boycott elections held in October 1985, nearly 70 per cent of the registered voters turned out at the polls. The calm general elections were an indication of the end of the political chaos created by Solidarity.[26]

In fact, according to some press reports, Deng Xiaoping, in a confidential report circulated to party cadres in the aftermath of the students' revolt in 1986, praised the Polish way of handling the crisis and of suppressing the opposition; in his view, China should do the same.[27] This change in the Chinese attitude can principally be explained by domestic considerations. The wave of discontent that had already emerged in China took a turn for the worse after the onset of the Polish crisis. Workers' discontent began to spread, and recurrent slow-downs, including strikes, affected a steel mill in Shanxi province and the electrical transformer plant in Kunming. Even worse was the demand of workers in a number of cities, including Shanghai and Wuhan, for the establishment of independent trade unions on the Polish model.[28]

The students' discontent continued even in the aftermath of the Polish crisis. Demonstrations took place in Sichuan and Shanxi provinces. And the Beijing dissident revue, *Tribune*, on 5 April 1981 sent its greetings to the Polish people. It declared:

> Dear Polish workers, you have by your struggles and strikes, obtained great victories and have become the focal point of the entire world. This victory has brought out the power of class unity and the new consciousness of this class. It has demonstrated that the new revisionist and privileged bureaucracy is only a paper tiger in the face of popular revolution. It has demonstrated that the democratic popular revolution is an inevitable trend of history. It has gone beyond national frontiers and acquired an international meaning.[29]

The Polish crisis was a major catalyst in making the leadership realize that China was no longer immune from spillover effects from any mass discontent in Eastern Europe. Now that Chinese society was in a state of flux, it had become more vulnerable in the face of any external discontent but more so from Eastern Europe simply because of the similarity of their socio-economic systems.

Therefore, following the Polish crisis, the CCP became much more prudent and jettisoned its earlier policies of welcoming discontent and of appealing to the East European population over the heads of the existing leadership. The whole Chinese policy since then is to work closely with the established governments and parties of the region, undoubtedly a dimensional change since the early sixties.

Economic factors

China was equally interested in building up economic relations with Eastern Europe. Now that the political barriers were tumbling down, economic interest in the area was becoming increasingly visible in Chinese declaratory and operational behaviour.

The advantages of forging ties with Communist countries are considerable. The first is monetary. China can have commercial exchanges without having to pay in hard currency—an advantage viewed as highly important, given that serious deficits are continually accruing with all the Western countries. The argument, often advanced, that barter trading deprives a country of exporting those goods to free currency areas does not really hold water since there is no guarantee that such goods will find the appropriate market in the free-currency areas.

A second advantage is technological. Since China is deeply interested in the transfer of technology, it was recognized that the socialist countries of Eastern Europe would be less reluctant to share their technology than the Western world, where both for reasons of strategy and competition a number of obstacles had been created for such transfers. East European technology of course is no match for the technology of the Western world. But in many sectors, what they have had to offer is more than adequate. The Czechs exported shoe-making equipment, spinning machines and technology for producing Tatra trucks, the Hungarians sent transmission cables, the Bulgarians exported technology for forklift trucks and the East Germans transferred technology for making refrigerator vans.[30] The importance of cooperation in the technological sector can be measured from the fact that science and technology meetings have been held jointly with the Soviet Union and East European countries. The first meeting was held in Bucharest in 1983 and the second in Moscow in May 1988.[31] The East European countries, furthermore, have taken on twenty-nine projects in China's 'spark plan', a programme started in 1985 to help China's rural economy with practical science and technology.[32] Periodic meetings between the State Science and Technology Commission (SSTC), of which State Councillor Son Jian is the chairman, and its counterparts in Eastern Europe have been institutionalized.

The third advantage is coordination for long-term cooperation. The socialist and planned economies of all these countries—notwithstanding all the changes—make it possible for them to conclude long-term agreements, thereby taking into

Table 10.2 China's total and net trade with East European CMEA countries 1980–8 (in US$ million)

		Bulgaria	Czech.	GDR	Hungary	Poland	Romania
1980	Total trade	67.57	201.27	263.61	114.61	232.12	1126.02
	Balance	−14.35	−32.96	42.29	−7.41	−24.56	−125.26
1981	Total trade	61.18	179.18	165.06	84.23	107.45	794.14
	Balance	−0.43	−24.82	−15.53	−17.35	−26.00	2.56
1982	Total trade	50.78	216.77	111.73	64.07	274.04	771.99
	Balance	0.53	57.92	31.17	4.28	−79.06	88.37
1983	Total trade	59.06	186.55	106.83	76.63	244.30	503.19
	Balance	11.40	−11.92	51.73	15.91	−65.28	19.53
1984	Total trade	42.09	283.26	147.75	112.68	226.81	710.86
	Balance	5.05	35.79	21.12	20.50	−19.65	174.91
1985	Total	39.54	421.33	208.03	192.22	461.18	757.02
	Balance	18.08	0.15	63.13	41.58	74.28	130.04
1986	Total trade	102.60	551.70	336.09	343.87	962.58	714.88
	Balance	27.65	112.67	9.24	−0.72	−41.78	−122.63
1987	Total trade	107.72	566.12	302.75	319.46	770.23	760.80
	Balance	−28.37	25.73	25.27	−107.62	79.94	−88.99
1988	Total trade	149.14	811.64	341.90	345.15	647.78	817.12
	Balance	60.37	54.60	63.52	29.16	23.65	−64.41

Source: Economic Commission for Europe

account the needs of each other and orientating their economies accordingly. China's State Science and Technology Commission, for example, has concluded long-term cooperation programmes spanning five years (1986–90) with Czechoslovakia, Bulgaria, Poland and East Germany. Long-term trade agreements have also been concluded with Poland, Czechoslovakia, Hungary and Bulgaria.[33]

The fourth advantage is the learning experience. Since most of the East European countries are undergoing a similar transition, China regards it as fundamental to study the changing East European models closely, to evaluate their significance, to avoid their mistakes and to find ways and means of applying the East European experience to their own model of growth. This trend, 'to learn from and make use of advanced foreign experience'[34], began in the late seventies and was considerably accelerated in the eighties.

All these factors have greatly contributed to the acceleration of Sino-East European ties in the trade sector. The agreed value of the five-year trade with the CMEA countries is US$12.5 billion thus averaging US$2.5 billion a year (see Table 10.2).

A peaceful international environment

By far the most important diplomatic innovation is the role China has assigned to Eastern Europe in generating a 'peaceful international environment'[35]. 'East

Europeans', declared Zhao Zhiyang in Bulgaria on 18 June 1987, 'are very concerned about the future of Europe and the world. They long for a stable international situation and strongly desire peace. They have contributed their share to the noble cause of maintaining peace and we appreciate their concern about world peace and their efforts to ease international tensions'.[36]

Clearly this is unprecedented, for never in the past did China consider the area to be in a position to do so. But with the arrival of Gorbachev in the Soviet Union, and with the beginning of a trend in the early eighties towards greater autonomy in the area, China increasingly considered that Eastern Europe might well be in a position to play a more autonomous and a more assertive role in European affairs.

After the mid-eighties, this became increasingly evident with China perceiving a three-level role for the Eastern bloc in the political sector. It was seen to have a role in the bilateral American-Soviet interaction on a wide spectrum of arms issues that concerned the Europeans. Second was its role in the confidence-building measures within the framework of the Helsinki accords. China now considers that East European countries—along with Western Europe—have a role to play in finding solutions to deadlocked situations. Third was its role in the Eastern Europe-Western Europe interaction. The development of economic relations, and the mutual political visits that were becoming increasingly frequent were viewed as a major development in the ongoing process of a real *entente* that would enlarge the contribution of all the Europeans to help 'check the super-powers' arms race and bring the world to peace and prosperity'.[37]

Western Europe

Western Europe in Chinese diplomatic strategy was more crucial than Eastern Europe. For one thing, it was far more powerful economically, far more stable politically and far more autonomous diplomatically. For another, through a process of unification it had acquired greater capability, to counter Soviet designs on Europe, to assist China in her modernization and to generate a peaceful international environment—all three major Chinese foreign policy goals in the eighties.

West European integration

The most important Chinese interest clearly was in West European integration. Much has indeed been said and written on the subject by Chinese political leaders, media commentators and scholars. Clearly, there was an element of continuity in Chinese foreign policy on the question, since as early as the seventies the Chinese leadership had given open support to West European unification.

But, three major significant modifications were introduced to this major foreign policy goal in the eighties. The first concerned Chinese motivations behind such a policy. The anti-Soviet dimension that originally generated Chinese interest in West European unification became less and less important.

If the Chinese media was still in the early and mid-eighties highlighting the vital importance of a unified Western Europe in the world's 'struggle against hegemonism, particularly against Soviet hegemonism',[38] it was assigning a more positive role to the area in the second half of the eighties—a role as an 'important promoter of the world's advance to a multipolar world'.[39] Although anti-Soviet dimension had not completely disappeared from Chinese thinking, it was no longer invoked with the same bluntness. Western Europe in the eighties was obviously viewed as something more important than as a mere counterweight to Soviet designs on Europe. The second major innovation is the establishment of an all-embracing supranational body. China clearly has become more sceptical of its real feasibility. The stress now is more on alliance, cooperation and coordination rather than on integration. One Chinese writer, belonging to the Foreign Ministry's Institute of International Studies, has even questioned its desirability. 'The road travelled by the Community over the past two decades,' in his view, 'shows that Western Europe's alliance can develop only by strengthening cooperation and coordination while adhering to the sovereignty of all member states and shunning supranational integration.'[40]

The third major innovation was the enhanced role China attributed to Western Europe in the acceleration of East–West relations and the consequent gain of wider autonomy by East European states from Moscow. Though China embraced this idea since the early seventies, it was only after the advent of Gorbachev that such an objective was viewed as something really feasible, and a West European role in its attainment was seen as crucial.[41]

Western Europe, thus, came to occupy a more basic position in overall Chinese diplomatic strategy than ever before; and in the new Chinese thinking Sino-West European cooperation also became more necessary and more important than previously. 'Because of its weak position and lack of strength, Western Europe', wrote one commentator, 'urgently needs allies outside the continent to help it to contend more effectively with the United States and the Soviet Union';[42] and it is for this reason and also 'to enhance its own safety and enlarge its manoeuvring room' that 'Western Europe pays considerable attention to China'.[43]

China therefore designed a three-pronged strategy *vis-à-vis* the region—a strategy of establishing a wide network of ties that would advance West European political integration, that would help China in her modernization and that would create the appropriate peaceful international environment.

One of the most important Chinese decisions of the eighties was systematically to establish a nexus of relations with the different political institutions of the European Community.

The European Commission

The focal point of Chinese interest is the European Commission with whom wide-ranging working relations have been established. In addition to an important diplomatic presence in Brussels and the Commission's representatives in Beijing, the most institutionalized component of this bilateral interaction is the annual meeting of the EC-China Joint Committee. This was stipulated originally in the 1978 bilateral trade agreement and repeated in the 1984 trade and

Table 10.3 High-level visits between China and the European Commission, 1980–8

Year	Name	Position
1981	Gu Mu	Vice-premier
1982	Etienne Davignon	Commissioner
1983	Wilhelm Haferkamp	Commissioner
1983	Chen Muhua	State councillor
1984	Zhao Ziyang	Prime minister
1985	Zhang Tuobin	State councillor
1985	Karl Heinz Narjes	Commissioner
1986	Wu Xuequian	Foreign minister
1986	Jacques Delors	President European Commission
1986	Lord Cockfield	Commissioner
1987	Willy De Clercq	Commissioner
1988	Li Tieying	Minister in charge of reforms
1988	Zhang Tuobin	State Councillor

cooperation agreement. So far five meetings have been held at the directorate level. Although the principal objective of these regular meetings is to assure a smooth operation of the trade and cooperation agreement, they have become a clearing house for the settlement of any economic and technical problem that may arise. In addition, they are increasingly used to decide on a host of procedural issues, including the organization of joint seminars, the establishment of training programmes and the arrangement of mutual visits. All in all, the Joint Committee has become a forum where practically everything non-political that concerns the two parties is discussed. The European Parliament has been encouraging the Commission and the Council to model the committee after the Sino-Japanese Joint Committee—in other words, to establish working parties that would help China find appropriate markets in the Community, and even to establish a regular secretariat to handle all liaison work and all business matters associated with the implementation of the Sino-EC agreement. For reasons that are not very clear both the Commission and the Council are apparently reluctant to enlarge the powers of the Joint Committee.

Another aspect of this ongoing Sino-European Commission interaction is the 1983 agreement 'to initiate high-level consultations in the interests of widening discussions to include all matters of mutual interest, thereby adding a new dimension to relations between China and the Community'.[44] Since most of the technical matters are aired and settled within the framework of the Joint Committee meetings, the new high-level periodic meetings were meant for exchanges concerning broader issues. This was confirmed by the first meeting that took place in Beijing in 1983 between Chen Muhua, the Chinese minister for trade and economic relations and Wilhelm Haferkamp, vice-president of the Commission where a wide range of international economic problems were discussed.

'High-level consultations' have regularly continued, the last one on 1 March 1988 between Commissioner Willy De Clercq, in charge of external relations and Zhang Tuobin, the Chinese minister for foreign economic relations and trade. (See Table 10.3).

The Commission also plays the role of an intermediary between China and the Community. It organizes meetings of European and Chinese experts to consult with each other. The three Sino–EC business weeks organized by the Commission in Brussels in 1981, 1985 and 1988 are examples of this activity. Other examples are the meetings held between Chinese officials and Community representatives such as in 1982 when China's newly reformed and decentralized foreign trade system was discussed.[45] Round-table discussions were also organized involving European and Chinese specialists in an exchange of technology on plastic processing in 1982,[46] on methodological problems pertaining to scientific and technical issues[47] and on issues related to investments in China in 1987.[48] There are also training programmes organized by the Commission for the Chinese. The wide-ranging programme covers such diverse sectors as statistics, language interpretation, energy, etc. The most important example is the training centre for economic cadres that was established in Beijing in March 1985. This programme, which offers an MBA course, began with thirty-five students and is expected to become a major centre in management training—an area in which there is a serious shortage of qualified personnel to run Chinese industries.[49]

European expertise has also been supplied for the modernization of some sectors of Chinese industry. In fact, the EEC has become a major supplier of technology to China—technology which is far more sophisticated than any coming from Japan or the United States. The Commission, for example, has used advanced know-how to evaluate the modernization needs of two pharmaceutical, five chemical and three food-processing factories and to assist the Chinese energy programme.[50]

The European Parliament

China also established relations with the European Parliament—another important catalyst for West European integration, describing it as a body that was 'helping to further integration'.[51] Initiatives taken included some important visits such as that of Emilio Colombo (president of the European Parliament) in January 1979, Deng Yingchao (Chairperson of the National People's Congress) in June 1980, Simone Weil (president of the European Parliament) in July 1981, a European parliamentary delegation in September 1981 and Denkert (president of the European Parliament) in June 1984.

If the consolidation of relations with the European Commission was considered to be vital from all points of view, relations with the European Parliament were thought to be important from a political angle. First of all, the European Parliament, in the aftermath of direct elections, has not only acquired greater weight and prestige, but has probably become the most integrating element within the European Community—at least this is how the Chinese see it. Second, the overall record of the European Parliament has been more political than any other community institution. On most of the major issues

pertaining to foreign affairs, there seems to be a large consensus of opinion
between the European Parliament and China. Yang Shangkun, vice-chairman of
the Standing Committee of the National People's Congress, underlined this point
in the speech he gave at a banquet for the European Parliament in September
1981. He declared: 'On the major international issues—Afghanistan, Kampuchea
and the Middle East—the European Parliament, anxious to safeguard world
peace, has condemned the aggressors and defended the cause of justice.
We appreciate and admire this stance'.[51] Third, the Parliament, having become
'fully aware of the political importance of China as a potential partner of
the European Community',[52] has consistently supported developing ties with
Beijing.[53] In fact it has consistently urged the Council and the Commission
towards greater Sino-EC *entente*. Recent examples of this are the resolutions that
were passed in 1984 and 1987. In its 1984 resolution it proposed, among other
things: (a) the establishment of a Community diplomatic mission in Beijing;
(b) the convening of a standing conference of Chinese and Community representatives 'as a forum for regular dialogue on subjects of mutual interest';[54]
(c) the formation of an additional Joint Committee of EC and Chinese experts 'to
tackle economic problems';[55] (d) the establishment of working parties and
pressure groups 'to encourage small- and medium-sized firms and state under-
takings to associate with· Chinese enterprises in fulfilling their commercial
objectives'.[56] In the 1987 resolution it called on the Commission and the Council
'to promote' China's accession to the GATT and 'to work in closer collaboration'
with China.[57]

The Council

The increasing politicalization of Sino-EC relations is also evident from China's
attitude towards the Council—the most powerful EC institution. Beijing took the
initiative of proposing regular consultations with that body within the framework
of its function of political cooperation. This was accepted by the Council in April
1983 and an agreement was reached to hold regular consultations every six
months between the political affairs director of the country having responsibility
over the Council deliberations and the Chinese ambassador to the country
concerned. The first of these meetings was held in Bonn in June 1983. In this
connection a recommendation was made by the European Parliament that such
consultations be upgraded to the ministerial level.[58]

The eighties thus witnessed a major transformation of Sino-EC relations.
A political dimension was added to what had primarily been economic relations
in the seventies.

Economic relations

Western Europe was also important economically because of the technological
benefits that China could reap. In contrast to the United States and Japan, the
West Europeans are apparently less hesitant in transferring sophisticated technology—a consideration that carries considerable weight in Chinese decision-

making in the economic sector. On numerous occasions, Chinese commentators have highlighted the importance of Western Europe 'as a main supplier of technology and capital equipment',[59] or 'as one of China's most important partners in science and technology'.[60] In fact, in the eighties, China concluded a number of very important economic agreements where state-of-the art technology was or is being transferred in the nuclear, automative, glass and tele-communications sectors.

There is considerable diversity in the West European involvement in the Chinese economy. A wide network of agreements have been concluded that range from the joint establishment of technical development projects in energy to agricultural sectors, to capital investment, loans, the establishment of training centres for personnel, the floating of bonds on the London and Frankfurt financial markets etc.

Politics is also a factor in economic relations. Western Europe clearly is much more acceptable as a partner than geographically contiguous and his-torically dominant Japan and the powerful United States whose superpower status does not dovetail with the Chinese objective of accelerating the multipolar trend within the international system. The political component in Chinese economic decision-making has become less important, but it is by no means totally absent. Often when economic decisions were taken in the eighties, the Chinese invariably took into account the possible political ramifications of an economic agreement.[61]

Economics relations have therefore considerably expanded with Western Europe in the eighties. Since the conclusion of the trade and economic agreement between China and the EC, the volume of trade has more than doubled to $11.6 billion in 1987, making the Community China's third major partner after Hong Kong–Macao and Japan. (See Table 10.4).

The pattern of cooperation has also become very broad. It has become indeed very wide-ranging, particularly in technical aid. The latest such example is $92.9 million assistance that the Community is providing to China's dairy industry between 1988 and 1992. It is the largest EC project since agricultural cooperation began in 1984, and is expected radically to overhaul and develop the whole industry. An interesting sidelight of this assistance is that all the income China will derive from the 50,000 tons of milk—donated by the EC—will be used to provide loans for further development of the dairy industry.[62]

The other important sector of cooperation is in manufacturing where a number of technically well-equipped and highly visible industries have been set up in China: consider the Shanghai–Bell Telephone Equipment Manufacturing company—a joint venture involving the Belgian company in $100 million capital investment. Consider also the $160 million Volkswagen project to manufacture 60,000 Santana cars and 100,000 engines a year by 1990. There is also a glass factory, run in cooperation with Britain's Pilkington Glass Company, which has the capacity to produce 50,000 standard crates of glass using a floating process.

Transfer of capital resources also increased. From EC countries, it was more in terms of loans, most of which were government loans. Of the $5.8 billion that China received in 1987 as government loans, $1.22 billion emanated from EC

Table 10.4 China's trade with the EC 1976–85 (US$ million)

		1976	1977	1978	1979	1980	1981	1982	1983	1984	1985
EC 10	**E**	**1274.6**	**792.4**	**1490.5**	**2103.1**	**1734.0**	**1894.4**	**2044.9**	**2755.4**	**3508.3**	**6533.9**
	I	**1346.7**	**859.0**	**929.0**	**1318.2**	**1883.6**	**2283.7**	**2334.2**	**2665.1**	**3210.6**	**3801.9**
	B	**−72.1**	**−66.7**	**+561.9**	**+784.9**	**−149.6**	**−389.4**	**−289.3**	**+90.3**	**+297.7**	**+2732.0**
Of which:											
West Germany	E	638.4	437.5	778.4	1089.0	823.3	909.5	870.5	1211.8	1329.3	2888.9
	I	275.6	246.9	277.5	375.4	562.0	663.5	681.4	828.5	1038.6	1095.5
	B	+362.8	+190.6	+500.9	+713.6	+261.3	+246.0	+189.1	+383.3	+290.7	+1793.4
France	E	354.4	83.5	155.2	247.3	218.7	246.0	351.8	496.7	396.3	1027.8
	I	196.9	163.5	165.3	221.3	307.7	414.9	402.4	432.0	490.6	579.7
	B	+157.5	−79.8	−10.2	−26.0	−89.0	−168.9	−50.6	+64.8	−94.3	+448.1
Italy	E	127.0	68.8	147.7	203.4	185.2	291.1	214.2	298.7	572.2	1042.1
	I	157.8	141.3	156.8	287.5	315.2	360.0	435.3	466.9	553.1	774.0
	B	−30.8	−72.5	−9.0	−84.1	−129.9	−68.4	−221.1	−168.2	+19.1	+268.1
Netherlands	E	40.1	45.5	103.4	116.5	106.5	86.0	67.9	148.9	219.6	326.2
	I	90.4	82.7	98.5	114.1	197.1	220.8	208.5	212.5	264.1	329.0
	B	−50.3	−37.2	+4.9	+2.4	−90.5	−134.8	−140.6	−63.6	−44.5	−2.8
Belgium-Luxemburg	E	40.7	41.5	159.5	95.2	75.1	104.0	213.1	250.5	317.3	364.7
	I	53.0	38.8	38.3	61.7	143.1	166.7	147.9	147.3	160.5	209.5
	B	−12.3	+2.7	+121.2	+33.5	−68.0	−62.7	+65.1	+103.2	+156.9	+155.2
United Kingdom	E	62.9	95.3	137.2	329.4	282.5	215.8	182.7	272.0	536.8	671.8
	I	538.1	155.6	163.6	214.8	287.5	376.6	374.5	435.8	536.3	623.4
	B	−475.1	−60.3	−26.4	+114.6	−5.0	−160.8	−191.8	−163.8	+0.6	+48.4
Ireland	E	0	0.7	1.0	2.8	1.8	1.3	4.5	4.9	9.2	17.2
	I	4.6	3.6	4.1	5.9	8.0	9.1	8.1	10.4	15.6	15.5
	B	−4.6	−2.9	−3.1	−3.1	−6.2	−7.8	−3.6	−5.5	−6.4	+1.7
Denmark	E	9.5	14.4	6.3	16.9	31.6	31.5	137.6	66.5	94.1	133.8
	I	26.9	24.7	23.3	30.4	45.1	53.9	54.6	101.6	123.3	146.3
	B	−17.4	−10.3	−17.0	−13.5	−13.5	−22.4	+83.1	−35.1	−29.2	−12.5
Greece	E	1.5	5.1	1.8	2.5	9.1	9.0	2.4	5.2	33.4	61.2
	I	3.5	2.1	1.6	6.9	17.8	18.5	21.2	30.2	28.5	28.9
	B	−2.0	+3.0	+0.2	−4.4	−8.7	−9.5	−18.8	−25.0	−4.9	+32.3

Note: E = Exports of EC etc. to China. I = Imports of EC etc. from China. B = Balance of trade.
Sources: EC, 1976–84: Commission (1984b), Table 7; EC, 1985: Computer printout provided by Eurostat office, Brussels (March 1985).

countries.[63] Furthermore of the nineteen loans offered to China in 1988, nine were given by EC countries and four by other European countries.

Direct foreign investments, on the other hand, have been trailing behind—and this despite the fact that China made considerable efforts to pass legislation to attract direct investment. The EC has been particularly remiss in this sector—far behind Japan and the United States; of the total figure of $2.58 billion invested in China in 1987, only $80 million came from the EC.

Deceleration of relations

Sino-EC economic interaction is slowly undergoing some change. Though it is continuing to expand, some degree of deceleration is increasingly becoming evident, particularly when one compares trade performance of other developed countries. In terms of absolute figures, the total volume of trade between China and the EC is less than between China and Japan and between China and the Hong Kong-Macao Region. Even the Community's actual share of total Chinese trade has settled down to around 10–11 per cent (See Table 10.5.). This is a poor performance in that the Community's share of total world trade approaches 20 per cent (excluding trade between member-states) considerably more than the United States (15 per cent) and Japan (8 per cent), and yet both these nations have a larger share of Chinese trade than the Community. In addition, the Community's share has declined since the late seventies when it averaged 15–16 per cent.

Trade deceleration is also applicable to non-EC West European countries. In this case too, the rate of expansion has been slower than with Japan and the United States. This mid-eighties' development has been attributed to a wide range of temporary factors: to China's readjustment policies, to the European recession and to the general confusion generated by China's new decentralization policies, as a result of which European businessmen do not know 'whether they should go to the provinces or to the centre, and which organization they should address in order to obtain the quickest and most effective results'.[64]

The importance of these elements is undeniable; all of them have contributed in various ways to the relative slow growth of Sino-EC trade-relations. However, it is questionable whether there are not other more fundamental factors that have contributed to this situation. Could it not be argued that the factors listed above are only temporary in nature and that Sino-EC trade-relations have really reached a plateau with no real prospects of any dramatic improvement?

Five factors appear to support this hypothesis. First of all, it is accepted that the EC countries are generally less competitive than Japan and the United States on a wide range of items. The Chinese leadership has often emphasized this consideration, though it has been rather reticent about giving it much publicity.[65] One recent example of Chinese concern about this was an article by Li Shude (director of the third department for regional affairs, Ministry of Foreign Economic Relations and Trade) in which he expressed the hope that European 'products, technology and equipment will be more competitive'.[66]

Since China's economic decisions are now less influenced by political considerations than previously, it is less likely that China will seek to expand trade in

Table 10.5 The European Community's* share of total Chinese trade 1975–84

	Percentage share of Chinese exports (EC imports)	Percentage share of Chinese imports (EC exports)	Percentage share of total Chinese trade
1975	11.4	19.1	15.5
1976	21.9	21.7	21.8
1977	12.9	12.5	12.7
1978	12.1	17.4	14.9
1979	13.2	18.4	16.0
1980	14.4	12.3	13.3
1981	11.6	9.6	10.6
1982	10.2	10.4	10.3
1983	10.7	11.5	11.1
1984	10.1	10.4	10.2

Source: European Commission, *European Information, External Relations.*

* The data relates to a European Community of Ten.

directions where economic considerations remain less favourable. The lack of any competitive edge in most of the industrial and agriculture sectors in the EC can be attributed to a number of factors. First of all, the compulsory overhead social costs are considerable. Western Europe is ahead of the United States and Japan in this respect. Paradoxically, what was viewed as a considerable social achievement a few decades ago is now considered a great burden for an economy that wishes to remain competitive.

Furthermore, since 1974 Western Europe has opted for the present as against the future. Although it accelerated the process of increasing the purchasing power of its population, it ignored a very important rule for an effective market economy—the rule of pumping back capital in the growth sector. Finally West European companies are still not flexible enough to adapt to a constantly changing economic environment, the most important characteristics of which are mobility, competition, efficiency and structural adaptability. The Americans and the Japanese realized all this long ago.

In addition, there is yet another handicap. There is apparently a growing tendency among West European companies to make technological arrangements with multinationals based outside Europe rather than with their own European counterparts. Summing up this generally rather pessimistic West European situation, a French industrialist declared:

> Certainly economic forecasts are dangerous. With enough patience and time, the Cassandra cries will one day be proved true. But in the meantime, I am sure of one thing. If the American and Japanese growth rates continue to develop at the rate of more than 4 per cent during the next two to four years, and Europe continues to stagnate at between 0 and 2 per cent, there will be no European industries left, except for some scattered vestiges of large historical monuments and beaches for American and Japanese tourists.[67]

Though this is perhaps a very harsh assessment of the current West European situation, it can hardly be challenged, considering the relative economic stagnation of the area.

Secondly, there is a growing protectionist trend in the Community which will probably become even more serious when the single Community market comes into effect after the end of 1992. Despite the formal commitment to free trade, there is increasing evidence of even more rigid protectionism than before.

Consider the textile agreement concluded in March 1984 between China and the EC.[68] Though there was 10 per cent increase in one specific category, the agreement on the whole is more restrictive than the 1979 textile agreement in that five important items have now been added to the list on which import restrictions have been imposed; and in that thirty-four additional categories of restrictions were imposed in certain regions of the Community. The new anti-fraud clause in the protocol imposed even greater limitations regarding procedures for the control of products. It is more than likely now that Spain and Portugal have become members of the Community that even greater restrictions will have to be imposed on textile imports since both of these countries are major textile producers, generating even greater difficulties for the ailing textile industry of some of the original members of the Community. The third textile agreement, concluded on 9 December 1988, is no better in this respect. If anything, it is still more restrictive. Though it has increased the Chinese quota, new restrictions, on the other hand, have been imposed on a wide sector of textile items that did not exist in the earlier agreement. Besides, quotas have been imposed on a number of textile products that were not restricted before.[69] Consider also the 1984 cooperation agreement to replace the 1978 agreement. While the former is much broader than the latter, in that the Community has been allocated new powers to accelerate cooperation, the restrictive clauses are identical. Attempts to make them more liberal were unsuccessful. It is significant, however, that there is one provision in the cooperation agreement which—at least in its terminology—is more restrictive than the preceding trade agreement. Whereas under article 4 of the 1978 agreement both the parties agreed that they 'will accord' (EC) or 'will give' (China) favourable consideration on the liberalization of imports, the corresponding article in the new agreement (article 5) differs slightly in that China will increase imports and the EC will 'strive' to increase imports.[70]

A series of restrictive measures including anti-dumping have also been taken against some of the Chinese products. While anti-dumping measures were still in operation in some cases (lithium carbonate and hydroxide, syrup of pears), or had been stopped after assurance from the Chinese that they would respect prices (alarm clocks, saccharin), there were two cases in which anti-dumping duties were definitely imposed—on oxalic acid and magnesite.[71] A more recent example was the imposition of duty on potassium permanganate.[72]

Thirdly, the disappointing performance of Sino-EC economic relations can also be attributed to the embargo by COCOM. Though restrictions are now less strict on China than on the Soviet Union, none the less there are still certain items that cannot be sold to China, or for which permission is required.[73]

Fourthly, the organizational framework of the EC—as it is constituted—creates serious problems regarding prompt decisions. Invariably, the decision-making process on economic issues gets bogged down because the wishes of each of the twelve highly individualistic member-states have to be taken into account and incorporated in the final decision before any steps can be taken. The situation is rendered even more complex by the fact that the member-states formulate their own national policies and conclude their own bilateral cooperation agreements. With such an inherently disadvantageous situation it becomes difficult for the Community to compete effectively with its main competitors—Japan and United States.

Fifthly, the reappearance of the Soviet Union as China's important economic partner could also prove problematic for Sino-EC economic relations. Trade between the two countries is continuing to grow and the present exchanges are considered by both to fall 'far short of the trade potential'.[74]

So Sino-EC economic deceleration in the eighties was due to both transitory and basic factors. Though the removal of the transient factors would certainly improve the prospects for economic relations between the two partners, real acceleration may prove problematic until some of the basic reasons have been effectively tackled.

Peaceful international environment

Western Europe is also perceived as a major element in generating a peaceful international environment both as an area and as an actor. As a geographical entity it is important because Chinese thinking in the eighties underlined the argument that a global conflict could only originate from the region where the superpowers have been in a state of armed confrontation, and where a blow up between them could irreversibly escalate into a global confrontation. Interestingly, Chinese thinking in the eighties slowly moved away from the view that an equilibrium in armed confrontation enhances the chances of peace, and is evolving towards the opposite view that it really enhances the dangers of war.

Western Europe is also considered as an actor in the generation of a peaceful international environment at the governmental and the non-governmental levels. With their ongoing process of integration, the Chinese see the West European states as 'trying to promote both the American–Soviet and East–West talks on disarmament to curb the superpowers' arms race'.[75]

The West European population is also viewed as an important element for the creation of a peaceful international environment. A plethora of articles and commentaries appeared in the Chinese press and journals in the eighties which highlighted the development of 'a widespread popular movement' that can 'no longer be ignored'.[76] and which has come to constitute a major roadblock to any global conflict. 'Since the beginning of this decade', declared another observer, 'the anti-nuclear peace movement has been gaining momentum in the developed capitalist countries'.[77]

It is important to note that all this is really new in Chinese thinking: in the past—particularly in the seventies—when the whole basis of Chinese foreign policy rested on anti-Sovietism, all such movements were suspect and often characterized as instruments of Soviet foreign policy.

The new focal point—West Germany

Within the broad framework established for Western Europe, the Federal Republic of Germany has emerged as the focal point of Chinese diplomacy. If in the fifties it was Great Britain, in the sixties it was France and in the seventies once again Britain that was placed in such a position, in the eighties Chinese interest shifted to West Germany.

This does not of course mean that both Britain and France were placed 'on the backburner' in Chinese diplomacy, that both of them had no role to play and no aid to give. It simply means that in their evaluation of the rapidly changing West European situation, the Chinese concluded that it was in their interest to make an extra effort to cultivate Bonn—perhaps a little more than London and Paris.

But why West Germany? What are the factors that influenced the Chinese decision? And why do they consider West Germany as 'one of the more powerful forces of this divided continent, both in economic and political terms'?[78] Clearly West Germany was perceived as a crucial country for the attainment of the three foreign policy goals that China had designed for the eighties.

First of all, there is security, a sector that has both military and political aspects. On the military front China was indeed struck by the important fact that the Federal Republic had gradually and unobtrusively built the best West European conventional army, comprising forces of 495,000, equipped with some of the most sophisticated weapons. With the increasing recognition of the importance of conventional weapons and conventional warfare in NATO's 'flexible response' strategy,[79] West Germany's role as a front-line state, situated in the heart of Europe, could only be seen as continuing to increase. A conventional army of this size would of course have been no match for the Russians, but then none of the armies of Western Europe, alone or together, would have been able to contain a massive Soviet attack without American support. What the new Bundeswehr could do was to make a purely conventional attack increasingly costly for the Soviet Union. The precise West German mission within overall NATO strategy has been to prolong the fighting long enough to permit both sides to decide whether they were prepared to commit themselves to the terrible uncertainties of a nuclear war.

In this connection, it is useful to mention that in a conversation Helmut Schmidt had with Hua Guofeng during the latter's visit to Bonn in 1979, he stated that in his view, 'in a war, the German forces will be more combative'. For this reason China 'would like to have a long-term development of our relations with the Federal Republic', for the latter, even if strong, 'will never attack China'.[80]

West Germany is also a major element in the political aspects of West European security. In the rapidly changing European picture—brought about by the advent of Gorbachev—where the military dimension is becoming less important, the capacity of West Europeans to unite is, in the final analysis, their strongest defence. West Germany, with its economic clout, is perceived as a key

Table 10.6 Trade between China and West
Germany 1980–7 (in US$ million)

1980	1,773
1981	2,007
1982	1,884
1983	2,356
1984	2,696
1985	4,492
1986	4,416
1987	4,228

Source: Statistisches Bundesamt, Wiesbaden

element. Not only has Bonn continued to insist that the integration of West European nations must remain an important objective, but that the Common Market must first of all set budget priorities for those projects that really enhance European unity.[81]

The role of West Germany is confirmed by this French commentator:

Without the FRG, Western Europe becomes an empty shell. Without the FRG West European frontiers become obscure and uncertain. Without the FRG 'West European integration' are empty words. Without the FRG, West European defences become one more myth created by dying civilizations that are fearful of their fate.[82]

Modernization

West Germany also became a key country in China's economic modernization. As a highly industrialized nation possessing sophisticated technology, West Germany is generally perceived by the Chinese as a country that would be in a position to make a crucial contribution to China's modernization. In fact it has been doing just that as China's biggest European trade partner, and fourth in world-wide trade after Japan, Hong Kong and the United States, (see Table 10.6). More than 300 agreements were concluded with included *inter alia* licensing, co-production and joint-venture agreements.[83] Many are quite prestigious, involving considerable capital investment, and including high-tech projects with major implications for the Chinese economy in general.

Consider the $160 million Volkswagen–Shanghai tractor automobile joint-venture agreement, concluded in 1984, to produce Santana automobiles and engines in Shanghai. The corporation's total fixed assets had reached $270 million by the beginning of 1988, and in the month of May of the same year an agreement was concluded with the Chinese authorities to issue bonds worth 19.5 million yuans to individuals and enterprises in China in order to acquire updated technology to produce 60,000 cars and 100,000 engines by 1990.[84] The importance of the project can be gauged from the fact that the Sino-German factory has already become the leading car producer in China, that 80 per cent of the components and spare parts used by the company will be produced in China by 1994[85] and that cars produced in this factory are meant for the domestic market. Considering that the Chinese government decided to make car manufacture one of the main sectors of the economy[86] and, at the same time, to limit car production to the six existing makers,[87] the impact of such a leading enterprise on the Chinese economy can only be enormous.

To take another example — there is the billion dollar deal concluded in August 1987 between Messerschmitt-Bolkow-Blohn and the China Aero-technology Import-export Corporation for the joint development of a new plane that will carry 60–85 passengers mainly on regional flights. The MBB officials have estimated the international market for the planes to be about 900 in the 1990s, without counting the Chinese market.[88] The commercial plane, powered by two fuel-efficient prop fan engines at the rear, is expected to become operational in 1995.

Another interesting example worth mentioning of Sino-West German cooperation is container ships — undoubtedly a crucial sector for trade — where through a network of contracts, credits and subsidies between West German companies, China and the Federal government a large container ship industry is being set up in China. A container-ship factory has been established in Shanghai by a West German company, where West German orders are placed; at the same time the Chinese have placed an order for fifteen large container ships with West German shipyards which are heavily subsidized by the West German government.[89] This mutual interaction, largest of the kind in this sector, has permitted China to acquire up-to-date technology, and equally a German-built fleet of container ships.[90]

There are numerous other agreements, orders, joint ventures etc. through which the Federal Republic is heavily involved in China, including a $160 million Luftansa/CAAC agreement (1987) to establish an aircraft maintenance centre, a $328 million agreement (1988) to construct a 100MW high-temperature nuclear reactor and the $359 million Mannesmann Demag AG/CNTIC contract to establish a TPY steel pipeline plant (See Table 10.7).

There has also been a considerable increase in the Chinese presence in West Germany. An important China Trade Centre was established in February 1985 in Hamburg. This was 'China's first comprehensive trading enterprise in Western Europe'.[91] Another one was set up in Frankfurt (1987) 'to promote economic, trade and technical exchanges with West Germany and other West European countries'.[92] In addition to the government sponsored commercial presence in FRG, many Chinese companies have set up their own autonomous offices. Seventeen companies, for example, have offices in Frankfurt and more than twenty of them are established in the state of Nordrhein Westfalen. [93]

Although China has been generally disappointed by the limited flow of modern technology from the developed countries, the Federal Republic, comparatively speaking, has been singled out as 'China's number one technology supplier'.[94] Up to the summer of 1987 over 200 contracts, for example, were approved to

Table 10.7 Sino–FRG agreements 1980–8 involving $100 million or more

Company/institution	Product/plant/technology	Value	Date	Type
NA/JIANGXI	Joint company to offer consultations, technical guidance, low-interest loans, for navigation and highway construction in Jiangxi	$194 million	September 84	Joint venture
Deutsche Lufthansa AG & other German companies/Beijing Municipal Govt.	Beijing Lufthansa Centre, multipurpose business complex including 600-room hotel	$215.3 million	January 87	Joint venture
Messerschmidt-Bolkow-Blohm FRG/CATIC	First stage feasibility study for joint venture to produce MCP-75 passenger aircraft	$130 million	August 87	Joint venture
	Production stage	$870 million	August 87	
Mercedes Benz MORINCO, No. 1 & No. 2. Machinery Plant, Baoton, Nei Monggol	Supply product information and manufacturing technology to produce 14 types of trucks	$180 million	May 88	Contract
Lufthansa Airlines/CAAC	Aircraft maintenance centre	$160 million	October 87	Joint venture
Deutsche Babcock Mannesmann & others/Ministry of nuclear industry	Joint construction of 100MW high-temperature nuclear reactor	$328 million	March 88	Consortium
FRG, HK & Australia/Beihai, Guangxi	Establish steel mill	$700 million	June 88	Joint venture
Mannesmann Demag AG/CNTIC & Tianjin	Build 500,000 TPV steel-pipe plant	$359 million	June 86	Contract
Siemens AG & AEG Telefunken AG	Electronic equipment for steel rolling plant	$120 million	February 85	Contract
Volkswagenwerk AG/Shanghai Tractor-Automobile Co.	Produce Santana cars	$160 million	October 84	Joint venture

introduce technological innovations including a hot-rolling strip steel mill for the second construction phase of the Shanghai Baoshan Iron and Steel complex and a high-speed wire-rolling mill for the Manshan Iron and Steel complex. Statistics also show that about half of China's imported technology has come from West Germany.[95]

Peaceful international environment

When the Chinese thought about striving to create a peaceful international environment in Europe, West Germany was considered to play a crucial role. Situated in the heart of Europe, and fearful of becoming a battleground for East–West conflict, West Germany—more than any other West European country— has become a major proponent of nuclear disarmament and the strongest supporter of *détente* with the Soviet Union. The Chinese, who rallied to these objectives in the eighties, saw a much greater foreign-policy convergence with Bonn than with anyone else in Western Europe. 'The new situation of *détente* between the East and West,' wrote a Chinese political commentator, 'has made West Germany readjust its policy in the light of its national interest. It talks of the elimination of the threat of war, the assurance of peace and security, and the realization of the reunification of the two Germanys'.[96]

Owing to its powerful economic position West Germany was also perceived as a key element in bringing about a real disengagement of Eastern Europe from the Soviet Union,[97] without really upsetting the latter. Particular stress was laid on what West Germany managed to do since *Ostpolitik*, inaugurated in the seventies, to push East Germany to make 'concessions on emigration and the human rights problem, in order to accentuate national identity and create conditions for reunification in future'.[98]

West Germany has also become a major centre of the peace movement—once again more than any other country of Western Europe. The Chinese completely abandoned their previous critical position of these movements, which were suspected of pro-Sovietism in the seventies, and came to view them as important and acceptable pressure groups for maintaining the peace momentum.

Thus in its three major foreign policy goals China has focused a great deal of attention in seeking out West German contacts at different levels and in different sectors. But what is perhaps important in Sino-West German relations is the inter-party interaction. Though the CCP had expressed willingness to interact with most West European democratic and left-wing parties, the Federal Republic was once again a significant focal point of Chinese political initiatives with particular attention given to developing relations with the Social Democratic Party (SPD).

Interest in the SPD was the result of the complete reversal in China's perception of the international situation, a turnabout that jettisoned the anti-Sovietism of the preceding period, and that viewed peace, complete disarmament, and East–West *détente* as new normative goals in foreign policy. The measure of the change can be discerned from the fact that during the preceding two decades the SPD was systematically berated for its more outgoing policies towards the Soviet Union and Eastern Europe.

Within the new broad framework there were three factors that specifically moved the Chinese to pay more attention to the SPD than they had ever done before—precisely the factors that had turned them against it in the past. One is the fact that it is an important left-wing political force in West German politics, has been in the forefront for thirteen years, has close links with the trade unions, and has acquired substantial influence among the social democrats at the European level. Some Chinese writers have shown great interest in the SPD's capacity rapidly to adapt itself to changing domestic socio-economic conditions, particularly the remarkable manner in which it abandoned its Marxist tendencies at its special congress in Godesberg in November 1959.[99] It is that capacity to change that made it possible for the party to remain a political force in the sixties. A Chinese commentator, writing in 1988, thought that the SPD would have to once again 'make readjustments both in theory and practical policies so as to adapt itself to the changing situation and come back to power again'.[100] While analysing the SPD role in German politics, Chinese writers have in effect established a link between change and capacity to survive in politics.[101]

The second factor is its open, active and flexible policies towards Eastern Europe, and the support it extended to the further acceleration of the multipolar trend in the international system, towards the eventual elimination of all nuclear weapons and to an accelerated Third World development.[102] All of these goals seemed to converge with the new Chinese thinking; and in this connection, it is important to note that during their visits to China in September 1982 and May 1984 respectively, Egor Bahr and Willy Brandt, the two chief architects of such policies, were lauded for having designed them.

The third factor for the CCP, which was rapidly becoming pragmatic in the economic sector and which still needs a new model, was the SPD's evolution and its espousal of policies that combine social justice with a market-orientated economy—an obvious source of attraction for China.

The CCP, therefore, took some initiatives to establish institutionalized relations with the SPD. After some initial reluctance from the West German party, an agreement was finally reached, during Brandt's China visit in May 1984, for the two parties to organize regular and high-level consultations.[103] The first such meeting took place in November 1985 when a CCP delegation, led by Politburo member Hu Qili visited West Germany at the invitation of the SPD. After five days of talk Hu declared that the two parties had 'common interests and many common or similar views on major international issues'.[104]

Conclusion

The eighties witnessed a major transformation in China's foreign policy. Practically everything changed: the Chinese perception, the Chinese strategy, the Chinese diplomatic style and the Chinese leadership.

Clearly the preponderant innovation related to the Soviet Union. China abandoned her anti-Sovietism—a stance that had underpinned her foreign policy for two decades. The consequences of what was the most importance change in the eighties were indeed considerable: every aspect of international affairs in which China was closely involved underwent a sea change. In many ways it was a *volte-face*, especially regarding Europe. West European integration, for example, was still important, but no longer urgent. East European disengagement was desirable but was no longer vital. East–West *détente*, nuclear disarmament and peace—hitherto all suspect and all frowned upon—were actively encouraged.

Within this new broad framework that was slowly emerging, the Federal Republic of Germany became a focal point of Chinese diplomacy in Europe. In the changing Chinese perception, West Germany had acquired the necessary clout efficaciously to meet Chinese needs in the economic sector, to play a more important role than other Europeans in satisfying China's security concerns and to generate the appropriate peaceful international environment so essential for accelerated economic development. Besides, in the ongoing 'multipolar' trend that was becoming increasingly visible, West Germany geographically placed as it is, economically powerful as it had become, and politically more confident as it was becoming, its future role in the whole of Europe could only be crucial especially with the inauguration of the new process of its unification with East Germany.

General conclusions

An examination of forty years of China's foreign relations have shown that Europe, through the years, has steadily acquired an important position in Chinese diplomatic strategy. This distant neighbour, at whose hands China had suffered innumerable humiliations for so many decades, finally re-emerged as an area in which the Chinese evinced considerable interest.

Although a number of factors contributed to this development, the principal one was that Europe presented a new picture of a continent that had acquired the capacity to establish some degree of equilibrium within the international system —an equilibrium that Beijing had begun to consider as vital in an asymmetrical world excessively dominated by the two superpowers.

The Chinese leadership had indeed—during these forty years—conjured up visions of a Sino-European partnership to achieve this equilibrium. Notwithstanding all the Chinese rhetoric in favour of alliance with the Third World, and in favour of close ties with Japan, Europe was none the less perceived as the most important and the most acceptable counterforce against 'superpower hegemony' —most important because of its growing economico-political power and most acceptable because of the absence of any actual or potential conflict with China.

If one were to take the four normatives (security, modernization, reunification and revolutions) that have heavily influenced China's foreign-policy behaviour during these forty years, it is difficult to escape the conclusion that Europe did and still does occupy a very crucial position for the successful achievement of most of them.

Consider China's security concerns. They have always been there, influencing its diplomatic initiatives, determining its reaction to the actions of others and even innovating its way of looking at the outside world. In fact, most of China's diplomatic reversals have been heavily guided by this objective. It caused China to ally itself with the Soviet Union just after the revolution, then prompted China to turn to the non-Communist world in order to forge a united international anti-Soviet front and finally led to the adoption of a non-aligned posture *vis-à-vis* the two superpowers—all for the sake of seeking maximum security.

What was Europe's importance in the enhancement of Chinese security? How did the Chinese perceive it? And what was the European response? First of all at no point in China's post-revolutionary history did the Chinese leadership ever consider that a security threat emanated or could emanate from Europe; for China knew that none of the European nations, singly or together, had the inclination or the capacity to threaten its security. Neither the British in Hong Kong, nor the Portuguese in Macao, nor even the French—during the early fifties—really ever worried the Chinese. They were of course against the European presence in the area, not for security reasons but because of their firm opposition to imperialism.

China, in fact, had conjured up visions of Sino-European partnership in the security sector. With the increasing resurgence of Western Europe as an

188

autonomous entity and with the increasing disengagement of some East European countries from the Soviet Union, China began to perceive Europe as a potential partner on Moscow's western flank.

Since the Chinese have a sense of history, and do tend to think in terms of decades and even centuries, it did not really matter that neither Eastern nor Western Europe were as yet ready or even capable of assuming such a role; what was vital for them was that the process of resurgence had begun and that the direction towards which Europe was heading was becoming clearer.

For China, the security dimension is the key element so far as the Soviet Union is concerned. Whatever may be the nature or the state of Sino-Soviet relations at any given point in time, the geopolitical reality of being contiguous to a powerful neighbour will always push China to seek counterbalancing nations or areas. And what could be a better counterbalance than Europe—a Europe which also had perpetual reservations regarding Russia in the past and Soviet Russia since 1917?

So the main thrust of Chinese diplomacy, since the Sino-Soviet dispute, has been to goad Western Europe to become more independent and more united, to encourage Eastern Europe to disengage and to push both of them to undo the partition of Europe.

This goal is probably one of the permanent fixtures of Chinese diplomacy to which it will always return no matter what her relations might be with the Soviet Union.

What about the Europeans? Do they think in a similar manner? As previously stated Europe has always had fears, first about Russia and then about the Soviet Union. In the past, the balance-of-power game used to be played out among the European powers themselves—including of course Tsarist Russia—since all of them felt the need to block anyone who became too powerful. But when Europe began to decline after World War I, and when Russia had extricated herself from the balance-of-power games after the Bolshevik revolution, Europe had to go beyond the continent and across the Atlantic to seek out the United States as a counterbalance to Soviet Russia. But now that Europe is becoming more powerful, more autonomous, and less partitioned, it may well become interested in also incorporating an increasingly powerful China in the balance-of-power game.

Europe's role in China's modernization has also been significant. Though China has forged economic ties with other countries and other areas, Europe occupies a special position in the Chinese strategy of building up her economy for three reasons.

The first is political. Europe is politically more acceptable than other developed countries. Though economic factors have clearly become more weighty in the Chinese decisional process, political considerations are by no means negligible. The fact that Japan has a colonial past, of which China was the principal victim, and that Japan has already made major inroads into the Chinese economy has often caused the Chinese leadership to forsake many sound and tempting Japanese economic proposals in order to avoid a greater Japanese presence. The economic power that Japan represents and the contiguous economic position it occupies should make Japan an even more important economic partner. But China has apparently concluded that a policy of diversification of economic relations was a vital and necessary objective in order to avoid undue economic pressures from any one country—most of all from Japan. The United States' superpower status plus a number of political discords have probably constrained China from going too far in her economic interactions with the United States.

The second reason is technological. The Europeans have focused their attention on the manufacturing sector, with a far greater willingness to transfer sophisticated technology than the other developed countries.

The third—and more recent—reason for a greater interest in Europe is ideological. Having abandoned the economic system it believed in for more than thirty years, China is in search of a new model—a model that would respond more effectively to its needs, and that would not, at the same time, symbolize a total denial of the past. In this connection too, Europe—both Eastern and Western—would be relevant to the new Chinese needs: Eastern Europe, because it finds itself in the same position as China in so far as some of the countries are carrying out new experiments that represent a mixed economic and a more pluralistic political system; and Western Europe, because many socialist parties through the years have successfully worked out solutions to major social issues within the framework of political and economic pluralism. Though China continues to insist that it will find its own solutions, what Europe has to offer in this connection can hardly be ignored.

Europe is equally important for the successful achievement of the third foreign-policy goal—the goal of integrating outlying areas of Taiwan, Hong Kong and Macao. There is, first of all, neither any dispute nor any differences regarding the integration of these areas to the mainland. Unlike the United States, none of the European countries have really contested China's right to integrate Taiwan. In fact the two European powers (Britain and Portugal) that have a presence in Hong Kong and Macao have successfully concluded accords with China under which the two areas would be integrated with the mainland within a certain time frame. In many ways, the long negotiations with Great Britain and Portugal helped China to establish 'the one country—two systems' concept by clearly indicating in the agreements the levels of autonomy these areas would enjoy even after formal integration.

The fourth normative goal of encouraging revolutions abroad is perhaps the only Chinese objective in regard to which Western Europe has not been attributed with any significant role. The stress was more on revolutions in the Third World, where the potential for radical change was perceived as far greater than anywhere else. Although this objective was certainly important during the Maoist period, and a great deal of Chinese external activity was influenced by this consideration, it was apparently abandoned in the eighties. The measure of Chinese abandonment of this goal can be discerned from the fact that China no more considers itself as a part of the international communist movement, and now believes only in bilateral interaction with other communist parties based on non-interference in each other's affairs.

Europe thus has occupied an important position in China's foreign policy during most of the last forty years of China's relations with the outside world. And there is every reason to believe that this pattern of behaviour will continue in the future—even more so when China becomes more assertive in international affairs.

Epilogue: the events of Tiananmen Square

The May–June 1989 events of Tiananmen square were indeed a major landmark in post-1949 Chinese history. They were important because they included massive anti-establishment demonstrations, and because they were severely repressed by the Chinese government. None of this was entirely new, for such events had occurred in the past; what was distinctive was its massive nature and the severity with which the demonstrations were repressed.

What has been the effect of all this on Sino-European relations? Have they been severely jolted and for how long? Undoubtedly, China's relations with most of the developed world were seriously affected. In the immediate aftermath, mutual recrimination became the order of the day and interactions in all sectors were severely curtailed if not totally suspended.

'Tiananmen Square' coincided with three important developments: Gorbachev's visit to Beijing, in France the bicentenary celebrations of the French revolution, and the commencement of the rumblings of discontent in Eastern Europe.

Gorbachev's visit to China had brought a large number of journalists to the country to cover what was generally perceived as a major event. However, when the 'Tiananmen Square' events occurred, the Western media's focus was shifted to these events, resulting in a massive flow of dramatic images on the world's television screens and of press dispatches. The power of the media was confirmed by this high-voltage publicity. The link between media diffusion and political behaviour became increasingly evident from the severe European reaction. Public opinion criticized the repression, and practically all the West European governments—though varyingly—condemned it, suspending many of their interactions with the Beijing government. Even the European Commission of the European Community—normally not used to casting political judgements— reacted by cancelling the visit to Brussels of Zheng Tuobin, the Chinese foreign trade minister, who was to co-preside over the EC–China mixed commission and who was to hold high-level meetings with Community leaders.[1] At the same time, the European Commission expressed its 'consternation' and 'shock' at the 'brutal repression' that the Beijing population had undergone.[2]

The second important event that coincided with 'Tiananmen Square' was the bicentenary celebration of the French revolution. The French government, having decided to focus its celebrations on what the revolution represented in terms of human rights, came to the forefront to condemn the Chinese repression, blocked all high-level visits, suspended aid, and stopped the conclusion of any economic deals. Even more significant was the French decision to give asylum to Chinese dissidents who had managed to escape from China, and to accord them the right to establish an organization in Paris (the Federation for Democracy in China) the announced purpose of which was to achieve 'peacefully, reasonably and non-violently' a respect for fundamental rights, for social justice and for the development of private economic initiatives.[3]

191

The third important coincidence was the rumbling of discontent in Eastern Europe. A process of political and economic pluralism was already under way in Poland and Hungary, and was spreading out to other areas of the region where conservative East European governments were holding back on liberalizing the Communist regimes. The trend on the whole was for change, and grass-roots pressure was indeed building up. Even East Germany—where the Chinese vice prime minister, Yao Yilin, was dispatched to participate in the anniversary celebrations of the German Democratic Republic—was moving away from the orthodox line.

China's isolation was thus total. If Western Europe had reacted severely, Eastern Europe had also failed to show any support or any sympathy.

But is all this permanent? Can the Sino-European crisis of 1989 continue indefinitely? If one accepts the argument that inter-state relations are never immutably bad or eternally good, the currently soured Sino-European relations cannot be expected to continue indefinitely. At some point the current tensions will have to end, and the basic determinants that influence the foreign-policy behaviour of nations will once again reassert themselves, over the provisional and tentative factors that now prevail—until such time as another crisis reappears on the horizon.

Notes

Chapter 1

1. Most of the official declarations pertaining to foreign policy underlined China's determination to ally itself with the Soviet Union and on berating the United States; for details, see reports made to the three sessions of the Chinese People's Political Consultative Conference in 1949, 1950 and 1951. Documentation available in supplements to *People's China* for the three years.
2. See Mao Zedong, 'On the people's democratic dictatorship', in his *Selected Works*, vol. IV, Beijing, Foreign Languages Press, 1961, p. 415.
3. See, for example, 'Premier Zhou Enlai's Political Report to the Third Session of the First National Committee of the Chinese People's Political Consultative Conference', 23 October 1951; supplement to *People's China*, no. 10, 16 November 1951.
4. Anna Louise Strong, 'The Thought of Mao tse-tung', *Amerasia*, no. 6, 1947, pp. 161–2.
5. For details, see vol. IV of Mao's *Selected Works*, op. cit.
6. Supplement to *People's China*, op. cit., p. 4.
7. Mao Zedong 'On New Democracy', *Selected Works of Mao Zedong*, vol. II, Beijing, Foreign Languages Press, 1965.
8. Anna Louise Strong, op. cit., p. 162.
9. *Yugoslav Survey*, no. 8, 1962, p. 1507.
10. Liu Suinian and Wu Qungan (eds), *China's Socialist Economy: An Outline History (1948–1984)*, Beijing: Beijing Review, 1986.
11. Prinson Meunier, *Le chincom ou la république populaire de la Chine face à l'embargo occidentale (1949–1957)*, Paris, Cahier d'études chinoises, no. 7, 1958.
12. For some details, see Humphrey Trevelyan, *Worlds Apart, China 1953–5, Soviet Union 1962–5*, London, Macmillan, 1971.
13. Ibid., p. 54.
14. *The Common Progamme and Other Documents of the First Plenary Session of the Chinese People's Political Consultative Conference*, Beijing, Foreign Language Press, 1950, p. 19.
15. Humphrey Trevelyan, op. cit., p. 51.
16. Ibid, p. 51.
17. Part of a communication sent by Swiss diplomatic representative in Stockholm to Berne on 21 February 1950, *Swiss Federal Archives B 22, 21 Cha*.
18. Note from Swiss legation in London to Berne of 23 August 1950, *Swiss Federal Archives B 22, 21 Cha*.
19. This was confirmed by the Chinese chargé d'affaires on his arrival in New Delhi where he established contact with only those European missions with whom his country had 'diplomatic relations'; see notes from the Swiss legation in New Delhi to Berne on 16 August 1950, *Swiss Federal Archives B 22, 21 Cha*.
20. Personal notes.
21. Humphrey Trevelyan, op cit., p. 30.

Chapter 2

1. For details, see *Khrushchev Remembers*, New York, Bantam Books, 970, p. 533. While Khrushchev, writing about the period, was underlining the weakness of the Vietminh position, the Western analysis was doing just the reverse, i.e. underlining their own weakness.

2. For the details about the Chinese requirements under the five-year plan, see *First Five Year Plan For Development of the National Economy of the People's Republic of China in 1953–1957*, Beijing, Foreign Languages Press, 1956.
3. Speech given by Zhou Enlai in Beijing on 30 April 1952 to representatives of the Chinese diplomatic missions abroad; for the text, see Zhou Enlai, *Selected Works*, Vol. 2, Beijing, Foreign Languages Press, 1984, pp. 85–93, (in Chinese).
4. *Foreign Office File 371/110216*, letter from Humphrey Trevelyan to Anthony Eden dated 31 August 1954, p. 5.
5. This statement was made by Nan Hanchen, Chairman of the Chinese arrangements Committee for the Moscow Conference; partial text in *New Times*, no. 12, 1952.
6. View expressed by British economist, Alec Cairncross, in his articles 'The Moscow Economic Conference', *Soviet Studies*, no. 2, 1952.
7. Liu Suinian and Wu Gungan, *China's Socialist Economy: An Outline History, 1949–1984*, Beijing, Beijing Review, 1986, p. 61.
8. Text in *Survey of the Chinese Mainland Press*, no. 433, 1952, pp. 14–15.
9. For details about Chinese policy in Geneva, see François Joyaux, *La Chine et le réglement du premier conflit d'Indo-Chine*, Paris, Publications de la Sorbonne, 1979.
10. *Xinhua News Bulletin*, 17 June 1954.
11. François Joyaux, op. cit.
12. Ibid.
13. He. de Galard, 'La Chine a-t-elle les clés de la paix', *France Observateur*, 24 June 1954, p. 6.
14. *New Statesman and Nation*, 24 July 1954, p. 90.
15. For details, see François Joyaux, op. cit.; also see Robert F. Randle, *Geneva 1954: The Settlement of the Indo-Chinese War*, Princeton, Princeton University Press, 1969; Percy Jucheng Fang and Lucy Guinong Fang, *Zhou Enlai: A Profile*, Beijing: Foreign Languages Press, 1986.
16. A British Embassy report seems to suggest this point; see *Foreign Office, File 371/110248*.
17. Heinrich Bechtoldt 'The Federal Republic of Germany and China: Problems of Trade and Diplomacy' in A.M. Halpern (ed.), *Policies Towards China: Views From Six Continents*, New York, McGraw-Hill, 1965.
18. 'Les relations franco–chinoises (1945–1973)', *La Documentation Française: notes et études*, Paris, 1973.
19. A note prepared by the economic and financial section of the French foreign ministry, partial text in François Joyaux, op. cit., p. 153.
20. Peter Cheng, *A Chronology of the People's Republic of China from October 1, 1949*, Totowa, N.J., Littlefield Adams, 1972.
21. Liu Suinian and Wu Qungan, *China's Socialist Economy: An Outline History (1949–1984)*, Beijing, Beijing Review, 1986, p. 61.
22. Heinrich Bechtoldt, op. cit.
23. *New York Herald Tribune*, 15 March 1954.
24. Ibid.
25. Arthur A. Stahnke (ed.), *China's Trade with the West: A Political and Economic Analysis*, New York, Praeger Publishers, 1972.
26. Ibid.
27. For Dulles' Statement, see *Department of State Bulletin*, 11 January 1954, p. 54.
28. See Alexander Eckstein, *Communist China's Economic Growth of Foreign Trade*, New York, Mcgraw Hill, 1966.
29. *France Observateur*, 24 June 1954, p. 10.
30. Pierre Mèndes-France, *Oeuvres complètes*, Vol. III, *Gouverner c'est choisir, 1954–1955*, Paris, Gallimard, 1986.

31. Ibid.
32. *Foreign Office, File 371/110216*; Note of 24 November 1954 addressed by the Foreign Office to the British Embassy in Washington, p. 1.
33. Ibid, pp. 2–4
34. *Foreign Office, File 371/122626*, minutes of discussions within the Foreign Office, p. 1.
35. David C. Wolf, 'To secure a convenience: Britain recognizes China', *Journal of Contemporary History*, no. 2, 1983, p. 320.
36. Liu Suinian and Wu Qungan, op. cit., p. 60.
37. Jack Dribbon, 'The British people want friendship in China', *People's China*, 16 July 1952, p. 33.
38. 'Sino-British Trade', *People's China*, 1 August 1952, p. 4.
39. See *Qian Duansheng*, 'Chinese–British Friendship', *People's China*, 16 August 1954.
40. For details see *Xinhua News Bulletin*, 4 May 1954.
41. Chi Chooting, 'The vast possibilities of Chinese–British Trade', *People's China*, p. 23.
42. *Foreign Office, File 371/110195*, note from the British Embassy to Foreign Office.
43. *Foreign Office, File 371/110248*, note from the British Embassy to Foreign Office.
44. *Foreign Office, File 371/110247*, note from the British Embassy to Foreign Office, p. 5.
45. *Renmin Ribao*, 15 August 1954.
46. *Foreign Office, File 371/110247*, op. cit., p. 3.
47. Ibid., p. 4.
48. Ibid.
49. *Foreign Office, File 371/110248*, note from the British Embassy to the Foreign Office.
50. *Foreign Office, File 371/120999*, minutes in the file.
51. Ibid., p. 3.
52. *Foreign Office, File 371/122626*, minutes of the discussion, p. 5.
53. *Foreign Office, File 371/110216*, note from the British Embassy to Foreign Office, p. 1.
54. Ibid., p. 2.

Chapter 3

1. Edward Crankshaw, *The New Cold War: Moscow v. Pekin*, London, Penguin Books, 1963, p. 53.
2. Ibid, p. 56.
3. For details, see Heman Ray, *China and Eastern Europe*, New Delhi, Radiant, 1988.
4. 'On historical experience concerning the dictatorship of the proleteriat', *Renmin Ribao*, 5 April 1956.
5. *L'Unita*, 26 June 1956.
6. See text of Soviet–Yugoslav Declaration of 20 June 1956 in Robert Bass and Elizabeth Marbury (eds), *The Soviet Yugoslav Controversy, 1948–58: A Documentary Record*, New York, The East Europe Institute, 1959, p. 57.
7. For texts of the Soviet statements on the question, see *The Anti-Stalin Campaign and International Communism*, New York, Columbia University Press, 1956, p. 10.
8. Cited in Heman Ray, op. cit., p. 9.
9. For details, see Flora Lewis, *A Case History of Hope*, New York, Doubleday, 1958, p. 182.
10. See R. Knox's articles in *The Observer*, 25 May 1957 and the *New York Times*, 18 April 1957.

11. Flora Lewis, op. cit., p. 183; for details of the Chinese policy see Jacques Levesque, *Le conflit sino-soviétique et l'Europe de l'Est*, Montreal, Les Presses de l'Université de Montreal, 1970; also see 'La Chine face aux événements d'octobre' in Pierre Kende et Krysztof Pomian (eds), *La deuxième révolution d'octobre*, Paris, Editions du Seuil, 1978.

12. *Xinhua News Bulletin*, 21 October 1956.

13. *New York Times*, 11 January 1957.

14. *Polemic on the General Line of the International Communist Movement*, Peking, Foreign Languages Press, 1965, p. 38.

15. Jacques Levesque, 'La Chine face aux evenements d'octobre', op. cit.

16. François Fejto, *Chine–URSS La fin d'une hegemonie: les origines du grand schisme communiste 1950–1957*, Paris, Plon, 1964, p. 163.

17. *Khrushchev Remembers*, New York, Bantam Books, 1971.

18. See 6 September 1963 statement of the editorial departments of *Renmin Ribao* and *Hongqi*, text in the *Polemic on the General Line*, op. cit.

19. The information was given by Gyorgy Heltai who was the Director of the Hungarian Ministry of Foreign Affairs at the time; see Jacques Levesque, 'La Chine face aux evenements d'octobre 1956' op. cit; also see his chapter 'Imre Nagy au Parlement' in *Histoire du soulèvement hongrois 1956* (sous la direction de P. Gosztony), Paris, Editions Horvath, 1971.

20. *Renmin Ribao*, 1 November 1956.

21. The principles are: (a) mutual respect for each other's territorial integrity; (b) mutual non-aggression; (c) mutual non-interference in each other's affairs; (d) equality and mutual benefit; (e) peaceful co-existence. These principles were first enunciated in a statement made by the prime ministers of India and China.

22. *Renmin Ribao*, 1 November 1956.

23. Ibid.

24. *Polemic on the General Line of The International Communist Movement*, op. cit., p. 69.

25. *Shih Chih Shin*, 30 November 1956; English text in *Extracts of China Mainland Magazine*, no. 64, 1956, p. 10.

26. *Polemic on the General Line of the International Communist Movement*, op. cit., p. 69.

27. *Renmin Ribao*, 5 November 1956.

28. Ibid.

29. *Xinhua News Bulletin*, 6 November 1956.

30. *Renmin Ribao*, 21 November 1956.

31. *Polemic on the General Line of the International Communist Movement*, op. cit., p. 61.

32. Khrushchev suggests in his memoirs that Liu Shoaqi, with whom Soviet leaders had discussions, appeared as hesitant as the Soviet leaders; N.S. Khrushchev. op. cit.

33. O.B. Borisov and B.T. Koloslov, *Sino-Soviet Relations 1945–1973: A Brief History*, Moscow, Progress Publishers, 1975, p. 71.

34. Leopold Labedz, 'The small leap sideways', *China Quarterly*, no. 3, 1960, p. 98.

35. For details about the Polish press see *Notes et études documentaires*, No. 3238, *Documentation français* November 1965.

36. Tamas Ascel, 'Hungary: glad tidings from Nanking', *China Quarterly*, no. 3, 1960, p. 94; Zhu De's (vice president of the PRC) visit to Hungary, 14–16 January 1956 according to the British Foreign Office 'was built up by the Hungarian authorities as a great occasion in tribute to the Communist regime in China', *Foreign Office, File 371/ 120887*.

37. On this question, Khrushchev wrote, 'Whichever course we choose we would not be pursuing nationalist goals, but the internationalist goal of fraternal proleterian

solidarity. To make sure that all countries understood us correctly on this point, we decided to consult with the other socialist countries—first and foremost with the fraternal Communist Party of China', *op. cit.*, p. 459.

38. *More on the Historical Experience on the Dictatorship of the Proletariat*, Peking, Foreign Language Press, 1957, pp. 35 and 37.

39. There had been another important visit to Eastern Europe by a delegation of the National People's Congress led by Peng Zhen. It spent two and a half months between 13 November 1956 and 1 February 1957 visiting the Soviet Union, Albania, Bulgaria, Czechoslovakia, Romania and Yugoslavia.

40. See Sino–Soviet Joint Communiqué, *Izvestia*, 19 January 1957.

41. *Notes et Documents* no. 2395, p. 15.

42. Ibid.

43. Joint Communiqué in *Xinhua News Bulletin*, 23 April 1957, p. 10.

44. See Zbigniew Brzezinski, *The Soviet Bloc: Unity Conflict*, New York, Praeger, 1961, pp. 281–2.

45. See Joint Communiqué, text in *Xinhua News Bulletin*, 23 April 1957.

46. Erwin Weit, *Dans l'ombre de Gomulka: Histoire que nous vivons*, Paris, Editions Robert Lafont, 1971, pp. 287–8.

47. Mao Zedong, *Selected Works* vol. V, op. cit., p. 365.

48. Ibid., p. 359.

49. *Tribuna Ludu*, 16 May 1957, cited in Hemen Ray, op. cit., p. 19.

50. Ibid., pp. 19–20.

51. This was the case of East Germany; for details see Erwin Weit, op. cit., p. 54.

52. Zhou Enlai's remarks on 27 March 1957, while reporting on his East European trip, cited in Brzezinski, op. cit., p. 282.

53. Text in *Documentation française: notes et étude documentaire*, no. 2451, 20 August 1958, p. 50.

54. The Yugoslav Ambassador to Moscow stated in his memoirs that Khrushchev was very angry with Kardelj's speech, even more than with Tito's famous speech in Pula; for details, see Veljko Micunovic, *Journées de Moscou 1956–1958: un ambassadeur de Tito au Kremlin*, Paris, Robert Lafont, 1979, pp. 174–5.

55. *Renmin Ribao*, 11 December 1956.

56. Ibid.

57. See *Report on Hungary: The Hungarian Revolution as Presented to the Chinese Public*, Hong Kong, China Viewpoints, 1957. Also see *Xinhua News Bulletin* of the period during the events.

58. Personal notes.

59. Robert R. Bowie and John A. Fairbank, *Communist China 1955–59: Policy Documents with Foreword and analysis*, Cambridge, Mass., Harvard University Press, 1962, p. 291.

60. See Janos Radvanyi, 'The Hungarian Revolution and the Hundred Flowers Campaign' *China Quarterly*, No 43, 1970.

61. For details, see Roderick MacFarquhar, *The Origins of the Cultural Revolutions I: Contradictions Among the People 1956–57*, London, Oxford University Press, 1960.

62. See *Long Live Leninism*, Peking, Foreign Languages Press, 1960, p. 60.

63. See Veljko Micunovic, op. cit..

64. *In Refutation of Modern Revisionism*, Peking, Foreign Languages Press, 1958, p. 45; for details regarding Sino–Yugoslav relations of the period see Wu Xiuguan, 'Les rapports sino-yougoslaves—mémoires d'un diplomate vétéran' *Beijing Information*, 5 December 1983.

65. *In Refutation of Modern Revisionism*, op. cit., p. 9.

66. Hemen Ray, op. cit., p. 28.

67. Brzezinski, op. cit., p. 282.
68. Edward Crankshaw, op. cit., 1963, p. 63.
69. Erwin Weit, op. cit., p. 287.
70. *Xinhua News Bulletin*, 25 May 1958. p. 29.
71. Hemen Ray, op. cit., pp. 28 ff.
72. See Peter Cheng, *A Chronology of the People's Republic of China*, Totowa, NJ, Littlefield Adams, 1972.
73. Hemen Ray, op. cit.
74. Ibid.
75. Cited in ibid., p. 31.
76. Ibid., p. 31.
77. Ibid., p. 31.
78. Ibid., p. 39.
79. Ibid., pp. 39–40.
80. See W.C. Griffith, (ed.), op. cit., vol. 2.
81. *Khrushchev Remembers*, op. cit., vol. 2, p. 324.
82. *Pravda*, 12 June 1958; also see *New York Times*, 12 June 1958.
83. Khrushchev specifically mentions about pressing the Bulgarians to abandon their plans of following the Chinese model of communes; see his *Memoirs*, op. cit., p. 326.
84. *Pravda*, 28 January 1959.
85. See *Khrushchev Remembers: The Last Testament*, vol. 2, London, Penguin Books, 1977, pp. 273–5.
86. For details see Hemen Ray, op. cit.
87. Peng Dehuai: 'Pages from Reminiscences', *Far Eastern Affairs*, no. 1, 1988, p. 133.

Chapter 4

1. *Peking Review*, no. 52, 1959, p. 21.
2. Wang Suren, 'Break-up of EFTA Negotiations', *Hongqi*, no. 14, 1958, p. 26.
3. *Peking Review*, no. 52, 1959, p. 21.
4. Wang Suren, op. cit., p. 26.
5. Personal notes.
6. Favourable Reports on the EEC sent by Huan Xiang to Beijing were seen and approved by Mao Zedong; personal notes.
7. See Declaration of the Soviet Foreign Ministry of 16 March 1957, text in *Europa Archiv*, 11 December 1957.
8. Institut de L'Economie Mondiale et des Relations Internationales, 'De la création du Marché Commun et de L'Euratom', text in Bernard Dutoit, *L'Union Sovietique face à l'integration européenne*, Lausanne, Centre de Recherche Européenne, Ecole de HEC, University of Lausanne, 1964, pp. 41–5.
9. For the text of the statement, see *Cahiers du Communisme*, no 4, 1959.
10. Personal notes.
11. Alexander Eckstein, *Communist China's Economic Growth and Foreign Trade*, New York, McGraw Hill, 1966, p. 307: also see Wolfgang Bartke, *China's Economic Aid*, London, C. Hurst, 1975.
12. For details, see Sidney Klein, *Economic Aspects of the Sino-Soviet Dispute: The Road Divides*, Hong Kong, International Studies Group, 1966.
13. Cited in *An Economic Profile of Mainland China*, Washington DC, US Government Printing Press, 1967, vol. 2, pp. 591–2.
14. Cited in Edgar Snow, *Red China Today: The Other Side of the River*, New York, Random House, 1970, pp. 584–5.

15. Liu Suinian and Wu Qungan, *China's Socialist Economy. An Outline History 1949–1984*, Beijing, Beijing Review, 1986.
16. Partial text in ibid., p. 271.
17. Based on author's close examination of the news bulletins of the two years.
18. A study of the *People's Daily* has been done by Stephen Kux, '*The Chinese Perception of Western Europe, 1961–1981: A Content Analysis of the People's Daily*', thesis submitted to the University of Zurich in 1982.
19. Based on author's close examination of the two publications.
20. *International organizations*, Beijing, 1961, pp. 1176–82 (in Chinese).
21. *The Historical Experience of the Dictatorship of the Proleteriat*, Beijing, Foreign Languages Press, 1959, p. 15.
22. Fang Zhenxiang, 'Some questions regarding the current developments of imperialist contradictions', *Hongqi*, no. 5, 1963, p. 7.
23. Ibid, p. 1; also see Liu Xemoi, 'Behind the interdependence between the US and Europe', *Hongqi*, no. 18, 1962, p. 9.
24. Ibid.
25. Fang Zhenxiang, op. cit.
26. *Xinhua News Bulletin*, no. 4954, 8 August 1962, p. 3.
27. Yao Yensheng, 'Sword and shield: rift between the US and its NATO allies over nuclear weapons control', *Peking Review*, no. 24, 1962, p. 10.
28. Ibid., p. 11.
29. Zhang Zhenya, 'Western conflicts in the mirror of Brussels', *Peking Review*, no. 6, 1963, p. 5.
30. Liu Xemoi, op. cit., p. 9.
31. *Peking Review*, no. 4, 1964, p. 10.
32. *Xinhua News Bulletin*, 2 February 1963.
33. Ibid.
34. Fang Zhenxiang, op. cit., p. 2.
35. Ibid.
36. See Zhou Yan, 'Britain and the Common Market', *Xinhua Monthly* (in Chinese); Zhen Ya, 'The rebuff Macmillan received and cooperation between the so-called "free countries" ', *Hongqi*, no. 10, 1962; Liu Xemoi, 'Behind the interdependence between US and Europe', no. 18, *Hongqi*, no. 18, 1962; Wang Suren, 'Break-up: EFTA negotiations', *Hongqi*, no. 14, 1958.
37. Zhang Zhenya, op. cit., p. 6.
38. *Peking Review*, no. 4, 1964.
39. Mao's remarks to the French Parliamentary delegation in January 1964, cited in Jacques Marcus, *The Peking Papers*, New York, Dutton, 1967, p. 287.
40. *New York Times*, 24 February 1964.
41. Cited in *L'Humanité*, 21 February 1964.
42. Roger Garside, *Coming Alive: China After Mao*, New York, Mentor, 1982, p. 3.

Chapter 5

1. Personal notes.
2. Cited in Edgar Snow, *Red China Today: The Other Side of the River*, New York, Random House, 1970, pp. 584–5.
3. For details, see Allan J. Barry, 'The Chinese food purchases', *China Quarterly*, 1961, no. 8.
4. Personal notes.
5. Ibid.

6. Ibid.
7. Edgar Snow, op. cit.; Felix Greene, *China*, New York, Ballantine, 1961; Jules Roy,*Le voyage en chine*, Paris: René Julliard, 1965; K.S. Karol, *La Chine de Mao: l'autre communisme*, Paris, Robert Laffont, 1966.

    This is by no means an exhaustive list, for there were some others including Hugo Portisch, editor of the Vienna *Kurier*, whose book (in German, 1965) was subsequently translated into English and entitled *Red China Today*, Greenwich, Conn. Fawcett, 1966.
8. *Peking Review*, no. 39, 1961, p. 22.
9. Ibid.; also see his article in *The Sunday Times*, 15 October, 1961.
10. Ibid.
11. Ibid., June 1960.
12. Hewlett Johnson, *The Upsurge in China*, Peking, Foreign Languages Press, 1961, p. 368.
13. François Mitterrand, *La Chine en défi*, Paris, Julliard, 1961, pp. 64–5.
14. For Lu's visit to England, see V. Wolpert, 'Minister Lu in London, 1961', *Far Eastern Economic Review*, no. 6, 1963.
15. Ibid., p. 314.
16. *La Documentation Française, Notes et Études*, nos. 4014–5, 1973.
17. Ernst Majonica, *Bonn–Peking: Die Beziehungen des Bunderepublik Deutschland zur Volkesrepublik China*, Stuttgart, Verlag W. Kohlhammer, 1971.
18. Ibid.
19. *The Economist*, 12 January 1963, p. 136.
20. Ernst Majonica, op. cit.
21. *Far Eastern Economic Review*, 20 February, 1964.
22. See V. Wolpert, op. cit.
23. *The Times*, 21 December 1963.
24. *Far Eastern Economic Review*, 1 August 1963.
25. The total value of exports from Britain to China in this sector was £3,032,000; see Colina MacDougall, 'Trade fair at Canton', *Far Eastern Economic Review*, no. 11, 1963.
26. *Peking Review*, no. 45, 6 November 1964, p. 4.
27. Daniel Tretiak, 'Spring fair at Canton', ibid., no. 16, 4 June 1964; also see Colina Macdougall, 'Britain's Peking Fair', nos. 12 and 20, 1964.
28. For details see Colina Macdougall, 'Eight plants for Peking', *Far Eastern Economic Review*, no. 4, 21 January, 1964; also see Percy Timberlake, 'China as a trading nation'? in Neville Maxwell (ed.), *China's Road to Development*? Oxford, Pergamon, 1975; Sidney Klein, *Politics vs Economics: Foreign Trade and Aid Policies of China*, Hong Kong, International Studies Group, 1968.
29. Lin Haiyun, 'China's growing foreign trade', *Peking Review*, no. 4, 22 January 1965, p. 9.
30. *Renmin Ribao*, 21 January 1964. The articles insisted 'that the domination of the intermediate zone plays a more and more important role in the global strategy of the United States'.
31. See Shi Chin 'Kennedy's peace strategy exposed'. 'Shih Chin' is a pseudonym that was presumably used by a leading Chinese figure. Under this name, he wrote an important series of articles on China's foreign policy in 1972. See his, *On Studying World History*, Peking, 1973 (in Chinese).
32. See 'More on the Differences between Comrade Togliatti and US', *Peking Review*, nos.10–11, 1963.
33. 'A Proposal concerning the General Line of the International Communist Movement', *Peking Review*, no. 25, 1963.
34. Editorial in *Renmin Ribao*, English text in *Peking Review*. 24 January 1964.

35. Edgar Faure, *Le serpent et la tortue: les problèmes de la Chine Populaire*, Paris, Julliard, 1957, p. 126.
36. Ibid., p. 51.
37. See Feng Lin, 'De Gaulle's Algerian policy', *Peking Review*, 30 March 1962.
38. Jacques Marcuse, *Peking Papers*, New York, Dutton, 1967, p. 288.
39. François Mitterrand, *La Chine au Défi*, Paris, Julliard 1961, p. 30.
40. Peter Cheng, *A Chronology of the People's Republic of China from October 1 1949*, Totowa, NJ, Littlefield Adams, 1972, p. 169.
41. For the Chinese positions, see Chinese Foreign Ministry (eds), *Contemporary China's Foreign Policy*, Beijing, World Affairs Press, 1985, (in Chinese).
42. See his press conference of 29 July 1963; text in Charles de Gaulle, *Discours et message: pour l'effort août 1962 – décembre 1965*, Paris, Plon, 1966.
43. Maurice Couve de Murville, 'Un voyage en chine', *Politique étrangère*, 1971.
44. Edgar Faure, op. cit.
45. Faure's host, who gave the speech at the banquet was Xi Ruo, chairman of the Chinese People's Institute of Foreign Affairs; partial text in *Peking Review*, no. 44, 1 November 1963, p. 5.
46. *Le Monde*, 25 January 1964.
47. 'Relations franco–chinoises 1945–73', *Documentation française*, op. cit., p. 29.
48. *Documentation française*, op. cit.
49. Full text in ibid., p. 53.
50. Ibid.
51. This was done through an interview given by Zhou Enlai to the chief correspondent of *Agence France Presse*, text in *Bulletin d'information de l'ambassade de la République Populaire de la Chine*, no. 158, Berne, 19 February 1964.
52. Jacques Guillermaz, 'Le généralisme tel que je l'ai connu', *Le Monde*, 1 April 1985.
53. Charles de Gaulle, op. cit., pp. 178–9.
54. *Documentation française*, op. cit., Maurice Couve de Murville, the French Foreign Minister, had declared before the Foreign Affairs Commission of the National Assembly that France would not take the initiative to break off relations with Taipai, see *Le Monde*, 24 January 1964.
55. Stephen Erasmus, 'General de Gaulle's Recognition of Peking', *China Quarterly*, April–June 1964, p. 167.
56. *Documentation française*, op. cit.
57. *Agence France Presse*, 18 December 1963.
58. *New York Times*, 10 January 1964.
59. François Fejto, 'France and China: The Intersection of the Two Grand Designs' in A. M. Halpern, *Policies Towards China: Views from Six Continents*, New York, McGraw Hill, Co, 1965, p. 63.
60. *Le Monde*, 28 January, 1964.
61. Ibid.
62. Ibid.
63. The Chinese nationalist mission in Paris created some difficulties. It had refused to evacuate the Embassy premises. Force had to be used to expel them on 14 March 1966.
64. Huang Zhen, the Chinese Ambassador, was vice-foreign minister, and Lucien Paye, representing France in China, was the former education minister.
65. Sydney Klein, *Politics Versus Economics: The Foreign Trade and Aid Policies of China*, Hong Kong, International Studies Group, 1968, p. 131.
66. *Documentation Française*, op. cit., p. 32.
67. In 1964 the United Nations' General Assembly did not pronounce on China's admission. But one can discern the shift if one compares the voting behaviour in 1963

and 1965. In 1963, out of a total of 111 members, 57 voted against, 41 for, with 13 abstentions. In 1965 out of a total of 117, 47 voted against, 47 for and 23 abstained.

68. 'Far Eastern round up', *Far Eastern Economic Review*, 20 February 1964, p. 408.

69. V. Wolpert, 'German taboo', *Far Eastern Economic Review*, 20 February 1964.

70. Heman Ray, 'Die ideologische Achse Peking–Pankow'. *Aussenpolitik*, no. 12, 1960.

71. See for example, Hsi Linsheng, 'West German Militarism on the March', *Peking Review*, 6 April 1962.

72. Roger Garside, *Coming Alive: China After Mao*, New York, Mentor, 1982, p. 3.

73. *Xinhua News Bulletin*, 20, 23 and 30 January; 1 and 28 February 1963.

74. *Xinhua News Bulletin*, 2 February 1963, p. 10.

75. Ibid.

76. *L'Humanité*, 21 February 1964.

77. For details see Ernst von Majonica, 'Die Volkesrepublik China und die deutsche frage', *Europa-Archiv*, No. 17, 1971; also see *Frankfurter Allgemeine Zeitung*, 5 May 1964, and Harry Hamm, *Das Reich der 700 millionem: Begegnung mit dem China von heute*, Dusseldorf, Econ., 1965, p. 306.

78. Arthur A. Stahnke, 'Sino–West German trade', in Arthur A. Stahnke (ed.), *China's Trade with the West: A Political and Economic Analysis*, New York, Praeger, 1972.

79. For details, see Ernst von Majonica, *Bonn–Peking. Die Beziehungen des Bunder-republik Deutschland sur Volksrepublic China*, Stuttgart: W. Kohlhammer, 1971, pp. 101–2.

80. Personal notes.

81. For details of the German interpretation, see Ernst von Majonica, op. cit.

82. See Gerhard Schröder, *Mission ohne Auftrog: Die Vorbereitung der Diplomatischen Beziehungen Zwischen Bonn und Peking*, Bergisch Gladback, Lübbe, 1988.

83. Personal notes.

84. For details, see Stahnke, op. cit.

85. *Department of State Bulletin*, 11 April 1966, p. 567.

86. Ibid, 28 February 1966, p. 317.

87. *New York Times*, 1 August 1966.

88. Stahnke, op. cit., 153.

89. Ibid, p. 151.

90. See Bonn press release dated 19 March 1966, published by the West German Information Office in New York.

91. Ernst von Majonica, op. cit., p. 24.

92. *Pekin information*, 22 February 1965, p. 23.

93. Ibid., p. 24.

94. *Peking Review*, 16 April 1965, p. 19

95. Ibid., 16 April 1965, p. 4 and 23 April 1965, p. 25.

96. Ibid.

97. 'Commentateur', 'La macedoine de Wilson', *Pekin information*, 12 July 1965.

98. The Chinese government attacked the British government for having released four Taiwan citizens who had intruded into the Chinese waters off the coast of Kwantung and Fukien provinces on a sabotage mission instead of detaining them, *Peking Review*, 3 September 1965, p. 8.

99. Editorial in *Renmin Ribao*, text in *Peking Review*, 18 December 1965, p. 17.

100. The American-backed resolution to the effect that replacing Taiwan's representative by that of Beijing was 'an important question' and therefore requiring a two-thirds majority first came up in 1961.

101. *Peking Review*, 8 November 1960, p. 23. In 1964, Mao Zedong also spoke to this effect and declared that Beijing was in no hurry to receive the British Ambassador. 'The Chinese', he is reported to have added 'can wait for another 15 years'; see Jacques Marcuse, *The Peking Papers*, New York, Dutton, 1967, p. 288.

102. *China Topics*, 29 January 1970.
103. Ibid.
104. *China Topics*, 29 January 1970, p. 2.
105. Ibid.
106. Alain Peyrefitte, *Quand la Chine s'éveillera . . . le monde tremblera, Regards sur la voie Chinoise* Paris, Fayard, 1973, p. 59.
107. Ibid.; also see André Malraux, *Antimemoires*, Paris, Gallimard, 1967.
108. Cited in Alain Peyrefitte, op. cit., p. 60.
109. See Charles de Gaulle, *Discours et messages pour l'effort 1962–65*, Paris, Plon, 1970.
110. 'Memorandum of Comrade Togliatti', August 1964, for complete text see *Global Digest*, no. 4, 1965.
111. Georges Marchais *Le socialisme pour la France, Cahiers du Communisme* February – March 1976.
112. See 'Les divergences entre le camarade Togliatti et nous'; 'Encore une fois sur les divergences entre le camarade Togliatti et nous'; and 'D'ou proviennent les divergences? reponse a Maurice Thorez et d'autres camarades', in *Proletaires de tous les pays unissons-nous contre l'ennemi commun*, Peking, Foreign Languages Press, 1963.
113. Remark made by Mao Zedong to André Malraux, see André Malraux, *Antimemoires* op. cit., p. 543.
114. Editorial in *Zeri i popullit*, 6 January 1965, published in *Peking Review*, No. 6, 1965.
115. Editorial comment on the meeting in *Renmin Ribao and Hongq*; English translation in *Peking Review*, No. 13, 1965.
116. 'Bankruptcy of Europe's new scabs', *Renmin Ribao*, 4 May 1967; English translation in *Peking Review*, No. 20, 1967.
117. Ibid.

Chapter 6

1. *Miscellany of Mao Zedong Thought*, Washington, DC: Publication Research Service, 1974, p. 20.
2. Tang Tsou, 'The Cultural Revolution and the Chinese political system', *China Quarterly*, no. 38, 1969, p. 79.
3. Expression used by Liu Suinian and Wu Qungan, *China's Socialist Economy: An Outline History, (1949–1984)*, Beijing, Beijing Review, 1986, p. 340.
4. Mao Zedong declared in 1967: 'the foreign policy is formulated by me and implemented by Premier Zhou', cited in Thomas Robinson (ed.), *The Cultural Revolution in China*, Berkeley, University of California Press, 1971, p. 354.
5. Vietnam reportedly was the only issue on which there was a discussion at the upper echelons of the CCP.
6. For details, see 'Chen Yi and the Cultural Revolution', *China Topics*, YB 455, 10 January 1968.
7. Published in the Beijing's Foreign Language Institute journal, *Red Flag*; text in *China Topics*, p. 3.
8. Ibid, p. 3.
9. For details, see Percy Jucheng Fang and Lucy Guinong, *Zhou Enlai: A Profile*, Beijing, Foreign Languages Press, 1986, p. 191.
10. 'Life in the Chinese Diplomatic Service', *China Topics* YB439, 18 September 1967.
11. *Peking Review*, no. 25, 1967.
12. Ibid.
13. Radio Free Europe, Poland, Item no. 2225/68.

14. 'The Chinese silence on East European developments', *Radio Free Europe Research* Communist Area, China Foreign Relations, 11 April 1968.
15. *Eastern Europe*, No 3, 1967.
16. Ibid.
17. Ibid, p. 31.
18. Ibid.
19. *Reuters*, 29 March 1964.
20. Cited in Hemen Ray, *China and Eastern Europe*, New Delhi, Radiant Publishers, 1988, p. 74.
21. Ibid.
22. Cited in ibid., p. 76.
23. 'Chinese endorsement of pre-Peking Polish CP', *Radio Free Europe Research*, China Foreign Relations, 20 September 1968.
24. Cited in Hemen Ray, op. cit., p. 75.
25. Complete text in *Peking Review*, no. 34, 1968, p. 10.
26. For details, see Elez Biberaj, *Albania and China: A Study of Unequal Relations*, Boulder, Westview Press, 1968; also see Enver Hoxa, *Reflexions sur la Chine*, 2 vols, Tirana, Editions '8 Nantori'. 1979.
27. *Peking Review*, 11 June 1965.
28. Peter R. Prifti, *Socialist Albania since 1944: Domestic and Foreign Developments*, Cambridge, Mass. MIT, 1978.
29. Elez Biberaj, op. cit.
30. Ibid.
31. See Enver Hoxa, vol. I, op. cit.
32. Ibid., pp. 250–1.
33. *Peking Review*, 27 October 1967, p. 15.
34. China's reduced interest in Romania can be discerned from the very little coverage that was given to Romanian developments. An analysis of *Xinhua* during March 1968 reveals that during the month the Chinese news agency carried twenty-nine items related to Albania but only one concerning Romania; see 'The Chinese silence on East European developments', *Radio Free Europe Research*, op. cit.
35. Cited in Hemen Ray, op. cit., p. 110.
36. *Xinhua News Bulletin*, 23 June 1966.
37. *Xinhua News Bulletin*, 23 August 1968.
38. Cited in Hemen Ray, op. cit., p. 152.
39. For details, see Enver Hoxa, op. cit., Vol. I.
40. *Peking Review*, 3 February 1967, p. 30.
41. Ibid, p. 30.
42. Ibid, p. 30.
43. *Survey of the Mainland Press*, 7 February 1967.
44. *Peking Review*, 3 February 1967, p. 30.
45. *Le Monde*, 4 February 1967.
46. *Peking Review*, 16 June 1967, p. 25.
47. *Peking Review*, 9 June 1967, p. 31.
48. For details, see *China Topics*, 7 June 1967.
49. *Xinhua News Bulletin*, 31 January 1967.
50. Ibid.
51. Ibid., 2 February 1967, p. 10.
52. *Peking Review*, 1 September 1967.
53. *The Polemic on the General Line of the International Communist Movement*, op. cit. p. 23.
54. 'Bankruptcy of Europe's new scabs', *Peking Review*, 12 May 1967, p. 10.

55. 'Sino–Belgian relations', *China Topics*, YB558 Int rels-Bel. 1 December 1970.
56. Ibid.
57. Klaus Mehnert, *Peking and the New Left: At Home and Abroad*, Berkeley, University of California Press, 1969, p. 62.
58. *Peking Review*, 1967, p. 18.
59. Ibid.
60. *Peking Review*, 1967.
61. For details, see Klaus Mehnert, op. cit.
62. Ibid., p. 64.
63. Ibid.
64. *Peking Review*, 1968, p. 10.
65. Paul Hollander, *Political Pilgrims: Travels of Western Intellectuals to the Soviet Union, China and Cuba 1928–1978*, New York, Oxford University Press, 1981, p. 187.
66. Mario-Antonietta Mocciocchi, *Deux mille ans de bonheur*, Paris, Grasset, 1983, p. 385.
67. See Percy Jucheng Fang and Lucy Guinong, *Zhou Enlai: A Profile*, Beijing, Foreign Languages Press, 1986, pp. 167–8.

Chapter 7

1. Clare Hollingworth, *Mao and the Men Against Him*, London, Jonathan Cape, 1985, p. 177.
2. Ibid, p. 177.
3. Liu Suinian and Wu Qungan, *China's Socialist Economy: An Outline History (1949–1984)*, Beijing, Beijing Review, 1986, p. 340.
4. *Peking Review*, no. 48, 1968, p. 12.
5. For details, see Michael Y.M. Kau (ed.), *The Lin Piao Affair: Power Politics and Military Coup*, White Plains, NY, International Arts and Sciences Press, 1975; also see Philip Bridgham, 'The Fall of Lin Piao', *China Quarterly*, no. 55, July–September, 1973.
6. *China Topics*, 30 September 1967, p. 4.
7. Ibid.
8. Clare Hollingworth, op. cit.
9. Speech by Fu Sheng, chairman of the Provincial Revolutionary Committee of Heilongjiang on Harbin Radio on 6 August 1969, cited in *Comparative Communism: An Interdisciplinary Journal*, nos. 3 and 4, 1969, p. 149.
10. Some writers have suggested that beginning in September 1968 'a shift in Chinese rankings of the US and the Soviet Union as primary enemies took place as, for the first time, the Soviet Union overtook the US as the main target of Chinese hostility'; for details on this shift based upon a close study of the *Peking Review*, see Linda D. Dillon, Bruce Burton and Walter C. Sodurlund, 'Who was the principal enemy? Shifts in official Chinese perception of the two superpowers', *Asian Survey*, no. 5, May 1977.
11. Ibid.
12. Brezhnev's speech to the Fifth Polish Party Congress on 12 November 1968, *Pravda*, 13 November 1968.
13. For details see Harrison Salisbury, *The Coming War between Russia and China*, London, Pan Books, 1969.
14. Ibid.
15. *Pravda*, 8 June 1969.
16. *Xinhua News Bulletin*, 28 June 1969, p. 15.
17. *Peking Review*, no. 19, 1969.

18. Lin Biao's report to the Ninth Congress, *Peking Review*, Special Issue, 28 April 1969, p. 29.
19. Ibid, 29.
20. From a document identified as 'Outline of education on situation for companies' issued by the PLA Kunming military region in April 1973. This document was obtained by Taiwan intelligence and published in *Issues and Studies*, June 1974.
21. Lin Biao's report to the Ninth Congress of the Party, op. cit., p. 26.
22. Ibid, p. 26.
23. Henry Kissinger, *White House Years*, Boston, Little, Brown, 1979, p. 764.
24. Ibid.
25. In January 1964 the *Renmin Ribao*, editorial, commenting on Mao's statement about the struggle of Panama against the United States, included only Western Europe, Oceania and Canada in the 'second intermediary zone'.
26. See Deng Xiaoping's speech at the Sixth session of the UN General Assembly in April 1974. The expression, 'second world', was used in a broader sense to include all the developed countries; full text in *Peking Review*, no. 16, 1974.
27. See 'Le république populaire de Chine et les "cinq centres" ', in *Annuaire de Tiers Monde*, 1975.
28. Shi Jun 'On studying some history of the national liberation movements', *Peking Review*, no. 45, 1972, p. 8.
29. *Peking Review* no. 2, 1973.
30. *Peking Review* no. 3, 1973.
31. *Peking Review* no. 23, 1971.
32. *Peking Review* no. 2, 1973, p. 19.
33. *Peking Review* no. 11, 1969, p. 26.
34. Ibid, p. 26.
35. 'The new tsars and the degeneration of the CPSU', *Xinhua News Bulletin*, 16 May 1969.
36. 'A black line running through two dynasties', *Peking Review*, nos. 35–6, 7 September 1973, p. 42.
37. Zhou Enlai's report to the national congress of the CCP, ibid., nos 35–6, 7 September 1973, pp. 22–4.
38. Ibid, 23.
39. Out of approximately a hundred complete plants purchased by the Chinese between 1972 and mid-1975, only eight were American. For details, see Alexander Eckstein, 'China's trade policies', *Foreign Affairs*, no. 1, 1975.
40. 'China's foreign trade', *Current Scene*, no. 9, 1975; also see *Financial Times*, 3 December 1973.
41. Clyde H. Farnsworth, 'China with energy potential seeks goods, arms in Europe', *International Herald Tribune*, 12 November 1975.
42. The director of the defence intelligence agency of the Pentagon had in fact suggested that China's programme to redeploy ICBM's was called off in mid-1973, *International Herald Tribune*, 26 February 1976.
43. For details about China's air power, see International Institute for Strategic Studies, *Military Balance 1975–76*, London 1975.
44. *Renmin Ribao*, 13 September 1970. In an article that appeared in *Renmin Ribao* on 22 December 1969, Willy Brandt's *Ostpolitik* was characterized as a dirty affair.
45. Ibid.
46. *Washington Post*, 27 May 1973.
47. *Renmin Ribao*, 7 November 1973.
48. *Renmin Ribao*, 20 December 1973.
49. 'The Harmel Report'. *The Atlantic Community*, no. 6, Spring 1968, p. 115.

50. According to Soviet publications, Zhou Enlai threatened West European countries that they 'should not count on maintaining equally good relations with both China and with the Soviet Union', I. Alexeyer, 'Peking's Europe policy', *International Affairs*, no. 1, 1976. p. 61.

51. For details, see Hemen Ray, op. cit.; also see Jerzy Lukaszewski, 'La Chine et L'Europe de l'Est', *Le Monde*, 24 February 1972 and articles on China and Eastern Europe in *La Nouvelle Chine*, no. 8, 1970.

52. *Peking Review*, no. 11, 1969.

53. *Peking Review*, no. 51, 1975, p. 10.

54. Ibid.

55. In an interview with a Yugoslav editor, Zhou Enlai said 'we are far away from Europe and as you know one of our proverbs says 'distant waters cannot quench fire', cited in Joseph O. Kun, 'China and Eastern Europe', *Radio Free Europe Research*, no. 10, 1970.

56. *International Herald Tribune*, 28–9 September 1968.

57. Jerzy Lukaszevski, op. cit.

58. See *Peking Review*, 1969, 1970, 1971, and 1972.

59. *Peking Review*, no. 34, 1969, p. 13.

60. Ibid.

61. *Peking Review*, no. 52, 1970, p. 17.

62. Ibid, p. 17.

63. Ibid.

64. *Peking Review*, no. 31, 30 July 1971, pp. 18–19.

65. Hemen Ray, *China and Eastern Europe*, New Delhi, Radiant Publishers, 1988.

66. The two countries also collaborated in the construction of a small military plane.

67. Ghita Ionescu, *The Break-up of the Soviet Empire in Eastern Europe*, London, Penguin Books, 1965, p. 140.

68. For details, see Elez Biberaj, *Albania and China: A Study of Unequal Alliance*, Boulder, Westview, 1986.

69. Ibid.

70. For example, see the texts of messages and speeches on the Twenty-sixth anniversary of Albania's liberation, *Peking Review*, no. 49, 1970.

71. Enver Hoxa, *Reflexions sur la Chine*, vol. I, op. cit., p. 476.

72. For details, see next chapter.

73. For background details, see *Yugoslav Survey Quarterly*, no. 1, February 1972.

74. A Yugoslav commercial delegation headed by the deputy chairman of the Federal Chamber of Economy, Stojan Milenkovic, paid a visit to China from 26 October to 3 November 1970, ibid.

75. See Peter Cheng, *A Chronology of the People's Republic of China from October 1, 1949*, Totowa, NJ, Littlefield Adams, 1972.

76. *The Times*, 16 June 1971.

77. Ibid.

78. *Peking Review*, no. 25, 1971, p. 5.

79. Ibid., p. 4.

80. Ibid., pp. 17–18.
    Also see *Yugoslav Survey Quarterly*, no. 1, February 1972.

81. Enver Hoxa, vol. 1, op. cit.

82. For background information, see Paul Lendras, 'The taboos are breaking', *Financial Times*, 24 June 1971; also see Dan Morgan, 'The Balkan geopolitical potpourri', *International Herald Tribune*, 30 August 1971; F. Stephen Larrabee, *Balkan Security*, Adelphi Papers No. 135, London, The International Institute for Strategic Studies, 1977.

83. See 'Changing perspectives on the Balkans', *Radio Free Europe Research*, East Europe Bulgaria 31, 9 December 1971.
84. *Le Figaro*, 27 January 1976; *Le Monde*, 6 February 1976; *International Herald Tribune*, 7–8 February 1976.
85. Ibid.
86. *Xinhua News Bulletin*, 29 July 1971, p. 10.
87. Cited in Hemen Ray, op. cit., p. 157.
88. *Peking Review*, no. 20, 1971; and no. 23, 1972.
89. Jin Guping 'Sovereignty and independence of Balkan countries brook no encroachment', *Peking Review* No. 43, 1974, p. 19.
90. For partial texts of these articles, see *Radio Free Europe Research*, East Europe, Bulgaria 31, 9 December 1971, p. 5.
91. Interview granted to foreign policy editor of Zagreb daily *Vjesnik*, 28 August 1971; partial text in *Radio Free Europe Research Communist Area*, Yugoslavia Foreign Relations, 2 September 1971.
92. *Peking Review*, nos 35 and 36, 1973, p. 22.
93. Ibid., p. 24.
94. Ibid., p. 22.
95. For details see Harish Kapur, *China and the European Community: The New Connection*, Dordrecht, Martinus Nijhoff, 1985.
96. *Peking Review*, nos 35 and 36, 1973, p. 22.
97. Liu Suinian and Wu Oungan, op. cit., p. 346.
98. At the third and fourth National People's Congresses, Zhou Enlai proposed to modernize agriculture, industry, national defence, science and technology.
99. *Peking Review*, no. 23, 1971, p. 11.
100. *Peking Review*, no. 11, 1973, p. 3.
101. Ibid., no. 11, 1972, p. 3.
102. *Le Monde*, 12 July 1972.
103. See Helmut Schmidt, *Des puissances et des hommes*, Paris, Plon, 1987.
104. For background information, see Harish Kapur, *China and the EEC: The New Connection*, Dordrecht, Martinus Nijhoff, 1986.
105. According to British sources by March 1971, the Chinese had discreetly expressed the wish to establish diplomatic relations with the Economic Community. See M.J. de Saint-Blanquat, 'La République populaire de Chine face à l'Europe', *Revue de Marché commun*, no. 155, 1972.
106. *Peking Review*, no. 23, 1971, p. 23.
107. Ibid., no. 24, 11 June 1971, p. 15; according to an article in a Soviet publication in 1971, Zhou Enlai characterized the Common Market as a 'first step towards independence', V. Pavlov, 'Europe in Peking's Plans', *International Affairs*, no. 3, March 1972.
108. *Peking Review*, no. 27, 1971, p. 36.
109. *Peking Review*, no. 23, 1971, p. 23.
110. Zhou Enlai's interview with Neville Maxwell, *Sunday Times*, 5 December 1971.
111. *Peking Review*, no. 29, 1974.
112. Agreement between the Community and forty-six countries of Africa, the Caribbean and the Pacific, signed in February 1975.
113. *Peking Review*, no. 51, 1975.
114. Personal notes.
115. *Frankfurter Allgemeine Zeitung*, 13 January 1973.
116. *Le Monde*, 3 October 1973.
117. *Information*, no. 168, 1978.
118. For details, see Harish Kapur, *China and the EEC*, op. cit.

119. Harry Hamm, 'Peking und die Europaische Wirtschaftsgemeinschaft', *Frankfurter Allegemaine Zeitung*, 3 November 1973, p. 4.
120. *Avanti*, 20 November 1971.
121. *Le Monde*, 11 January 1973.
122. Cited in *Le Monde*, 15 June 1973.
123. C.L. Sulzberger, 'From China with love', *International Herald Tribune*, 5 February 1973.
124. See Foreign Minister Huang Hua's speech to the Thirty–third session of the UN General Assembly; *Renmin Ribao*, 10 October 1978.
125. *Peking Review*, no. 42, 1972.
126. Reporting on the Nixon–Heath talks of February 1973, the *Peking Review*, for example, quoted both leaders' statements that 'economic rivalry between the US and the Common Market must not be allowed to weaken Atlantic solidarity on the eve of major east-west negotiations'; Ibid., no. 6, 9 February 1973, p. 21; for similar declarations to US Congressional leaders in July 1972, see L. Bartalits and Jan H. Groenen, 'The People's Republic of China and Western Europe', in F. von Geusau Alting (ed.), *The External Relations of the European Community: Perspectives, Policies and Responses*, Farnborough, Hants, Saxon House, 1974.
127. Cited from an article in *Le Monde*, 22 April 1975.
128. *International Herald Tribune*, 1–2 November 1975.
129. *Issues and Studies*, June 1974.
130. *Peking Review*, nos. 35 and 36, 1973, p. 23.
131. For details, see Angela Stent, *From Embargo to Ostpolitik: The Political Economy of West Germany–Soviet Relations 1955–1980*, Cambridge, Cambridge University Press, 1982.
132. See joint statement in *New Times*, no. 8, February 1975.
133. *Peking Review*, nos. 35–6, 1973, p. 23.
134. Ibid., p. 22.
135. *International Herald Tribune*, 6 September 1973.
136. Joint editorial of *People's Daily, Red Flag, Liberation Army Daily* on 1 January 1970, full text in *Peking Review*, no. 1, 2 January 1970.
137. From the speech by Qiao Guanhua, head of the Chinese delegation to the Twenty-eighth session of the UN General Assembly on 2 October 1973, text in *Peking Review*, no. 40, 5 October 1973, p. 12.
138. Liu Suinian and Wu Qungan, *China's Socialist Economy: An Outline History, 1949–1984*, Beijing, Beijing Review, 1986, p. 375.
139. Ibid.
140. See Bernard D. Nossiter, 'China pay policy may spur deals with West', *International Herald Tribune*, 19 January 1973.
141. For details on Sino–British relations, see Robert Boardman, *Britain and the People's Republic of China 1949–1974*, London, Macmillan, 1976.
142. *Peking Review*, no. 9, 1973.
143. Full text of the communiqué in *Peking Review*, no. 11, 1972, p. 3.
144. See the Communiqué, ibid.
145. See *Peking Review*, No. 27, 1971; No. 46, 1971, and No. 50, 1971.
146. Ibid, p. 28.
147. C.L. Sulzberger, op. cit.
148. *Far Eastern Economic Review*, 18 November 1972, p. 9.
149. For details, see *China Topics*, 16 August 1972.
150. For details, see Derek Davies, 'Royle Progress', *Far Eastern Economic Review*, 10 June 1972.
151. Ibid., p. 20.

152. *Peking Review*, No. 24, 1973.
153. *Time*, 23 April 1973, p. 12.
154. Ibid.
155. *Financial Times*, 7 March 1973.
156. *New Times*, no. 8, February 1975.
157. Ibid., p. 25.
158. Ibid., p. 25.
159. *Xinhua News Bulletin*, 26 May 1974.
160. Ibid., 21 April 1974, p. 10.

Chapter 8

1. *The Times*, 16 September 1977.
2. 'Chairman Mao's theory of the differentiation of the three worlds is a major contribution to Marxism–Leninism', *Peking Review*, no. 45, 4 November 1977.
3. Ibid., 22 May 1978, p. 10.
4. Michel Tatu, 'M. Deng propose à Washington la formation d'une coalition', see *Le Monde*, 30 January 1979; also see James Reston, 'When strangers meet', *International Herald Tribune*, 1 February 1979.
5. From an article that a Japanese paper, *Jinmin Shimbun*, published on Mao's 'three world' strategy and published by the Hsinhua News Agency; partial text in Fedor Burlatsky, *Mao Tse-Tung: An Ideological and Psychological Portrait*, Moscow, Progress Publishers, 1980, p. 355–6.
6. Jin Guping, 'The Munich tragedy and contemporary appeasement', *Peking Review*, no. 50, 9 December 1977.
7. Ibid.
8. Ibid.
9. See Roy Medevedev's article in *Moscow News*, reproduced in *Hindustan Times*, 10 October 1988.
10. *Peking Review*, 10 September 1978, p. 10.
11. Paul Lendvai, 'China's second front in Europe', *Financial Times*, 1 September 1978.
12. Josip Broz Tito, 'De bonnes relations avec tous les pays sans egard aux differences', *Questions Actuelles du Socialisme*, nos. 11–12, November–December 1976.
13. *Xinhua News Bulletin*, 30 August 1977, p. 30.
14. Mihajlo Saranovic, 'La Chine entre elle-même et le monde', *Questions Actuelles du Socialisme*, no. 9, September 1978, p. 12.
15. Mention is made to Tass attack in an article by the 'Commentator' in the *Renmin Ribao*, 13 September 1978; full text in *Renmin Ribao*, no. 38, 22 September 1978.
16. See Paul Lendvai, op. cit.
17. *Peking Review*, no. 38, 1978, p. 10.
18. From Tito speech at the Banquet, text in *Xinhua News Bulletin*, 30 August 1977, p. 44.
19. Josip Broz Tito, op. cit., p. 4.
20. From Huo Guofeng banquet speech during Tito's visit to Beijing, full text in *Xinhua News Bulletin*, 30 August 1977, p. 39.
21. Text of the speech in *Background in China*, 26 December 1977, p. 20.
22. Hemen Ray, *China and Eastern Europe*; New Delhi, Radiant Publishers, 1988.
23. *Peking Review*, 20 August 1978, p. 13.
24. *Ji Dengkuei*'s report on Hua's visit to Yugoslavia to the Standing Committee of the National People's Congress on 15 September 1978, *Peking Review*, no. 38, 22 September 1978, p. 4.

25. Paul Lendvai, op. cit.
26. *Peking Review*, no. 38, 1978.
27. For details, see Nina Halpern, 'Learning From Abroad', *Modern China*, no. 1 January 1985.
28. Ibid.
29. Roger Garside, *Coming Alive: China After Mao*, New York, Mentor, 1982.
30. Mihajlo Saranovic, op. cit.
31. For details, see Enver Hoxa, *Reflections on China*, Vol. II, 1973–1977, Tirana, the '8 Nentovi' Publishing House, 1979.
32. Ibid., p. 544.
33. Partial text in Biberaj, *Albania and China: A Study of Unequal Alliance*, Boulder, Westview, 1986, pp. 126–8.
34. Ibid.
35. Ibid.
36. Ibid.
37. *Peking Review*, no. 21 1978, p. 23.
38. *Le Monde*, 29 September 1977.
39. Cited in ibid.
40. Cited in ibid.
41. Cited in ibid.
42. *Renmin Ribao*, 29 January 1977.
43. Ji Jing 'The reform of the economic system in Hungary', *Economic Management*, no. 6, 1979 (in Chinese); also see Du Liwei and Wei Yunlang, 'Hungary's reform of the price system and price adjustment', *Economic Management*, no. 11, 1979 (in Chinese).
44. Li Shuhua, 'The historical background and the main contents of the new economic system being carried out in Hungary', *World Economy*, no. 12, 1979 (in Chinese).
45. Interview granted to *Le Figaro*, 3 November 1976, *Renmin Ribao*, 1 May 1978.
46. Cited in G. Apalin and U. Mityoyev, *Militarism in Peking's Policies*, Moscow, Progress Publishers, 1980.
47. *Frankfurter Allgemeine Zeitung*, 28 September 1978.
48. S.K. Ghosh, 'Debate on military modernization in China', *News Review on China, Mongolia and the Koreas*, February 1977, pp. 65–7.
49. Ibid, p. 66.
50. See CIA Foreign Assessment Center, *Chinese Defense Spending*, Washington DC, CIA, July 1980.
51. For details, see David L. Shambourg, 'China's Quest for Military Modernization', *Asian Affairs: An American Review*, no. 5, May–June 1979.
52. Chine Vice Foreign Minister Yu Qian announced Chinese intention to purchase arms through an interview with Italian newspaper *Il Populo*; this interview was carried by *Manichi Daily News*, 19 June 1978. Deng made a similar statement to retired Japanese military officers visiting Beijing, *International Herald Tribune*, 24 October 1977. According to press reports, in his meeting with Woerner, the president of the German Bundestag's Defence Commission, Deng declared that 'arrangements' to this effect could be made with the industrialized countries. See *Le Monde*, 2–3 October 1977.
53. *New York Times*, 1 March 1978; *International Herald Tribune*, 24 October 1977; *Japan Times*, 7 May 1978; *Manichi Daily News*, 19 June 1978.
54. Victor Zorza, 'Peking Debates European Option'. *International Herald Tribune*, 21 December 1977.
55. Secretary of State Cyrus Vance's remarks on 4 March 1978 on the eve of his departure for China, *News Review on China, Mongolia and the Koreas*, March 1977. p. 20.

56. In fact, a precedent had already been established by the US sale of satellite installations that had been arranged for Nixon's visit; see Edith Lenort, 'China sets sale precedent', *Far Eastern Economic Review*, 18 March 1972.

57. William T. Tow and Douglas T. Stuart, 'China's military turns to the West', *International Affairs*, Spring 1981.

58. *Sunday Times*, 18 December 1977.

59. Ibid.

60. *Le Monde*, 26 June 1978.

61. *Neue Zürcher Zeitung*, 22 June 1978.

62. Frederick Bennett, *La Chine et la sécurité européenne*, Paris, Western European Union, 1978, p. 14.

63. Assembly of Western European Union, *China and European Security*: A report submitted on behalf of the General Affairs Committee by Mr Caro, Rapporteur, Document Paris: Western European Union, 1983.

64. Ibid, p. 4.

65. Ibid, p. 4.

66. *Le Monde*, 20 June 1978.

67. Ibid.

68. Apalin and Mityoyev, op. cit., p. 222.

69. *Observer*, 3 September 1978.

70. Tow and Stuart, op. cit.; also see James Callaghan, *Time and Change*, London, Fontana, 1988.

71. *Statesman*, 18 October 1978.

72. Ibid.

73. *Financial Times*, 24 November 1978.

74. Ibid.

75. James Callaghan wrote in his memoirs that this question was discussed at the Guadaloupe summit meeting in January 1968 (West Germany, Great Britain, the United States, France) and they all agreed that 'we should send similar replies to Brezhnev making clear that improving our lines with China did not imply that we were "playing the China card" against the Soviet Union', op. cit., p. 530.

76. *Observer*, 3 September 1978.

77. Ibid.

78. *Le Monde*, 5 May 1978.

79. James Callaghan, op. cit., p. 530.

80. For details see Harish Kapur, *China and the EEC: The New Connection*, Dordrecht, Martinus Nijhoff, 1986.

81. Ibid., p. 93.

82. Commission des Communautés Européennes, *Proposition d'un règlement (CEE) du Conseil relatif au régime commun applicable aux importations en provenance de la République populaire de Chine*, Com., 78396 final, 3 July 1978.

83. European Parliament Working Document, 198, 1978.

84. *Journal officiel des Communautés Européennes*, Législation L345, 31 December 1979.

85. For details, see 'The European Communities scheme for Generalized Preferences', *European Information External Relations* 18, March 1970.

Chapter 9

1. For details, see Eugene Pillsbury, 'Peace, disarmament, security: view from Beijing', *World Marxist Review*, no. 5, 1988, pp. 74–80.

2. The text of Hu Yaobang's report that dealt specifically with China's foreign policy appeared in *China and the World*, no. 3, 1983, Beijing Review, Foreign Affairs series.

3. Deng Xiaoping, *Fundamental Issues in Present-Day China*, Beijing, Foreign Languages Press, 1987, p. 3.
4. For the text of his speech, see *China and the World*, op. cit, p. 19.
5. This was a report named after the Belgian foreign minister which was submitted to NATO; for the full text of the report, see 'Harmel Report', *The Atlantic Community Quarterly*, no. 6, Spring 1968.
6. Ibid., p. 115.
7. Cited by Michael Parks, 'March away from Maoism troubling China's military', *International Herald Tribune*, 2 December 1980.
8. Jean Daubier, 'La Chine et l'URSS peuvent-elles modifier leurs relations?'*Le Monde Diplomatique*, June 1980.
9. For texts of these articles, see *The Polemic on the General Line of the International Communist Movement*, op. cit.
10. *Renmin Ribao*, 2 April 1980.
11. Wang Shuzhong, 'The post-war international system' in Harish Kapur (ed.) *As China Sees the World*, London, Pinter, 1987.
12. One of the recent examples was the dispatching of a ministerial delegation to Europe in 1989 to consult experts about how to handle China's rising inflation.
13. A. Doak Barnett, *The Making of Foreign Policy in China: Structure and Process*, Boulder, Westview, 1985.
14. For some details of his role see Harish Kapur, *China and the EEC: The New Connection*, Dordrecht, Martinus Nijhoff, 1986.
15. Personal notes.
16. David L. Shambaugh's review of Harish Kapur's *As China Sees the World*, in *China Quarterly*, 1988, p. 481.
17. Harish Kapur, op. cit.
18. Doak A. Barnett, op. cit.
19. Ibid.
20. Lucien W. Pye has argued that factionalism is less important in foreign affairs than in domestic affairs; see his *The Dynamics of Factions and Consensus in Chinese Politics: A Model and Some Propositions*, Santa Monica, Rand Corporation, 1980.
21. For some details regarding the functioning of the bureaucracy, see Kenneth Lieberthal and Michel Oksenberg, 'Understanding China's bureaucracy', *China Business Review*, November–December 1986.
22. 'Academia' is used in a broad sense to include persons attached to research institutes or to universities or to academic associations.
23. Personal notes.
24. *China Daily*, 17 September 1986.
25. Personal notes.
26. Deng Xiaoping, op. cit., p. 98.
27. Zhen Qimao, 'War and Peace: A Reappraisal', *Beijing Review*, No. 23, 1986.
28. For some details, see Zhou Zunnan, 'Theoretical basis for the adjustment of China's foreign policy', *Journal of Foreign Affairs*, no. 1, 1988 (in Chinese).
29. Deng Xiaoping, op. cit., p. 116.
30. Ibid., p. 69.
31. Speech by Zhao Ziyang to the Royal Institute of International Relations in Brussels on 5 June 1984; text in *Beijing Review*, no. 25, 1985, p. V.

Chapter 10

1. *China Daily*, 17 September, 1986.
2. The author had the opportunity of discussing Europe with many Chinese personalities from the academic world.

3. Ding Hong and Lao Guan, 'Resurgence of Western Europe' in Harish Kapur. *As China Sees the World*, op. cit., p. 62

4. Ibid.

5. Li Yiyan, *Soviet–European Relations under New World Situation* (unpublished paper written in 1987) p. 6.

6. Personal notes.

7. Ding Hong and Zhang Baoxing, *Opportunity Policy and Role on Western Europe in Present-day World* (unpublished paper written in 1987).

8. This expression was often used by Chinese scholars in their discussion with the author.

9. See *World Affairs* (in Chinese), No. 16, 1986.

10. Deng Xiaoping, 'Europe—a force for maintaining peace', *Beijing Review*, no. 2, 1988, p. 14.

11. Dai Yannian and She Duanzhi, 'Hungary: 20 years on', ibid., no, 39, 1988.

12. Michael Parks, 'China starting to renew links with East European countries', *International Herald Tribune*, 16 March 1983.

13. Deng Xiaoping, *Selected Works* (1975–1982), Beijing Foreign Languages Press, 1984, p. 300.

14. Ibid., p. 301.

15. *Le Monde*, 4 May 1983.

16. See Hu Yaobang's news conference on 11 May 1983; text in *Beijing Review*, no. 21, 1983, p. 16.

17. Michael Parks, op. cit.

18. China's vice-premier, Chi Pengfei, declared in an interview that 'recent experience in Poland has been an important lesson for us', ibid.

19. *China Aktuell*, December 1980.

20. *Beijing Gingnianbao*, 1 January, 1980, p. 11.

21. *Xinhua News Bulletin*, April 1981, p. 10.

22. *Renmin Ribao*, 16 June 1981.

23. *Beijing Review*, 28 September 1981.

24. See *Xinhua News Bulletin*, 16, 19 and 21 December 1981.

25. Manuel Lucbert, 'Pekin paraît accepter le fait accompli', *Le Monde*. 8 October 1982.

26. *Beijing Review*, 20 January 1986, pp. 12–13.

27. Daniel Southerland, 'Deng hails Poland's handling of dissent', *International Herald Tribune*, 27 February 1987.

28. Xu Xing, 'Le vent qui vient de Pologne', *Le Monde*, 12 July 1981.

29. Ibid.

30. Zhang Zeyu, 'China–Eastern Europe trade expansion', *Beijing Review*, ibid., no. 22, 1987.

31. *China Daily*, 19 February 1988.

32. Ibid.

33. *Beijing Review*, no. 22, 1987.

34. *Renmin Ribao* November 1987. For details, see 'Major lessons from East European reforms', *International Studies* (in Chinese).

35. Zhang Zeyu, op. cit.

36. *Beijing Review*, 29 June 1987, p. 15.

37. *Beijing Review*, 1988, p. 10.

38. Guo Fengmin, 'Basic ideas behind the foreign policies of West European countries', ibid., no. 5, 1982.

39. Ding Hong and Zhang Baoxiang, 'Opportunity, Policy and Role: on Western Europe's Role in Present-day World', paper written in 1987, Beijing, China Institute of Contemporary International Relations, 1987, p. 2.

40. Qian Nengxin, 'Western Europe's role in US–Soviet rivalry', *Beijing Review*, no. 31, 1986, p. 18.
41. Ji Yin, 'Western Europe: its foreign policy', *Beijing Review*, no. 2; 1984.
42. Ibid., p. 31.
43. Ibid, p. 31.
44. *Europe Information External Relations*, No. 76 1984, p. 6.
45. European Commission of the European Communities, 'The Reform of China's Foreign Trade System', Brussels, 27 July 1982.
46. *Europlats, General Report*, Mission to the PRC 14–13 October 1982, Brussels 1982.
47. *Activités: CEE–Chine en 1983*, Brussels, 1982.
48. *Europe Information*, External Relations No. 90/88, Brussels, March 1988.
49. Christian Tyler, 'China opts for business by degree', *Financial Times*, 8 March 1985.
50. For details about cooperation in the energy sector, see *Energy: Cooperation with China: A Contract Based on Trust with Tangible Results*, memo 70/87, Brussels, 18 June, 1987.
51. Directorate General for Committee and Interparliamentary European Delegations, *European Parliament Delegation for Relations with the National People's Congress of the People's Republic of China*, 2nd meeting report, 28 October 1981, DOC PE 75–240, p. 24.
52. Ibid., Doc 75–751 Bur/Ann, p. 1.
53. *Débats du Parlement européen*, 14 March 1979.
54. *European Communities, European Parliament Working Documents*, 1983–1984. Document I–1345 (1983), p. 29.
55. Ibid., p. 30.
56. Ibid., p. 30.
57. Ibid., 1987–1988, Document A2–56/87, 18 May, 1987, pp. 6, 13.
58. Ibid., Document I–1345 (1983).
59. Qiu Shiguan, 'On Sino-EC Trade and Economic Relations', 1988, unpublished paper, p. 1.
60. Yao Jingtang 'EEC ranks as biggest technology supplier', *China Daily*, 10 November 1987.
61. This was confirmed by major agreements concluded in September 1984 and March 1985 with Volkswagen and Peugeot for the production of automobiles in China. Though economic considerations were not absent while concluding these accords, the Chinese were none the less—according to *The Economist*—'anxious to link themselves with a European manufacturer because of the fear of becoming too dependent on the Japanese' (*The Economist*, 2 March 1985).
62. Qu Yingbo, 'EEC helps with Dairy development', *China Daily*, 25 November 1987.
63. Qiu Shiguan, op. cit.
64. *The reform of China's Foreign Trade System*, op. cit., p. 3.
65. Personal notes.
66. Li Shude, 'China–EEC economic and trade relations', *China's Foreign Trade*, no. 1, 1983, p. 11.
67. Jean Riboud, 'La gauche et le declin de l'Europe: Cassandre dans le vieux monde', *Le Monde*, 26 February 1985.
68. Commission of the European Communities, *Conclusion des négociations textiles CEE/Chine*, IP84 135, 5 April 1985.
69. For the text of the treaty, see *Official Journal of the European Communities*, L 380 vol. 31, 31 December 1988, Luxemburg 1988.
70. *Trade and Economic Cooperation Agreement between the European Economic Community and the People's Republic of China*, Brussels, 1984, p. 3.
71. *Mesures de défense commerciale prises à l'egard de la Chine*, Brussels, 29 October 1982.

72. Commission of the European Communities, *Proposal for a Council Regulation (EEC)*, *no. Com. (88)*, 256 final Brussels, 1988; *China Trade and Economic Newsletter*, no. 331, 1984.
73. For details, see Harish Kapur, *China and the EEC: The New Connection*, Dordrecht, Martinus Nijhoff 1986.
74. *Beijing Review*, no. 1, January 1985, p. 6.
75. Li Yiyan *et al*, 'Main West European Nations: Policies, Measures and their impact on disarmament', *Contemporary International Relations*, no. 1, 1988, p. 10 (in Chinese).
76. Ran Longbo, 'The Peace Movement in Western Europe', *West European Studies*, no. 1, 1986, p. 5.
77. Zhen Qimao, 'War and peace: a reappraisal', *Beijing Review*, no. 23, 1986, p. 10.
78. *Frankfurter Allgemeine Zeitung*, 31 July 1972.
79. See Andrew J. Pierre (ed.), *The Conventional Defense of Europe: New Technologies and New Strategies*, New York, Council on Foreign Relations, 1986.
80. Helmut Schmidt, *Des Puissances et des hommes*, Paris, Plon, 1988, p. 345.
81. This point is stressed in a sixty-page report presented to the government after a top-level review of Bonn's European policy; for details, see *International Herald Tribune*, 1 December 1975.
82. Jacques Guilleme Brulon, 'RFA, clé de l'Europe', *Le Figaro*, 4–5 February 1984.
83. For details, see 'China's Big European Friend', *Intertrade*, July 1987.
84. *Summary of World Broadcasts*, FF WOO 27, A/13 25 May, 1988.
85. 'Volkswagen in Shanghai', *New China Quarterly*, January 1987.
86. Ying Chenxiao and Jin Fulai, 'Beijing's four-wheel drive', *South*, November 1988.
87. For details, see *China Reconstructs*, April 1989.
88. *International Herald Tribune*, 7–8 August 1987.
89. *China Trade Report* December 1983.
90. Ibid.
91. Li Shude, 'China's Stronghold in Western Europe', *Intertrade*, April 1986, p. 27.
92. *China Daily*, 9 September 1987, p. 1.
93. Ibid., 11 July 1988.
94. Hao Qi, 'In Good Faith', *Intertrade*, July 1987, p. 16.
95. Ibid.
96. Wan Shuya, 'US differs with West Germany on Major Defence Issues', *Beijing Review*, no. 34, 1989, p. 10.
97. Zhu Weige, 'Current Policy of the Federal Republic of China', *International Studies* no. 3, 1989 (in Chinese).
98. Li Yiyan, 'Soviet–European Relations under New World Situation' (1987), unpublished paper, p. 8.
99. Pan Qichang, 'On the Godesberg Programme of the Social Democratic Party of Germany', *West European Studies*, November 1988.
100. Ibid., p. 89.
101. Ibid.
102. For details on the SPD policies, see Matthew A. Weiller, 'SPD Security Policy', *Survival*, November–December 1988.
103. *Xinhua News Bulletin*, 22 November 1985.
104. Ibid., p. 20.

Epilogue

1. Commission of the European Communities, *Press Release*, 1P(89) 1989.
2. Ibid.
3. *Le Monde*, 26 September 1989.

Bibliography

Official and semi-official documents

China

Foreign Languages Press
On the Historical Experience of the Dictatorship of the Proleteriat, Beijing, 1956.
More on the Historical Experience of the Dictatorship of the Proleteriate, Beijing, 1957.
In Refutation of Modern Revisionism, Beijing, 1958.
Long Live Leninism, Beijing, 1960.
Prolétaires de tous les pays unissons-nous contre l'ennemi commun, Beijing, 1963.
The Polemic on the General Line of Soviet–US Collaboration pursued by the leaders of the CPSU, Beijing, 1965.
Struggle against Imperialism and Revisionism to the Very End: A Collection of Documents from the Visit to China of the Albanian Party and Government Delegation, Beijing, 1966.
The Tenth National Congress of the Communist Party of China, Documents, Beijing, 1973.
Resolution on CPC History (1949–81), Chinese Document, Beijing, 1981.
The Twelfth National Congress of the Communist Party of China, (1982), Beijing, 1982.
The Second Session of the Sixth National People's Congress (May 1984), *Main Documents*, Beijing, 1984.
Documents of the Thirteenth National Congress of the Communist Party of China (1987), Beijing, 1987.

Commission of the European Communities

'The People's Republic of China and the European Community', *Europe Information, External Relations*, Nos 106 (1975), 168 (1978), 13 (1978), 17 (1979), 42 (1981), 79 (1985), 90 (1988).
EC–China. A Statistical Analysis of Foreign Trade, Brussels, 1981.
The Reform of China's Foreign Trade System, July 1982, Brussels, 1982.

European Parliament

'Relations between EEC and the People's Republic of China', Debates of the European Parliament, *Official Journal of the European Communities*, Nos C157 (July 1975), 219 (July 1977), 233 (September 1978), 239 (February 1979), 243 (May 1979), 245 (September 1979), 284 (April 1982), 313/254 (April 1984), A–2–56/87 (May 1987).

Great Britain

Foreign Office File (FO) 371/110195 from Humphrey Trevelyan in Beijing to Foreign Office on 24 July 1954.
FO 371/110216 from Humphrey Trevelyan in Beijing to Foreign Office on 31 August 1954.
FO 371/110216 from Humphrey Trevelyan in Beijing to Foreign Office on 20 October 1954.
FO 371/110216 from Foreign Office to Sir R. Scott at British Embassy in Washington, 24 November 1954.

FO 371/110216 from Desmond Donnelly to Foreign Office, 27 November 1954.
FO 371/110247 from British Embassy in Beijing to Foreign Office, 20 August 1954.
FO 371/122626 from O'Neill in Beijing to Foreign Office, 27 February 1956.
FO 371/122626 Foreign Office minutes, 12 March 1956.
FO 371/122626 from C.T. Crowe in Beijing to Foreign Office, 13 March 1956.
FO 371/133344 from A.D. Wilson to Foreign Office, 10 December 1957.

West European Union

Assemblée de l'union de l'Europe occidentale, *La Chine et la sécurité européenne* (Report submitted on behalf of the General Affairs Committee by Frederick Bennet), Document 770, 16 May 1978, Paris, 1978.
Assembly of West European Union, *China and European Security* (Report submitted on behalf of the General Affairs Committee by Caro), Document 945, 18 May 1983, Paris, 1983.

Memoirs, autobiographies and collected works

Callaghan, James, *Time and Chance*, Glasgow, Collins, 1987.
Deng Xiaoping, *Selected Works of Deng Xiaoping 1975–1982*, Beijing, Foreign Languages Press, 1984.
—— *Fundamental Issues in Present-day China*, Beijing, Foreign Languages Press, 1987.
Eden, Anthony, *Memoirs* 3 vols, London, Cassell, 1960–5.
Gaulle, Charles de, *Discours et messages: Pour l'effort août 1962 décembre 1965*, Paris, Plon, 1966.
Hoxa, Enver, *Reflections on China*, 2 vols, 1962–77, Tirana, The '8 Nentori' Publishing House, 1979.
Kissinger, Henry, *White House Years*, Boston, Little Brown, 1979.
Khrushchev, Nikita, *Khrushchev Remembers*, 2 vols, New York, Bantam Books, 1971; vol. 2, London, Penguin Books, 1977.
Macciocchi, Maria-Antonietta, *Deux mille ans de bonheur*, Paris, Grasset, 1983.
Malraux, André, *Antimémoires*, Paris, Gallimard, 1967.
Manac'h, Etienne M., *Memoires d'extrême Asie: Une traversée de puissances invisibles Chine–Indochine 1972–1973*, Paris, Fayard, 1982.
Mao Zedong, *Selected Works of Mao Zedong*, Peking, Foreign Languages Press, 1965–70, 5 vols.
Mendès-France, Pierre, *Oeuvres complètes III—Gouverner c'est choisir 1945–1955*, Paris, Gallimard, 1986.
Micunovic, Veljko, *Journées de Moscou 1956–1958—Un ambassadeur de Tito au Kremlin*. Paris, Robert Lafont, 1979.
Schmidt, Helmut, *Des puissances et des hommes*, Paris, Plon, 1988.
Schröder, Gerhard, *Mission ohne Auftrag: Die Vorbereitung der Diplomatischen Beziehungen Zwischen Bonn und Peking* , Bergisch Gladbach, Lubbe, 1988.
Trevelyan, Humphrey, *Worlds Apart: China 1953–55 Soviet Union 1962–65.* London, Macmillan, 1971.
Zhou Enlai, *Selected Works of Zhou Enlai Volume I*, Beijing, Foreign Languages Press, 1981.
Wu Xiuauan, *Eight years in the Ministry of Foreign Affairs (January 1950–October 1958) Memoirs of a Diplomat*, Beijing: New World Press 1985.

Studies

General

Armstrong, J.D., *Revolutionary Diplomacy: Chinese Foreign Policy and the United Front Doctrine*, Berkeley, University of California Press, 1977.

Ahn, Byung-Joon, *Chinese Politics and the Cultural Revolution, Dynamics of Policy Processes*, Seattle, University of Washington Press, 1979.

Apalin, G. and U. Mityayer, *Militarism in Peking's Policies*, Moscow, Progress Publishers, 1980.

Barnett, Doak A., *The Making of Foreign Policy in China: Structure and Process*, Colorado, Westview Press, 1985.

—— China's Economy in Global Perspective, Washington DC, The Brookings Institution, 1981.

Camilleri, Joseph, *Chinese Foreign Policy: The Maoist Era and its Aftermath*, Oxford, Martin Robertson, 1980.

Chang, Paris, *Power and Policy in China*, University Park, Pennsylvania State University Press, 1975.

Cheng, Peter, *A Chronology of the People's Republic of China from October 1, 1949*, Totowa, NJ, Littlefied, Adams and Co., 1972.

Cottrell, Robert (ed.), *Tiananmen: The Rape of Peking*, London, The Independent 1989.

Eckstein, Alexander, *Communist China's Economic Growth and Foreign Trade: Implications for U.S. Policy*, New York, McGraw-Hill, 1966.

Etiemble, *L'Europe chinoise* vols I and II, Paris, Gallimard, 1988 and 1989.

Fang, Percy Jucheng and Lucy Guinong J. Fang, *Zhou Enlai: A Profile*, Beijing Foreign Languages Press, 1986.

Faure, Edgar, *Le Serpent et la tortue: les problèmes de la Chine populaire*, Paris, Julliard, 1957.

Fejtö, François, *Chine–URSS*, 1950–66, 2 vols, Paris, Plon, 1956 and 1964.

Feng-Hwa Mah, *The Foreign Trade of Mainland China*, Edinburgh, Edinburgh University Press, 1972.

Franz, Uli, *Deng Xiaoping: biography*, Paris, Compagnie 12, FIXOT, 1989.

Garside, Roger, *Coming Alive: China after Mao*, New York, Mentor, 1982.

Halpern, A.M. (ed.), *Policies towards China: Views from Six Continents*, New York, McGraw-Hill, 1965.

Hollander, Paul, *Political Pilgrims: Travels of Western Intellectuals to the Soviet Union, China and Cuba 1928–1978*, Oxford, Oxford University Press, 1981.

Hsüch Chün-Tu, *China's Foreign Relations: New Perspectives*, New York, Praeger, 1982.

Huck, Arthur, *The Security of China*, New York, Columbia University Press, 1970.

Joyaux, François, *La Chine et le règlement du premier conflit d'Indochine, Genève, 1954*, Paris, Sorbonne, 1979.

Ness, Peter Van, *Revolution and Chinese Foreign Policy: Peking's support for Wars of National Liberation*, Berkeley, University of California Press, 1971.

Ojha, Ishwer C., *Chinese Foreign Policy in an Age of Transition: The Diplomacy of Cultural Despair*, Boston, The Beacon Press, 1969.

Passin, Herbert, *China's Cultural Diplomacy*, London, The China Quarterly, 1962.

Peyrefitte, Alain, *Quand la Chine s'éveillera: regards sur la voie chinoise*, Paris, Fayard, 1973.

Pye, Lucien W., *The Dynamics of Factions and Consensus in Chinese Politics: A Model and some Propositions*, Santa Monica, The Rand Corporation, 1980.

—— The Dynamics of Chinese Politics, Cambridge, Mass, Oelgeschlager, Gunn and Hain, 1981.

Kapur, Harish, *The Awakening Giant: China's Ascension in World Politics*, Alphen aan den

Rijn, Sijthoff and Noordhof, 1981.
_____ *China and the EEC: The New Connection*, Dordrecht, Martinus Nijhoff Publishers, 1986.
_____ *As China Sees the World: Perception of Chinese Scholars*, London, Pinter, 1987.
Kardelj, Edvard, *Le socialisme et la guerre: au sujet de la critique chinoise de la politique de coexistence*, Belgrade, Maison d'édition Jugoslavija, 1960.
Karol, K.S., *La Chine de Mao: l'autre communisme*, Paris, Robert Lafont, 1966.
Lee, Ching Hua, *Deng Xiaoping: The Marxist Road to the Forbidden City*, Princeton, The Kingston Press, 1985.
Liu Suinian and Wu Qungan (eds), *China's Socialist Economy: An Outline History (1949–1984)*, Beijing, Beijing Review, 1986.
MacFarquhar, Roderick, *The Origins of the Cultural Revolution*, 2 vols, Oxford University Press, 1974 and 1983.
Medvedev, Roy, *China and the Superpowers*, Oxford, Basil Blackwell, 1986.
Mehnert, Klaus, *Peking and the New Left: At Home and Abroad*, Berkeley, University of California, 1969.
Meyer, Eric, *Pékin: Place Tian an men*, le Méjan, Editions Actes Sud, 1989.
Mitterrand, François, *La Chine au défi*, Paris, Julliard, 1961.
Randle, Robert F., *Geneva 1954: The Settlement of the Indo-Chinese War*, Princeton, NJ, Princeton University Press, 1969.
Roy, Jules, *Le voyage en Chine*, Paris, Julliard, 1965.
Salisbury, Harrison E., *Tiananmen Diary: Thirteen Days in June*, London, Unwin Paperbacks, 1989.
Schram, Stuart R., *The Political Thought of Mao Tse-tung*, London, Penguin, 1969.
_____ (ed.) *Mao Tse-tung Unrehearsed: Talks and Letters 1956–1971*, London, Penguin, 1974.
Snow, Edgar, *Red China Today*, New York, Random House, 1970.
Wang Gungwu, *China and the world since 1949: The Impact of Independence, Modernity and Revolution*, London, Macmillan, 1977.
Yahuda, Michael, *Towards the End of Isolationism: China's Foreign Policy after Mao*, London, Macmillan, 1983.
Zagladin, V. (ed.), *Europe and Communists*, Moscow, Progress Publishers, 1977.
Zagoria, Donald, *The Sino–Soviet Conflict, 1956–1961*, Princeton, NJ, Princeton University Press, 1962.

Western Europe

Actafev. G.B. *et al.* (eds.). *Kitaii i Kapitalisticheskie strani europi*, Moscow, Izdatelctvo Nauka, 1976.
Belde, Klaus, *Das Bild der Bundesrepublik Deutschland in der Pekinger 'Volkszeitung'* (1949–1973), Hamburg, Helmut Buske Verlag, 1978.
Boardman, Robert. *Britain and the People's Republic of China 1949–1974*, London, Macmillan, 1976.
Claisse, Alain *et al.* Les relations entre la France et la République de chine 1945–1973 *La Documentation française, notes et études*, Paris, La Documentation Française, 1973.
Dever, Matthew Bedford, 'China, West Europe and Detente 1969–1984', MA thesis, University of Virginia (unpublished), 1985.
Ferraz, Gonzalo Bescos, *'La chine et l'Europe: théorie et pratique—La position chinoise à l'egard de l'Europe depuis 1949 jusqu'à la Révolution culturelle'*, diploma thesis, Graduate Institute of International Studies, Geneva, 1983 (unpublished).
Jacoviello, Alberto, *L'hyothèse chinoise*, Paris, Seuil, 1973.

Kux, Stephan, 'The Chinese Perception of West Europe 1960–1981: A content analysis of the People's Daily,' a thesis presented to obtain the graduate degree of the University of Zurich, 1982 (unpublished).

La Chine en construction, Chine–France: 20 ans d'échanges amicaux, Special Issue, 27 January 1984.

Luard, Evan, Britain and China, London, Chatto and Windus, 1962.

Majonica, Ernst, Bonn–Peking: Die Bezichungen der Bundesrepublik Deutschland zur Volkesrepublik, Stuttgart, W. Kohlhommer, 1971.

Porter, B.E., Britain and the Rise of Communist China: A Study of British Attitudes 1945–54, Oxford, Oxford University Press, 1967.

Ruediger, Machetzki. Deutsch–Chinesische Bezichungen Ein Handbuch, Hamburg, Institut fur Asienkunde, 1982.

Stahnke, Arthur A. (ed.), China's Trade with the West: A Political and Economic Analysis, New York, Praeger, 1972.

Stephenov, A.I., FRG i Kitaii, Moscow, Mezhdunavodnie Otnoshenia, 1974.

Eastern Europe

Biberaj, Elez, Albania and China: A Study of an Unequal Alliance, Boulder, Westview, 1986.

Brzezinski, Zbigniew. The Soviet Bloc: Unity, Conflict. New York, Praeger, 1961.

Fejto, François. Chine–URSS 1950–1966, Paris, Plon, 1964 and 1966. 2 vols.

Gosztony, P., (ed.), Histoire du Soulèvement Hongrois 1956, Paris, Editions Horvath, 1971.

Hamm, Harry, Albania: China's Beachhead in Europe, New York, Praeger, 1963.

Kende, Pierre et Krzysztof Pomian, La deuxième révolution d'octobre, Paris, Editions du Seuil, 1978.

Levesque, Jacques, Le conflit sino–soviétique et l'Europe de l'Est. Montreal, Montreal University Press, 1970.

Lewis, Flora, A Case History of Hope: The Story of Poland's Peaceful Revolutions, New York, Doubleday, 1958.

Radvanyi, Janos, Hungary and the Superpowers—The 1956 Revolution and Realpolitik, Stanford, Hoover Institution Press, 1972.

Ray, Heman, China and Eastern Europe, New Delhi, Radiant Publishers, 1988.

Weit, Erwin, Dans l'ombre de Gomulka: histoire que nous vivons, Paris, Editions Robert Lafont, 1971.

Articles

General

Aslanov, R, and B. Bolotin, 'Maoists groupings in the West suffer ideological and political defeat', Far Eastern Affairs, no. 3, 1980.

Chen Qimao, 'War and Peace: a reappraisal', Beijing Review, no. 23, 1986.

Craincross, Alec, 'The Moscow Economic Conference', Soviet Studies, no. 2, 1952.

Goncharov, S. and A. Vinogradov, 'The Evolution of PRC's foreign policy concept', Far Eastern Affairs, no. 5, 1988.

Gittings, John, 'China's foreign policy: continuity or change', Journal of Contemporary Asia, no. 2, 1972.

Huan Xiang, 'China is its own master in foreign affairs', China and the World, no. 3, 1983.

_____ 'Relative detente befalls the world', Beijing Review, no. 1, 1989.

Joyaux, François, 'Revolution culturelle et politique extérieure chinoise', *Politique étran-gère*, no. 1, 1968.

Krivtsov, V. 'The Maoists' foreign policy strategy', *Far Eastern Affairs*, no. 3, 1978.

Lei Jenmin, 'Trade with capitalist countries', *People's China*, 16 January 1954.

Leng Shao-chuan, 'China and the international system', *World Affairs*, no. 4, 1976.

Liebethal, Kenneth, and Michael Oksenberg, 'Understanding China's bureaucracy', *The Chinese Business Review*, November–December 1986.

Steiner, H. Arthur, 'Mainsprings of Chinese communist foreign policy', *American Journal of International Law*, no. 1, 1950.

Volokhova, A., 'Zhou Enlai and Chinese diplomacy', *Far Eastern Affairs*, no. 5, 1988.

Xie Yixian, 'China's foreign policy: a 1980s' tune-up', *Beijing Review*, nos 7–8, 1989.

Xing Shugang, Li Yunhua and Liu Yingna, 'Changing balance of Soviet–US power', *Beijing Review*, no. 19, 1983.

Yee, Herbert S., 'Schools of thought in the literature on Chinese foreign policy behaviour', *China Report*, May–June 1979.

Young, Mun Kim, 'The Role of Ideology in Chinese foreign policy: the theory and practice of the three worlds'. *Journal of East Asian Affairs*, 1981.

Zhang Baoxiang, Lu Yao Kun and Sun Jianrong, 'A new era for the development of East–West relations', *Contemporary International Relations*, no. 3, 1988 (in Chinese).

Zheng Fangkun, 'China holds symposium on peace', *Beijing Review*, no. 23, 1986.

Zhou Zunnan, 'Theoretical basis for adjustment of China's foreign policy', *Journal of Foreign Affairs College*, no. 1, 1988 (in Chinese).

Zheng Weizhi, 'Independence is the basic canon: an analysis of the principles of China's foreign policy', *Beijing Review*, no. 1, 1985.

Western Europe

Alexeyev, I. 'Peking's European policy', *International Affairs*, no. 1, 1976.

Biegel, Alfred, 'The Sino–West European connection', *Military Review*, no. 1, 1976.

Bouc, Alain. 'Peking now wants a united Europe', *The Atlantic Community*, no. 2, 1970.

Braine, Bernard, 'China and the European Community', *China Now*, no. 76, 1976.

Bressi, Giovanni, 'China's foreign policy: Western Europe'. *European Review*, Spring 1973.

—— 'China and Western Europe'. *Asian Survey*, no. 10, 1978.

Brick, Philip, 'The politics of Bonn–Beijing normalization 1978–84', *Asian Survey*, no. 7, 1985.

Broadbent, K.P., 'China and the EEC: the politics of a new trade relationship'. *The World Today*, no. 5, 1976.

Bunkar, Bhagwan Sahai. 'Sino–French diplomatic relations 1964–81', *China Report*, January–February 1984.

Chang Tai-lin, 'Les relations entre la république de Chine et la France', *La Chine libre*, September–October, 1988.

Chien Twansheng 'Chinese-British friendship' *People's China*, 16 August 1954.

Dreyer, Peter. 'The China trade: will EEC agreement mean increased business?', *European Community*, no. 1, 1978.

de Dubnic, Vladimir Reisky, 'Germany and China: the intermediate zone theory and the Moscow treaty', *Asia Quarterly*, no. 4, 1971.

Ding, Yuanhong, 'Vicissitudes in West European-US Relations', *China and the World*, no. 4, 1983.

Fang Zhengxiang, 'Some questions on the current development of imperialist contradic-tions', *Hongqi*, no. 5, 1963.

Erasmus, Stephen, 'General de Gaulle's recognition of Peking', *China Quarterly*, April–June 1964.

Findorff, W.B., 'China and the European Community', *Aussenpolitik*, no. 2, 1973.

Gorce, Paul Marie de la, 'Les relations entre la Chine et l'Europe occidentale', *Etudes internationales*, no. 1, 1970.

Grossman, Bernhard, 'Peking–Bonn: a substantial non-relations', *Pacific Community*, no. 1, 1970.

Gu Junli, 'Preliminary political analysis of Western European situation', *West European Studies*, November 1988.

Guo Fengmin, 'Basic ideas behind the foreign policies of West European countries', *Peking Review*, nos. 4 and 5, 1983.

Houtmans, Pierre, 'La Chine et l'Europe entre la stabilité et les risques d'une troisième guerre mondiale', *Studia Diplimatica*, no. 4, 1979.

Hubert, Agnès, 'Le sens du rapproachement CEE–Chine: pragmatisme commercial et alliance stratégique', *Revue du Marché Commun*, no. 211, 1977.

Jen Kuping, 'The Munich tragedy and contemporary appeasement', *Peking Review*, no. 5, 1979.

Ji Yin, 'Western Europe: its foreign policy', *Peking Review*, no. 31, 1986.

Larin, A. 'Britain in China's foreign policy', *Far Eastern Affairs*, no. 3, 1979.

Li Cong. 'Prospects for economic development in Western Europe', *West European Studies*, no. 1, 1986.

Liu Ximu, 'Behind the so-called interdependence between US and Europe', *Hongqi*, no. 8, 1962 (in Chinese).

Liu Youhou, 'East meets West', *Intertrade*, no. 5, 1987.

Liu, William H. 'Britain's China Policy', *China Report*, nos. 5 and 6, 1978.

Li Yiyan *et al*, 'Main West European nations: policies, measures and their impacts on disarmament', *Contemporary International Relations*, no. 1, 1987 (in Chinese).

Lomykin, Vitaly, 'Who is helping Peking in its military build-up?', *World Marxist Review*, no. 2, 1982.

Louren, Erhard, 'Bilaterale Aussenwirtschschaftsbeziehungen zwischen der Volkes-republik China und der Bundesrepublik Deutschland', *Osteuropa*, no. 7–8, 1988.

Milligan, Stephen, 'EEC–China Trade Pact', *European Community*, no. 6, 1978.

Pan Qichang, 'On the Godesberg Programme of the Social Democratic Party', *West European Studies*, November 1988.

Philip, Brick. 'The politics of Bonn–Beijing normalization 1982–84', *Asian Survey*, no. 25, 1985.

Qian Nengnin, 'Western Europe's role in US–Soviet rivalry', *Beijing Review*, no. 31, 1986.

Ran Longbo, 'The Peace Movement in Western Europe', *West European Studies*, no. 1, 1986.

Redmond, John and Zhou Lan, 'The European Community and China: new Horizons', *Journal of Common Market Studies*, no. 2, 1986.

Sa Na, Chiu Kipen and Shen Yungxiong, 'Defence of national independence and second world countries', *Peking Review*, no. 5, 1978.

Strauss, Lothar, 'China und die EWG', *Deutsche Aussenpolitik*, no. 12, 1978.

Ting Hong and Yang Jingshuang, 'West European defence cooperation: past, present and future', *Contemporary International Relations*, no. 3, 1987 (in Chinese).

Tow, William T. and Douglas T. Stuart, 'China's military turns to the West', *International Affairs*, no. 2, 1981.

Tran, Ngoc Bich. 'Chine/CEE: quel avenir', *Sudest Asie*, no. 32, 1984.

Vent, Hans Myron Henning, 'The Bonn–Peking connection: overview of the trade and treaty relations', *Issues and Studies*, no. 12, 1975.

Wan Shuyn, 'US differs with West Germany on major defence issues', *Beijing Review*, no. 34, 1989.

Wang Shu, 'How China–FRG entered into diplomatic relations', *Journal of Foreign Affairs College*, April 1988 (in Chinese). Wang Yange, 'France–West Germany cooperation at a new stage', *Contemporary International Relations*, no. 2, 1988 (in Chinese).

Wilson, Dick, 'The People's Republic of China and the European Community', *Europe Information*, no. 17, 1979.

Wolf, David C. 'To secure a convenience: Britain recognizes China—1950', *Journal of Contemporary History*, no. 2, 1983.

Weiler, Mathew A., 'SPD security policy', *Survival*, November–December 1988.

Xing Hua, 'Europe after the INF Treaty', *Beijing Review*, no. 13, 1988.

Yang Zhan Lin, 'US and the Common Market', *Peking Review*, 30 March 1962.

Younger, Kenneth, 'The Western attitude to China', *China Quarterly*, no. 10, 1962.

Yurkov, S., 'China and Western Europe', *Far Eastern Affairs*, no. 4, 1979.

Zang Churzheng, 'An analysis of the economic and trade relations between China and EEC', *New China Quarterly*, July 1986.

Zhang Baoxiang, Lu Yaokun and Sun Jianrong, 'A new era for the development of East–West relations', *Contemporary International Relations*, no. 3, 1988 (in Chinese).

Zhu, Weige, 'The present state and the future of the Federal Republic of Germany', *International Studies*, no. 3, 1987.

_____ 'Federal Germany's policy towards the East', *Beijing Review*, no. 29, 1989.

Eastern Europe

Aczel, Tamas, 'Hungary: glad tidings from Nanking', *China Quarterly*, no. 3, 1960.

Andelman, David A., 'China's Balkan strategy', *International Security*, no. 3, 1979/80.

Chen Min, 'China and Eastern Europe: a new relationship based on realistic needs', *Jerusalem Journal of International Relations*, no. 1, 1989.

Du Defeng and Guo Giyong, 'Political structural reforms in four East European countries', *Contemporary International Relations*, no. 3, 1987 (in Chinese).

Dumesnil, Claude, 'Les relations entre la Chine et les pays de l'Est', *Revue du Marché Commun*, no. 2, 1975.

Dziewanowski, K., 'Communist China and Eastern Europe', *Survey*, no. 77, 1970.

Esslin, M.J., 'East Germany: Peking–Pankow Axis', *China Quarterly*, no. 3, 1960.

Halpern, Nina P., 'Learning from abroad: Chinese views of the East European economic experience, January 1977–June 1981', *Modern China*, no. 1, 1985.

Jen Juping, 'Sovereignty and independence of Balkan Countries brook no encroachment', *Peking Review*, no. 43, 1974.

Kun, Joseph C., 'Chinese communist reaction to Czechoslovak crisis', *Radio Free Europe Research*, China No. 2, 1968.

_____ 'China's changing relations with Eastern Europe', *Radio Free Europe Research*, no. 0754, 1970.

_____ 'Nepszabadsag' offers Hungarian view of Chinese events', *Radio Free Europe Research*, no. 1213, 1971.

_____ 'A survey of Yugoslav–Chinese relations', *Radio Free Europe Research*, no. 1442, 1972.

_____ 'China's trade with Eastern Europe: built in limitations', *Radio Free Europe Research*, no. 1750.

Labedz, Leopold, 'Poland: the small leap sideways', *China Quarterly*, no. 3, 1060.

Larrabec, F. Stephen, 'Changing perspectives on the Balkans', *Radio Free Europe Research*, Bulgaria, no. 31, 1971.

Morris, S.J., 'Chinese policy towards Eastern Europe', *Contemporary China*, no. 2, 1978.

Prybyla, Jan S., 'The China Trade', *Eastern Europe*, no. 3, 1967.
—— 'Albania's economic vassalage', *Eastern Europe*, no. 7, 1967.
Stankovic, Slobodan, 'Croatia's economic relations with China', *Radio Free Europe Research*, no. 1466, 1972.
Tretiak, David and Teliki Gabor, 'The uneasy alliance: the Sino–Yugoslav rapprochment and its implications for Sino–Albanian relations', *Current Scene*, 15 October 1977.
Zeng Shuzhi, 'Renewing old friendship—a visit to Eastern Europe', *China Reconstructs*, no. 10, 1987.
Zhu Weige, 'Current policy of the Federal Republic of Germany', *International Studies*, no. 3, 1989 (in Chinese).
Xu Xing, 'Le vent qui vient de Pologne', *Le Monde*, 12 July 1981.
Yu, Arsenev, S. Stepanov and V. Kukushikin, 'China's trade and economic relations with socialist countries', *Far Eastern Affairs*, No. 4, 1988, *Yugoslav Survey*, 'Yugoslavia and China', no. 10, 1962.
Yugoslav Survey 'Relations between Yugoslavia and the People's Republic of China', No. 1, 1972.

Journals and newspapers consulted

Asian Survey (Berkeley)
Beijing Review (Beijing)
China Aktuell (Hamburg)
China News Analysis (Hong Kong)
China Quarterly (London)
China Report (Delhi)
Contemporary International Relations (Beijing, in Chinese)
Current Scene (Hong Kong)
Far Eastern Affairs (Moscow)
Far Eastern Economic Review (Hong Kong)
Journal of International Studies (Beijing)
Foreign Trade (Beijing)
Red Flag (Beijing, in Chinese)
International Affairs (Moscow)
International Herald Tribune (Paris)
Intertrade (Beijing)
Issues and Studies (Taipei)
Joint Public and Research Service (Washington)
La Documentation française (Paris)
Le Monde (Paris)
La Nouvelle Chine (Paris)
New Times (Moscow)
People's China (Beijing)
Problems of Communism (Washington)
Radio Free Europe Research: Communist Area (Munich)
Summary of World Broadcasts: Far East (London)
Survey of China Mainland Press (Hong Kong)
Xinhua News Bulletin (Beijing)

Index